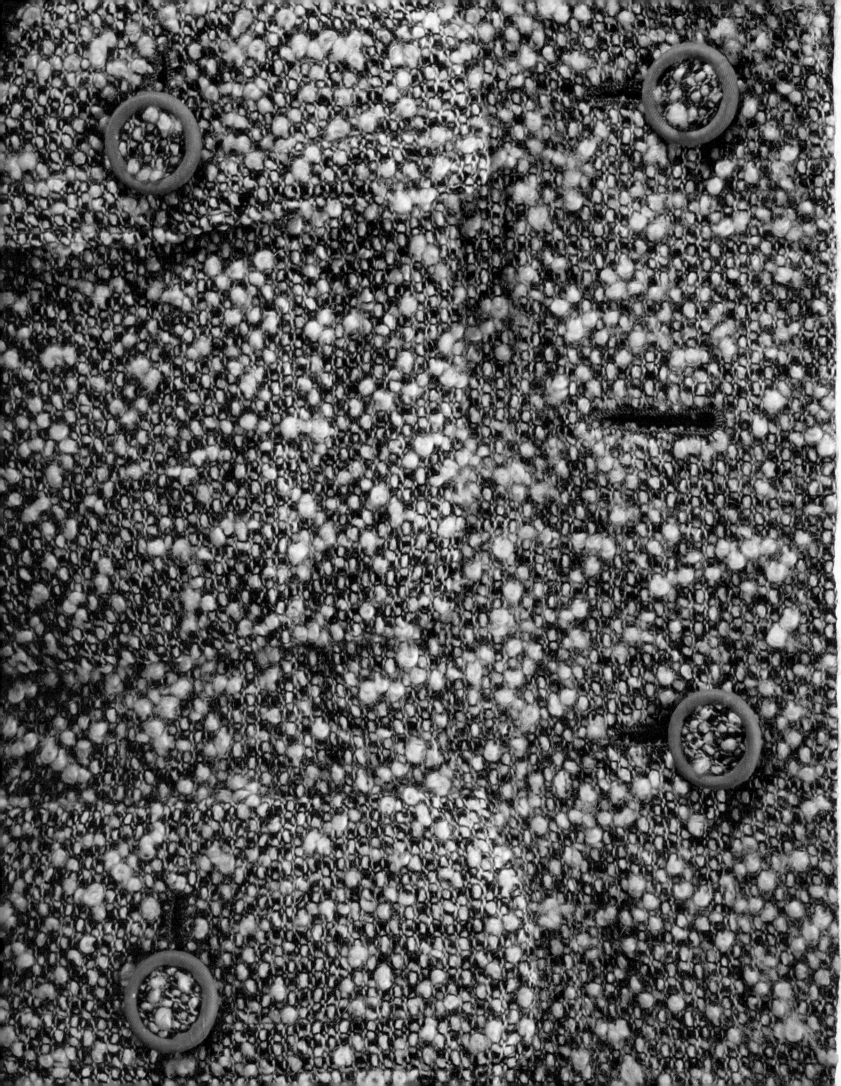

A TRIBUTE TO THE WORLD'S MOST ENDURING LABELS

LUXEFASHION

A TRIBUTE TO THE WORLD'S MOST ENDURING LABELS

LUXEFASHION

CAROLINE COX

Foreword by **CAMERON SILVER**

RUNNING PRESS
PHILADELPHIA · LONDON

A Quintessence Book

Copyright © 2013 Quintessence

ISBN: 978-0-7624-5111-1
Library of Congress Control Number: 2013943903

QSS: HEFN

9   8   7   6   5   4   3   2   1
Digit on the right indicates the number of this printing

This book was designed and produced by
Quintessence Editions Ltd.
230 City Road, London, EC1V 2TT

Senior Editor: Ruth Patrick
Designer: Dean Martin
Editorial Assistant: Zoë Smith
Picture Researchers: Sara DiGirolamo, Zoë Smith
Production Manager: Anna Pauletti

Editorial Director: Jane Laing
Publisher: Mark Fletcher

Running Press Book Publishers
2300 Chestnut Street
Philadelphia, PA 19103-4371
Visit us on the web!
www.runningpress.com

p2: Canvas heeled shoe by Salvatore Ferragamo
p4–5: Black reptile skin clutch bag by Gucci

Color reproduction by KHL Chromagraphics, Singapore
Printed in China by 1010 Printing International Ltd.

CONTENTS

FOREWORD

"What's in a name? That which we call a rose
By any other name would smell as sweet."
Romeo and Juliet (II, ii, 1-2)

What *is* in a name? Why are luxury consumers so seduced by brands whose names we sometimes can't pronounce, but whose products we wear? We forfeit our own initials to wear someone else's monogram because we are enthralled by luxury and legacy. However, we don't always know what makes the name so desirable. In this book, Caroline Cox gives us a tutorial on why these names matter and have remained relevant with the passing of time. I think of this book as the *Cliff's Notes* to the luxe life.

My love of luxury is very personal. When I was nineteen years old, I traveled to London where I couch surfed at a friend's apartment in Chelsea. I didn't have much cash, but I did manage to trek down Sloane Street and visit the Hermès boutique. Fortunately, I knew the "H" in Hermès was silent and I knew I needed to own something by Hermès. I purchased a Vision II agenda in black ostrich for £350 ($530). A seemingly absurd amount of money to pay considering my housing arrangement, but let's just say that agenda has outlasted my use of a calendar since switching to an iPhone for my diary. My Hermès Vision II remains in pristine condition, even though an agenda is a bit of an anachronism some twenty-five years after triumphantly purchasing it. That purchase got me hooked on luxury, much to my checking account's dismay.

In a world where luxury has become as ubiquitous as fast food, and fast fashion has made style accessible to the masses, heritage brands provide the consumer with a degree of certainty and timelessness amid a barrage of disposable excess and access. It's no surprise that 85 percent of women in Japan own a Louis Vuitton product, but I would argue most clients of Vuitton have no idea that the founder of this brand began as a luggage packer. In 1854, Louis Vuitton opened his eponymous *malletier* on Rue Neuve-des-Capucines where he eventually invented the first flat trunk. Vuitton may have started his career packing French couture, and now the house has come first circle, presenting its very own Parisian parade of men's and women's clothing designed by Marc Jacobs since 1998. Louis Vuitton and fashion are at the very core of this ultimate luxury brand.

Luxury does not necessarily have to be prohibitively expensive. I find luxury is determined by both quality and investment. Take, for example, the 100-year-old company L.L. Bean. Most famous for its hunting boots sold for less than $200, it represents the very best of its kind. That's luxury. It need not be a crocodile boot to be a luxurious purchase. However, a Lucchese alligator boot will set you back nearly $13,000 and represents the best of its kind, too.

Provenance is not easy to fake. Perhaps one reason why investors continue to resurrect fabled brands from yesteryear as luxury is about story telling, and what better way to entice the consumer than with waxing nostalgia through the history of a name associated with the rich and royal? As a purveyor of vintage couture at DECADES, our clients are drawn to the certainty of the past. Luxury never goes out of style; it is both in fashion and out of fashion, simultaneously. I often say, "If it was good 100 years ago, it's even better today." Whether it's a Lock & Co. hat or a pair of Mazarin socks, this book has us covered from head to toe by brands that really do what they do better than anyone else.

This book has me inspired to take a trip around the world and visit the headquarters of each highlighted brand. I have made a list of things I want and invite you to join me. We will go to Scotland for William Lockie cashmere and Milan for a Maglia Francesco umbrella. Naturally, my bespoke suit will be Gieves & Hawkes in London, and it won't be easy to choose between John Lobb or Rudolf Sheer & Söhne brogues. Let's end up near Moscow, scouring the intoxicating selection of Pavlovsky Posad's fine woolen shawls.

There's so much more in a luxury brand name than just an iconic and recognizable logo. These brands who have survived wars and revolutions, depressions and recessions, rationing and rarity, are a reminder that true luxury perseveres against the fads of fashion. Just like a surname that is passed on from generation to generation, the goods offered by these fabled houses are passed on much in the same way. That's what is in a name and it is the ultimate in luxury: a legacy.

Cameron Silver

Left: Surrounded by bolts of cloth, couturier Christian Dior discusses the fitting of an evening gown during the edit of a collection, *c.* 1950s.

INTRODUCTION   9

INTRODUCTION

A Louis Vuitton steamer trunk in an attic's cobwebbed eaves opens to reveal a peach silk satin *robe de style* by Lanvin, an exquisite handmade Charvet shirt, and a subtly cut black crêpe day dress by Coco Chanel. Such bespoke clothes evoke bittersweet memories resonating with times past and remain precious heirlooms to be handed down rather than disposed of after a season's wear. Yet today we live in a culture obsessed with the throwaway, with no time to develop any kind of meaningful relationship with our clothes, unable to understand the importance of vernacular skills and traditions, and the symbolism of design and pattern. With cheaper prices stimulating overconsumption, the crafted, handmade garment is increasingly under siege, yet the following pages show us that bespoke brands still exist today even in such a relentlessly accelerating climate of saturated multimedia.

Luxury brands with the reputation for artisanal excellence still remain, such as the couture house of Lanvin established in 1889 (see page 162); the French institution of Charvet, a men's outfitters situated on the Place Vendôme in Paris since 1838 and renowned for its Mur des Blancs, or "wall of whites," 400 fabrics in more than 100 different shades of white (see page 74); and Chanel, not only an innovative atelier since 1909 but also a preserver of couture's heritage (see page 190). In 1997, Chanel founded Paraffection, a subsidiary company set up to save and promote the history, craft, and manufacturing skills of artisan workshops, including the costume jeweler and button maker Desrues (est. 1929), millinery label Maison Michel (est. 1936), feather maker Lemarié (1880), and, most significantly, the historic embroidery house of Lesage founded in 1868 by Albert Michonet, who worked for Empress Eugénie and her couturier Charles Frederick Worth.

Evocative names such as Gieves & Hawkes (see page 24) and Borsalino (see page 114) have managed to survive and still light up the fashion world like lighthouses in a storm. There are other less well known brands, too, hidden gems that take their place alongside the global fashion powerhouses featured in the pages of this book. The Pavlovsky Posad shawl factory, for example, is more than 200 years old and one of heritage fashion's greatest survivors; the Russian Revolution, two world wars and Perestroika have yet to close its doors (see page 44). Today the work created at Pavlovsky Posad is regarded as an important folk art in its homelands, and each year designs are created by artists from the Pavlovo Posad School of shawl design, who use a combination of traditional designs, or *krok,* in new compositions in gouache that are then vetted by a panel represented by the Ministry of Culture and the Council of Folk Crafts for the Moscow Region. Painter Elena Zhukova says, "When we create new designs, inspiration is important but knowledge and experience are even more so— because these shawls are all about traditions that we have to respect." Family-owned company Ombrellificio Maglia Francesco, or Maglia (see page 104), was established in Italy by umbrella maker Francesco Maglia, who had

"Some people think luxury is the opposite of poverty. It is not. It is the opposite of vulgarity."
Coco Chanel

been making bespoke work since the age of fourteen in the mountain village of Montichiari in Lombardy. In 1856, he moved to the ancient university town of Pavia and founded his own-name company based in the Via Ripamonti, Milan, which is today run by the fifth generation of the family, Francesco and Giorgio. The constituent parts of their handmade umbrellas are made on the shores of Lake Como and assembled in their workshop in Milan. Swaine Adeney Brigg (see page 20), purveyors of the finest quality English leather goods, has its origins as an equestrian whip makers established in Marylebone Street, London, by saddler John Ross in 1760, and today make bespoke articles such as the London Suit Carrier crafted by a single artisan in the Cambridge workshop out of vegetable-tanned hand-finished English bridle leather.

It seems that after a decade obsessed with the throwaway and clothes with such built-in obsolescence that they fade and fray after little wear, that some of today's more canny consumers are making an alternative choice. Many are eschewing fleeting fashion, increasingly uneasy over its modes of production, in favor of brands with a history of great craftsmanship. Moreover, as resources dwindle, we need to be mindful of our choices, and the most sustainable way of buying fashion is buying well, by choosing goods of such superb quality that they will last a lifetime. Take the case of Dale of Norway, a firm that has been in existence since 1879 and maintains the country's knitwear heritage, which dates back to the ninth century. Dale continues to manufacture the traditional Setesdal *lusekofter* (sweater), with its distinctive inset raglan sleeves and pewter closures, in yarn that is so stable that its breaking strength is three times that of

"The craftsmanship is very much the same... I sometimes think that if my great-grandfather walked in he'd feel very much at home."
James Hunter Lobb

ordinary wool. Such knitwear is so durable that it can be passed down through the generations as a family heirloom, invoking memories of times past yet also mapping out a new autobiography of family history for the next generation. Thus, a brand such as Dale is featured in this book because it has intrinsic worth, a promise that has transferred across successive generations.

Heritage is not about banal retro styling or taking refuge in past glories; it is about brands with a solid backstory that still makes sense today. Brands such as Brooks Brothers and Chippewa are not just stories of various items of apparel; they encompass the history of the United States. Brooks Brothers was founded in 1818, the year that the refurbished White House opened its doors in a symbolic step toward independence after being looted and burned by the British army four years earlier. As the country shook itself free of colonial restraint, it began inventing its own traditions, including the sartorial, and Brooks Brothers, the United States' oldest clothing retailer, played a significant part. The Chippewa Shoe Manufacturing Company, set up in 1901 to cater to the demands of local loggers, was named after the local Native American Chippewa tribe who lived and traded fur pelts on the southern shores of Lake Superior.

This book is a unique tribute to the world's most hallowed fashion brands and comprises two sections: the first provides in-depth feature portraits of some of the finest brands, renowned labels, and those less well known; the second is an essential directory of a further 160 brands, contributing to the story of how artisans from all over the world have created exceptional objects of desire that have endured because of their superb quality, superior craftsmanship, and timeless design appeal. It will take readers on a captivating journey through Europe and North America, uncovering the most fabled creators, from Hermès of Paris and Lock of London through to legendary U.S. boot brand Lucchese. As Xavier Aubercy, the latest of his family to run the firm of fine Parisian shoemakers since 1935 puts it, "We draw our strength from the beauty of our profession, from the generation that went before us, and all the people for whom beautiful objects and craftsmanship are a passion or a dream. It's all this that gives us a sense of our accomplishments. This is the source of that extra something that we are so proud of."

PRE-NINETEENTH CENTURY

Many luxury fashion labels have extraordinarily long lineages surviving war, successive economic depressions, and changes in fashion and the patterns of fashion consumption. They embody the importance of artisanal skills, vernacular traditions, and high-quality materials that predate the effects of industrialization. The fashion system, as we know it today, emerged in the fourteenth century when the increasingly influential merchant class challenged the nobility as the arbiters of taste. As fashion emphasized cut and contour, tailoring and its associated disciplines came to the fore including drapery, and the making of fine shoes and hats.

Left: Detail of a vintage Gieves & Hawkes military uniform, showing the intricate stitching.

Right: The interior of the Lock & Co. shop, displaying a selection of classic gentlemen's hats and the firm's distinctive white hat boxes.

Below right: A reconditioned antique top hat, in "hatter's plush," a fine silk applied to felt and polished to give a glossy finish.

1676
LOCK & CO.

James Lock & Co. Hatters of 6 St. James's Street, London, is the oldest hat shop in the world with a roll call of celebrated customers, including the Duke of Wellington, Admiral Lord Nelson, Sir Winston Churchill, and film star Charlie Chaplin whose ubiquitous Lock & Co. Bowler is arguably movie history's most iconic hat. Two historic catastrophes affected the founding of Lock & Co., the Great Plague of 1665 and the Great Fire of London in 1666, both of which forced a general movement of the population away from the City and the River Thames into the West End, which began to develop as the center of luxury trades in London. George James Lock was the son of a family of coffee, chocolate, and tobacco importers, headed up by his father Sir John Lock, who lived in Goodman's Fields. In 1686, the Lock family consolidated its various concerns into a row of seven houses in St. James's Street, leased by George James Lock and set in the shadow of Henry VIII's former home, St. James's Palace. The houses were a business and a residence, with spaces rented out to other tradesmen and as private homes. It was a fantastic environment within which to trade; St. James's Coffee House was a notorious meeting place for the political wrangling of members of the Whig Party, many of whom came from the English landed gentry. It was only a short step from the coffee house to the hatter's to peruse the stock, thus Lock & Co. duly became the sartorial extension of the fashionable coffee house.

In 1747, George's grandson, James Lock, was apprenticed at the age of sixteen to hatter Charles Davis, also of St. James's Street. He stayed for seven years, learning the fundamentals of the craft, including felt-making, the name given to the method of turning beaver, rabbit, and hare fur into hoods that were then stiffened with shellac, steamed into shape, brimmed, and finished.

At this time, the embellished cocked hat held sway in aristocratic circles, and Lock historian Frank Whitbourn describes how "its complement of buttons, loops, tassels and cockades derived from military necessity; they served as means of identification in the field, and because they were fascinating in themselves, whatever their function, they were not discarded when fighting was done. The cockades, loops, buttons and tassels, as the order books testify, went to town."

After his indenture was up, James married Davis's daughter, Mary, and automatically became heir to the firm that he went on to inherit in 1759. In 1765, the business moved to new and more spacious premises at the other side of the road, at No. 6, the former domain of potter Peter Vanina, who used a kiln to fire popular earthenware figurines of well-known characters including William Shakespeare. Lock & Co. remains there today, and the back of the shop where steaming is carried out is still referred to as "the kiln." In 1794, James Lock, who had no living male heirs, went into copartnership, rather controversially, with his illegitimate son, George James. The company passed into a less fruitful period for a number of reasons: competition came from three other hatters in the same street; Mayfair rather than St. James's became a popular haunt, its pavements stalked by rakes and dandies following the fashionable influence of George "Beau" Brummell; George James was also somewhat profligate, living high off the hog with not enough means to sustain such a lavish lifestyle. Thankfully, when his son James took over the running of the debt-ridden business in the 1830s, it began to enter an era of prosperity with the newly established railways bringing in more customers from farther afield, an increase in military orders, and the festivities surrounding the coronation

LADIES
HATS
THIS WAY

Top: The original order and design sketches for Lord Nelson's two-cornered bicorne hat. **Above:** Charlie Chaplin, whose Bowler hat was part of his stage persona, is pictured in 1931. **Right:** The shop front of Lock & Co. on St. James's Street, London.

summer of 1838 when the young Queen Victoria was crowned, stimulating the demand for hats.

The cocked hat fell out of fashion in favor of the top hat, and James Lock created a gray version especially for Royal Ascot racing meet; Frank Whitbourn writes of how "it was an immediate success. Its privileged wearers became so jealous of it that they dared not keep it at home lest, between one Ascot meeting and the next, they should be tempted to give it a local airing, and find themselves expelled from Ascot forever. So after use, it became usual for a customer's Ascot to be tucked away in tissue paper at No. 6. Every year when Ascot came round once more to crown the Season, each hat was unfolded, as though it were the Gold Cup itself, and polished for its public appearance. The racing done, the hats were, so to speak, weighed-in back at the shop, bedded down again in their cardboard boxes, and then shelved like coffins in the family vault awaiting resurrection."

This was also the era of the Coke hat, today known as the Bowler hat, commissioned by Norfolk farmer William Coke in 1850 as an alternative to the top hat worn by his gamekeepers and groundsmen. The height of top hats meant that they were regularly swiped off by the overhanging branches of trees and blown off by gusts of wind, so a less tall, fitted hat was necessary. The prototype Coke or "hard fur felt in semi-rough finish," as it was known in the trade, was manufactured by the Bowler brothers of Southwark to Lock & Co.'s specifications. It was domed in appearance, fitted to the head, and hardened with shellac as well as thoroughly tested by William Coke at Lock & Co.—at one point he jumped on the hat to test how it coped with his weight, and the hat stood firm. The Coke was a huge success and was worn by all classes by the end of the century, but in the 1950s demand began to wane. More recently, this classic hat has found a new audience in hip-hop and in Northern Nigeria, where the male members of the wedding party sport a Bowler as a symbol of status and success.

James Lock had no successor on his death so his interests in the business passed to his nephew, Charles Whitburn, the son of his sister, Ann. In 1871, Charles and James Benning became partners, and since then the business has remained within the two families in an amicable relationship. The shop retains many of its original seventeenth-century features, including a listed "coffin"-shaped English oak staircase regularly visited by architectural students. Like many London buildings of this period, Lock & Co. was constructed with height but not width because of the prohibitive cost of land; when anyone expired on the higher floors, the coffin had to be winched down through the well of the staircase to the ground, hence the name.

Lock & Co.'s unassuming entrance belies the fact that it remains a treasure trove of traditional hats, what Diana Vreeland, then fashion editor of U.S. *Vogue* described in 1981 as "a paradise for men, just a paradise," and includes classic rabbit and beaver fur felt fedoras, straw boaters, soft-brimmed Homburgs, leather-banded French berets, and riding and dressage helmets. A cabinet set into the wall holds the order for Lord Nelson's two-cornered bicorne hat and another the bespoke pattern for Queen Elizabeth II's head shape, used by crown jewelers Garrard to size the coronation crown. Best-selling items include handmade, hand-blocked caps made to a customer's specification by one Mr. Gill, an expert artisan who has worked for the company for decades—his name is enshrined in the classic Gill cap. Lock & Co. sends lengths

of the best-quality Scottish wool, finest cashmere, and Harris tweed to Mr. Gill's workshop to be cut and "made up" or sewn together by his staff with the lining and cap constructed separately. The peak is put in and the cap lined out, after which it is put on the block by the master artisan who hand blocks and steams the cap to give it a much rounder shape so as to hug the head well; bespoke caps are cut with deeper backs to give an even closer fit. Lock & Co. also provides an aftercare service so that the fit remains true; managing director Sue Spencer explains, "When customers go shooting, the English weather means that caps can get soaked in a downpour of rain. Men tend to stick the wet cap on the radiator to dry when they get home and after they have done this a few times it starts to tighten up. We have a hat-stretching service where the cap is put on a block and steamed and stretched back to size." Lock & Co. also sells hat jacks that can be used by customers who live abroad to stretch their own hats.

It is said that the staff in the shop are so experienced that a customer's head measurements can be gauged immediately by eye, but if the shape appears a little more unusual, out comes the Conformateur, a measuring instrument with brass expanders invented in 1840 by

"The Conformateur registers the exact shape of the head so that a hat can be made to fit it precisely."

Conformateur patent

Left, clockwise from top left:
1. An original nineteenth-century Coke, today known as the Bowler hat, commissioned by Norfolk farmer William Coke in 1850 as an alternative to the top hat. 2. A selection of wooden Bowler hat blocks. 3. The Conformateur, a head-measuring device invented in 1840 and still used today. **Below:** Antique hats from the company's archives are displayed in the shop.

LOCK & CO. 19

Allié-Maillard. This beautifully engineered device in brass and ebony uses a system of levers and pushpins to, as the patent put it, "register the exact shape of the head so that a hat can be made to fit it precisely." The Conformateur is positioned on the head as if it were a hat and slowly pushed down, thereby expanding the pushpins so that they remain tight to the circumference of its shape. The top has a cork-lined lid containing a blank piece of paper with pins that mark out the measurements, thus creating a pattern that is removed and kept for reference. Lock & Co. has a fascinating selection of Conformateur measurements on display belonging to well-known customers including General Charles de Gaulle, writer Evelyn Waugh, actor David Niven, Field Marshal Montgomery, and the infamous aristocrat Lord Lucan.

The Conformateur remains an important piece of kit for hard hats, such as toppers and Cokes, which have to be fitted correctly or they will not sit properly. Sue Spencer explains: "Many people have a long, oval head shape and other hatters tend to give the customer bigger sizes of top hat to fit front to back. You end up with a gap at the sides. At Lock's we heat and mold the hat to fit and can customize a top or Bowler hat with an elegant curled brim to flatter the customer's face shape." Top hats cannot be steamed as it would watermark the silk, so they have to be held in front of direct heat; the shellac stiffening inside softens and then the block or jack is put in, a process executed entirely by "feel." Reconditioned and relined antique top hats are sold in beaver or "hatter's plush," a fine silk applied to felt and polished to give a mirrorlike finish. This is hard to replicate today so antique top hats remain much sought after, with those in the know at Ascot aspiring to the best sheen. The Voyager is Lock's modern innovation, a hat that can be rolled up when traveling because it is unlined and does not contain a "leather," the band that traditionally keeps a hat in shape; a band of softer grosgrain is used instead. The fur felt of the Voyager is taken from the soft underbelly of the rabbit making it naturally water repellent and ultra pliable.

Millinery was added to the portfolio in the early 1990s with a couture range designed by Sylvia Fletcher and handmade on the premises in materials such as finely stitched spiral pedal straw and the more open-weave sinamay straw, derived from the banana plant. Hats can be hand dyed to match outfits, and assistants are available to explain the dress etiquette for Royal Ascot, which fuels one of the shop's busiest times of the year. Collections are seasonal, following the custom of the fashion industry, whereas men's seasonal hats are stocked all year round.

Lock & Co.'s classic Panama hats are handwoven in Ecuador in different grades of Tequila palm fiber; the finest takes one person three months to weave, hence its £800 plus ($1,200) price tag. Smoking caps are also a feature of Lock's merchandise: the only gentleman's hat to be worn indoors. They are hand stitched from quilted silk velvet surmounted with a gold tassel from Hand & Lock, an embroidery firm in existence since 1767 which has a long tradition of working with couturiers Dior, Norman Hartnell, and Hardy Amies.

The business keeps its retinue of prestigious customers by being in the unique position of holding two royal warrants, for the Duke of Edinburgh and the Prince of Wales. Prince Charles wears the Turnberry cap; its distinctive width and protruding peak keep the rain out of his eyes while shooting at Balmoral Castle, Scotland, and he has it made up in the same tweed as his suits.

1750
SWAINE ADENEY BRIGG

Swaine Adeney Brigg, purveyors of the finest-quality English leather goods, originated as an equestrian whip-makers, established in Marylebone Street, London, by saddler John Ross in 1760. In 1769 the building was destroyed by fire, but by 1770 the company was reestablished in Piccadilly and became whip-maker to the royal family. In 1798, the business was sold to James Swaine, who had already established a reputation as foreman of a successful whip-makers in Holborn, and until 1825, whips remained the only retail product, which was not unusual in the days when the horse was the only means of transport. It was a seasonal trade, as the firm's historian Katherine Prior explains: "In London and other cities, April to July was the busiest time of year for sales of driving whips, as the smarter households renewed their equipage for driving out and making calls during the social season. Then August to October saw a burst of sales in riding whips, as the gentry took to their horses for the hunt season. November to March was traditionally the slack

Swaine had a mixed clientele that ran the gamut of coach drivers through to the most fashionable of Regency bucks, including the so-called "Prinny's Set" who were the notoriously libertine friends of the pleasure-loving

Prince Regent and included Frederick "Poodle" Byng, nicknamed after his constant canine companion. Whips ranged from the purely functional to dandified accessories and could be crafted from a range of materials, such as yew, bamboo, and baleen (whalebone), covered with catgut or pigskin. Sticks made from the evocatively named "rabbit-bitten" holly were particularly prized, named after the effect given to wood after it had been gnawed by the incisors of rabbits in winter. After the holly sticks had been polished, the imprint of the teeth marks gave a beautifully mottled effect.

In 1837, the company became suppliers of whips by royal appointment to the young Queen Victoria, whose fanciful flights of fashion had chased silver grips and ornate silver-gilt mounts. She was an expert horsewoman who, as custom dictated, rode side saddle on a quilted pigskin seat with a velvet-lined slipper stirrup; this gendered method of horse riding was instituted in the fourteenth century as chastity became highly valued during the era of feudal rule. Thus, when Anne of Bohemia journeyed across Europe in 1382 to meet her betrothed, King Richard III, she went sidesaddle sitting on a chairlike contraption with a front pommel for grip

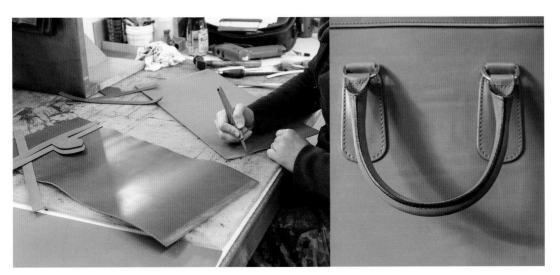

Far left: Craftswoman preparing the leather by scratching the surface before gluing. **Left:** Handle detail on a Pullman case in London Tan. **Above right:** Actor Patrick Macnee as John Steed of British 1960s television show *The Avengers*, with his whangee-handle Swaine Adeney Brigg umbrella.

and a rudimentary footrest. By the seventeenth century the custom had become so entrenched it was believed that only wanton women rode astride; a pommel was introduced at the front of the saddle around which the rider could hitch one knee for stability and assert a degree of control. This system was still in use in the nineteenth century and was followed by Queen Victoria when she went for regular canters across Windsor Great Park wearing a velvet riding habit and a top hat with a veil draped about the brim, accessorized with a Swaine whip.

In 1845, James Adeney joined the firm and it began to enter a period of international recognition after presenting at the Great Exhibition of 1851. This extravagant affair was held in London at the glittering glass Crystal Palace designed by Joseph Paxton and was a showcase for the best of design during the height of the British Empire. Swaine and Adeney showed a large selection of canes and whips, including one "mounted with gold and set with brilliants and rubies" for which they received a medal and their reputation soared with the attendant publicity. One visitor wrote that few gentlemen there "and possibly few of the ladies could have failed to admire the handsome show of riding whips by English, French, Belgian, Spanish, and American manufacturers," and those on show ranged from robust coachmens' whips to miniature models for children. When Swaine and Adeney showed at another exhibition in New York two years later, a journalist poetically opined: "Blessed is the steed on whose fleet flanks such whips are ornamentally applied!"

The advance of the railways and the concomitant decline in equestrian transport meant that Swaine and Adeney needed to add other products to extend their range, and they began to concentrate on hunting accessories, including horns, spurs, hunting knives, and presentation whips, as well as highly crafted walking sticks and umbrellas. The popularity of motoring in the early twentieth century presented another challenge, but the company responded with the manufacture of luggage, and, by the 1920s, high-quality handbags, document cases, and handmade leather gloves. Umbrellas continued to be an important part of their repertoire, with frames by Fox's of Stourbridge covered in handwoven silk, and handles and shafts made from materials as diverse as malacca cane or bamboo sheathed in kangaroo and ostrich

"Blessed is the steed on whose fleet flanks such whips are ornamentally applied!"
New York journalist, 1853

skin. Crooks could be carved from rhinoceros horn or in the whimsical shapes of terriers, otters, monkeys, or pheasants, most notably by August and Ferdinand Czilinsky, whose work is highly sought after today.

In 1943, the umbrella makers Thomas Brigg & Sons became part of the company, and it was rebranded Swaine Adeney Brigg. Today, Brigg umbrellas are still regarded as the "gentleman's umbrella" and have the reputation for never turning inside out in the wind because of their sturdy construction. Frames are made from oil-tempered steel with inner springs of nickel silver, and the covers are made from either nylon twill or the original English

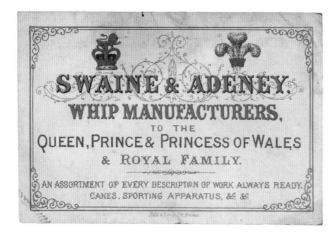

silk secured with hand-sewn lacquered metal tips. Handles can be commissioned in oak, stripped cherry, maple, and malacca, or covered with crocodile, lizard, and ostrich. Significantly, Briggs was the first umbrella maker to receive a royal warrant in 1893 and it continues to supply umbrellas to the royal family today.

The die-hard tradition of Swaine Adeney Brigg survived the fashionable fads of the 1950s and 1960s, and gained welcome publicity in 1962 when Patrick Macnee as the suave, impeccably dressed John Steed in *The Avengers* sported a Swaine Adeney Brigg black silk umbrella with a distinctive whangee handle. Whangee is a form of bamboo root derived from Asia that gains its unusual appearance from soil erosion on the sharp gradients on which it is grown while being exposed to the harsh elements. The bamboo root is sent to Swaine Adeney Brigg where it is bleached, boiled, and bent into a burnished handle, which is then attached to the Brigg shaft and frame. Steed's umbrella memorably concealed a sword that was brandished very deftly in many episodes of the popular television series, and his other umbrellas included one that concealed a sound recorder and a camera for undercover photography.

Swaine Adeney Brigg also had a starring role on film in the same decade, when James Bond carried a luxurious black leather attaché case in *From Russia with Love* (1963). This burnished *objet de luxe* came complete with a flat throwing knife, a 0.25 caliber AR7 folding sniper's rifle with an infrared sight, and twenty rounds of ammunition and gold coinage hidden away in the sides. In Ian Fleming's original Bond novels, a Swaine Adeney Brigg gadget-laden briefcase was standard issue for all 00 agents by Q Branch, complete with a distinctive red skiver lining, a thin soft leather made from the grain side of a split sheepskin. It is now one of the firm's most popular bespoke items. Other leather goods include the London Suit Carrier, made by a single artisan in the Cambridge workshop out of hand-finished traditional English bridle leather naturally tanned with plant extracts, and the Chesterford suitcase, with a bridle handle constructed using eight hand-sewn leather components and flexible board panels reinforced with a custom-made steel frame.

In 1996, the company incorporated hatmakers Herbert Johnson of New Bond Street, a company that also had a well-known foray into film after director Steven Spielberg and actor Harrison Ford visited its original premises at 13 Old Burlington Street in the 1980s. Spielberg was about to direct *Raiders of the Lost Ark* (1981), and the character of Indiana Jones played by Ford needed a distinctive hat that would mark the character's metamorphosis from archaeology lecturer to adventurer. They chose the Poet—a style launched in the 1890s— a tall-crowned, brushed, fur felt hat with a wide brim in sable brown and customized it to fit the physical demands of the role. The brim was made ovoid and was pulled down at the front to protect the eyes, leaving an uncluttered silhouette at the sides for the camera, and the ribbon trim was made thinner; 1½ in. (39 mm) instead of 2 in. (50 mm). The Indy hat is still available today, hand-cut using the original patterns created in collaboration with Spielberg and Ford. Swaine Adeney Brigg also retains the warrant to supply royal whips, most recently for six postilion riders accompanying the royal wedding carriage in 2011, described by Roger Gawn, director of the company, as: "extremely long, enabling the mounted postilion to tickle the carriage horses at the back." The company also repairs and hand delivers any of the objects it has supplied to the royal family over the years, including in 2011 the Prince of Wales's sporran. Tom Williams, manager of the St. James's shop remarks, "Without sounding glib about it, it's one of those things you get used to."

1771
GIEVES & HAWKES

Since 1495, when the first dry dock was built in Portsmouth, England, on the orders of Henry VII, the city has been home to the British naval forces. The Royal Navy was formally established in 1660 but there was no uniform as such until 1748, with the publishing of the tome *Uniform Regulations*; the many editions that followed set down the requisite regulation dress for officers and subalterns alike. The highest ranks of the Royal Navy were dressed by Meredith's of Portsmouth, a tailoring business founded on the High Street in 1785 by Melchisedek Meredith, who created bespoke garments for Admiral Lord Nelson and Flag Captain Hardy. His grandson, the well-known English novelist George Meredith described the popular tailor in 1860: "Mr. Melchisedek, whom people in private called 'the Great Mel,' had been the pride of the town. He was a tailor and he kept horses; he was a tailor and he had gallant adventures; he was a tailor and he shook hands with his

customers. Finally he was a tradesman and never was known to have sent a bill. Such a personage comes but once in a generation and when he goes, men miss the man as well as his money."

Meredith's was, in fact, the origins of a great tailoring dynasty, Gieves & Hawkes; after Melchisedek died leaving substantial debts, his successor and son, Augustus, ran the business for a short time and then sold out to an adjacent tailor in the High Street run by Joseph Galt. In 1882, Galt went into partnership with James Watson Gieve as Gieves & Galt, and the enterprising duo fitted out a company yacht with a fully functioning workshop and sailed off to the Crimea to cater to the needs of the officers stationed there, thus reviving Meredith's early relationship with the Royal Navy which was to hold the company in good stead. James Gieve became sole owner in 1887, and after his death in 1888, his two sons, James Watson Gieve and John Gieve, inherited the business.

In the early twentieth century, the threat of Germany's large naval resources galvanized Britain into pouring more money into its own sea power; a revised set of uniform regulations proved a boon to Portsmouth tailors, and James Gieve, sensing a huge business opportunity, set up a series of branches in all of Britain's main naval ports, and the firm started sending telegrams of congratulations to sea cadets after they had been accepted as entrants to the Royal Naval College on the Isle of Wight, including a note offering to fit them out for uniforms. A representative of the firm also met the new college entrants at the dockside before embarkation on the ferry to check their clothes were of the correct sartorial standard. Gieve's strategies were a success, and the bond with the navy was such that in 1911 his firm published a catalog that included a telegraphic

Above left: A portrait of James Gieve, who joined the company in 1852 as partner and became sole owner in 1887. **Above right:** The

No. 1 Savile Row premises of Gieves & Hawkes. **Right:** A bespoke suit in progress, for which the company is well-known.

Below left: A military crest from the Gieves & Hawkes archive. **Bottom left:** A page from the Hawkes customer ledger of 1835 itemizing the purchases made by Field Marshal the Duke of Wellington for his regiment. **Below right:** In 1748, the publishing of *Uniform Regulations* began the standardization of military dress.

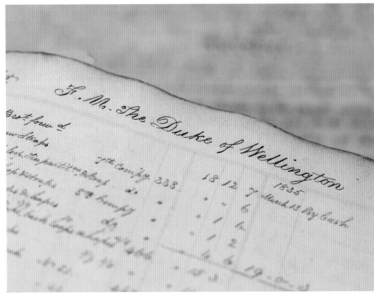

code "prepared to enable officers to telegraph their needs as economically as possible": "Alopecurus" meant "send at once a new regulation cocked hat; "Alpha" for a "new ball dress coat and gold lace trousers."

In 1903, Gieve opened premises in London at 21 George Street, specializing in full dress and ceremonial uniform; by 1912 it had moved to a larger building in South Molton Street, receiving the first of many royal warrants after fitting King George V as an officer in the Royal Navy. The need for uniforms during World War I meant long hours for the workers but huge profits for the firm; the company also developed an ingenious life-saving device: a vulcanized rubber ring that fitted into a naval waistcoat with a pocket containing a small flask of reviving brandy. After the war, the business expanded to include uniforms for naval staff employed on cruise ships and for the public schools Harrow and Winchester, among others. A grand outlet opened on Bond Street with a beautifully furnished lounge for customers, and business remained brisk throughout the next two decades.

In 1927, on the death of James Gieve, Rodney Watson Gieve joined the management of the company and the strong links with the navy were maintained. David W. Gieve, in his history of the company, tells of one occasion in Portsmouth when "a cruiser came into the harbor flying her paying-off pennant one Saturday morning. But when she had berthed, the paymaster commander was horrified to find that someone ashore had blundered, and there was no cash available with which to pay off the crew. Tempers were running high and the dockyard authorities were unable to help. So he betook himself to Gieves and asked for a loan on his personal account! A Gieves cheque for £27,000 was cashed; the crew was paid off, and the crisis averted. The loan was duly paid on Monday morning, and an armed guard was provided to escort the Admiralty's cash to the Manager's office."

During World War II, Gieves was fully mobilized to meet the demand for uniforms, but the positioning of its premises at Britain's naval bases meant many buildings were destroyed by Germany's strategic bombing campaigns; enemy planes buzzing over London scored a direct hit on the Bond Street store, obliterating the original building. In the 1950s, the market for bespoke uniforms began to change; the reductions in the armed services meant less demand both at home and overseas. Gieves hit back by introducing more ready-to-wear, including their iconic brass-buttoned navy blazer; by opening the first ladies' department in 1948; and, after a complete restructuring, by closing many of the branches outside London. Opportunity was to knock, however, in 1974 when Gieves formally joined with the tailoring firm Hawkes & Co. at the prestigious address of No. 1 Savile Row, the former home of the Royal Geographical Society.

Savile Row's history stretches back to the eighteenth century. In 1733, a London newspaper reported that "a new pile of buildings is going to be carry'd on near Swallow Street by a Plan drawn up by the Right Hon. The Earl of Burlington, and which is to be called Savile Street." By the end of the eighteenth century, tailors had begun to cluster around this area, including Thomas Hawkes, Henry Creed, and Meyer & Mortimer. As men's clothing began to depend more on cut and fit rather than on expensive embellishment after the influence of the celebrated English dandy George "Beau" Brummell, a tailor who could work cloth well with the proportions of the body was much sought after. In 1804, the *Dictionary of English Trades* ran, "A master tailor ought to have a quick eye, to steal the cut of a sleeve or the patterns of a flap, or the shape of a good trimming at a glance. Any bungler may cut a shape when he has the pattern before him but a good workman must make the clothes sit easy in spite of a stiff gaint or awkward air."

The enterprising Thomas Hawkes was born in Stourbridge and, with £5 in his pocket, came to London to find employment with Mr. Moy of Swallow Street, a manufacturer of velvet caps. Hawkes opened his own shop in Brewer Street in 1771 and became tailor to King George III and Prinny, the Prince of Wales. Hawkes's fame came from his way of "jacking" or hardening leather so it could withstand the swipe of a sword's blade, which garnered him important commissions from soldiers of the British Empire. Hawkes died in 1809 and the business continued with his son-in-law, Richard Moseley, as head. By 1860, the firm was being run by Hawkes's nephew, Henry Thomas White, who had specialized in the gold wire embroidery used in military uniform and invented the solar topee, a cork helmet worn as protection from the tropical sun, referred to today as the pith helmet. In his autobiography, journalist and explorer Henry Stanley wrote of how an African native of Ugogo "showed a marked interest in the stranger clad in white

flannels, with a Hawkes patent cork solar topee on his head, a most unusual thing in Ugogo."

With the joining of two historic tailoring dynasties, a legend was born—Gieves & Hawkes—whose flagship store, with its bespoke workrooms and extensive military archive, remains on the Row today; the business also retains a strong retail network of fourteen outlets within the United Kingdom and Far East. Bespoke remains the foundation, what the firm describes as "a priceless masculine experience" whereby an individual has a suit that is his or hers exclusively, one that will fit no other. At Gieves & Hawkes, the traditional skills of hand cutting, figuration, and tailoring are informed today by the aesthetic of modern styling. When a customer begins the process of ordering a bespoke suit, they are ushered into the Adam Room where a detailed consultation takes place with the cutter who has to have at least ten years experience before being allowed to take measurements. From these, a manila paper pattern is constructed that will remain permanently on the premises for any later orders. The pattern pieces are cut from cloth, and the jacket (called a coat in the trade), vest, and pants are sent to specialists in each garment with a trimmer in charge of the buttons, linings, and paddings. The components of the garments are basted or loosely stitched together in

visible white cotton, without pockets, buttons, or other finishings. At the first fitting, chalk marks are made on the cloth to show where an alteration is to be made, then the baste is removed and reworked for the forward fitting.

Savile Row historian Richard Walker gives a comprehensive account of what happens next: "The bespoke tailor is a sculptor in the way that he fashions a hollow shell to accommodate and flatter a particular body with all of its oddities, and one of his special skills is in molding the cloth into the contours by continual damping and shaping with a hot iron. The suit is given shape, bounce, and further individuality through umpteen unseen stitches worked into its innards, and it is that which is least noticed which takes most time— particularly the construction of the 'canvas,' which is the linen, felt, cotton, or horsehair interlining that forms the jacket's scaffolding. The interlinings are covered with hundreds of containing stitches, then sewn into the jacket in layers. As jacket and linings are stitched together, the tailor gently rolls the layers of fabric in his hand so that the finish will have 'life' and not appear too smooth and perfect."

All bespoke garments are hand finished, including edge stitching, the padding of lapels, and the construction of individual buttonholes, as well as the hand-sewn loop behind the lapel buttonhole to hold a blossom. All this work ensures that a bespoke suit will last much longer than a ready-to-wear example, and that the seams have enough inlay to allow adjustment if the body shape alters over time. In 2011, journalist Luke Leitch entered Gieves & Hawkes portals and described how "Fires roar, jazz tinkles, and there is a glassed shoe workshop within which you can see shoemakers Carréducker cobbling together lovely bespoke footwear. Instead of solely suits, suits, suits, there is now a classy (expensive too) selection of casual clothes, including soft leather pea coats, canvas kit bags, unlined cashmere mix jackets, jumpers, shirts, scarves— everything really. Visitors can have a haircut or a wet shave in the Gentlemans' Tonic in-house barber shop, or in another room browse through the barmy-but-fun selection of on-sale antiques (current stock includes an ejector seat)." The refit was supervised by chief executive John Durnin on behalf of owner Christopher Cheng Wai Chee of Hong Kong, whose goal is to "polish up the brand and put it back where it should be: at the top of the market."

Below: Robert Gieve (left) with one of the firm's cutters working on a page boy's uniform for the wedding of Prince Charles and Lady Diana Spencer in 1981.

Right: A navy herringbone single-breasted jacket with slanted pockets and peak lapel. **Far right:** A bespoke heritage-checked single-breasted jacket in flannel.

"A master tailor ought to have a quick eye, to steal the cut of a sleeve or the patterns of a flap, or the shape of a good trimming at a glance."

Dictionary of English Trades, 1804

1780
CHAUMET

Chaumet is the oldest of the grand jewelers on the prestigious Place Vendôme in Paris, with a name inextricably linked with those of Napoleon and Josephine, the house's best-known clients. The founder, Marie-Étienne Nitot was originally apprenticed to Auber, court jeweler to Marie-Antoinette, and thus had access to the wealthy aristocrats of the Versailles court, so when the jeweler opened his own business in 1780, it was relatively easy to build up an affluent clientele. After surviving the French Revolution (unlike many of his customers), Nitot's business continued until a chance encounter with Napoleon in 1802. The general's horse had become uncontrollable and Nitot, throwing caution to the wind, grabbed the reins and calmed it down. To show his gratitude, Napoleon appointed him his personal jeweler and Nitot went on to create many of the most important imperial pieces, including the consular sword set with the 140-karat Regent Diamond, the most valuable of all gems contained in the French crown jewels, which today resides in the Louvre.

Napoleon's attitude to jewelry was intensely political; the French crown jewels had been destroyed during the French Revolution with the monarchy itself, and, when he declared himself emperor, one of Napoleon's aims was to restore the sumptuous self-presentation of the Bourbon kings of Versailles, and by so doing give himself and his family an aura of majesty. A crown, robes, and any fabulous sartorial gesture were for Napoleon important trappings of power and indicators of social status and success, as well as a boost to the French economy by promoting the luxury trades. For his own coronation, Napoleon commissioned Nitot to create a new set of crown jewels including a gold coronation crown, or Crown of Charlemagne, set with cameos after the ancient crown of France destroyed in the French Revolution. The name also denoted Napoleon's identification with the medieval king and Roman Emperor Charlemagne.

Napoleon was also responsible for reviving the tiara; it had been a fashionable form of headgear when wrought from gold and worn low on the forehead by the empresses of ancient Rome, and was consequently a symbol of imperial power. Nitot made the elaborately garlanded diamond diadems and tiaras with rosettes and scrolling laurel leaves worn for the coronation of 1804; they were such a gorgeous means of displaying authority that a fashionable trend for the headgear swept across Europe among the aristocracy. A diadem designed for Napoleon's wife, Josephine, one of the most fashionable ladies of Paris, contained coral cameos and pearls set in gold with a lapis lazuli inlay with a portrait of Napoleon at the center. Jewelry historian Diana Scarisbrick describes how "Napoleon's enthusiasm was so great that he did not scruple to authorize the removal of eighty-two cameos and intaglios from the state collection of the Cabinet des Médailles in 1808, which Nitot et Fils mounted with quantities of pearls into a tiara with matching necklace, belt, and bracelets. Unfortunately it proved too heavy for the Empress Josephine to wear, but she enjoyed taking the parure from its box and discussing the subjects of the cameos with her friends."

Nitot also modeled a dazzling diamond and ruby parure for Napoleon's second wife, the Empress Marie-Louise, who took the place of Josephine after she failed to produce an heir. It was made up of a diadem, crown, necklace, a pair of earrings, and bracelets set with twenty-four rubies and more than 500 diamonds, a girdle, and a comb. Nitot's jewelry had the effect Napoleon desired; Honoré de Balzac in *La Paix du Ménage* (1830) evocatively described how in the French court, "Diamonds glittered everywhere—so much so it seemed as if the entire wealth of the world were concentrated in the salons of Paris. Never had the diamond been so sought after."

Since 1780, Nitot's establishment has passed through nine generations of jewelers. In 1815, for example, Jean-Baptiste Fossin, the workshop director, took over from Nitot's son, François Regnault, with all the requisite connections for the royal clientele, having worked on the Napoleonic commissions. He introduced a more obviously naturalistic style using designs incorporating grapes, cherries, diamond ivy leaves, bulrushes, and hawthorn set *en tremblant*, that is on springs so that they quiver when the wearer moves. In 1843, a reporter from the fashion magazine *Les Modes Parisiennes* visiting the opera described seeing "a whole crop of red currants in the blond hair of a beautiful foreigner: each of the currants amidst the green leaves was set with a large ruby. There were branches of red currants covering her white gros de Naples dress." Fossin also introduced elements of Renaissance and Medieval Revivalism into the design including the *ferronière*, a chain worn low on the forehead with a drop at the center, and the coronet, a small crown constructed of jewels affixed on a metal ring.

Fossin's successor, Jean-Valentin Morel, journeyed to England after the revolution and, after opening a London branch, became jeweler to Queen Victoria. Joseph Chaumet took over the house and gave it its definitive name in 1885; it was a huge success and Chaumet went on to make fabulous jewelry for most of the royal courts of Europe, including their trademark tiaras. The bandeau, a derivation of the tiara constructed of two half-circles with no upright elements, was also popular, inspired by the portrait of Napoleon's sister, Princess Pauline Borghese, by Robert Lefèvre, which depicted the sitter wearing a neoclassical muslin gown of minimalist simplicity with a flat bandeau of opals and cameos trimmed with diamonds. One bandeau of 1897 in the Chaumet Collection in Paris has seven feathers atop the house's trademark knife-blade wires, so thin as to be almost invisible and designed to intermingle with the natural osprey plumes cleverly set to conceal the wires.

Chaumet's international audience included Indian princes such as the Maharajah of Indore, who developed a taste for the pleasures of Paris; many were connoisseurs of jewelry bringing their finest pieces to the Place Vendôme to have the stones reset in light, supple platinum settings. A roster of U.S. names came too; heiresses whose wealth derived from the railways and steel and oil industries, dubbed the "buccaneers" by author Edith Wharton for their ability to attract husbands from an impoverished aristocratic dynasty. Successful matches included Consuelo Vanderbilt to the ninth Duke of Marlborough, Jennie Jerome to Lord Randolph Churchill, May Goelet, the daughter of a New York real estate tycoon, to the eighth Duke of Roxburghe, and Maude Burke from San Francisco who married Sir Bache Cunard, the shipping magnate. Whether in Europe or the United States, any putative bride wanted a gown by Charles Frederick Worth and a tiara by Chaumet. Tiaras became more lightweight with the use of platinum, a metal that had both strength and rigidity so the quantity of material used in settings could be very much reduced. Platinum did not tarnish like silver so could be used to create delicate white pierced filigree settings, creating maximum sparkle. Such work became an exquisite souvenir taken back to New York and displayed at the city's most important social events, further spreading the reputation of the company.

Chaumet was a pioneer of the aigrette, a headpiece that has become a defining fashion of the Belle Époque. The aigrette mirrored the plumage of the egret, with a gem to the front in the manner of a maharajah, and caught on after the director Sergei Diaghilev's production of *Scheherazade* in 1910 featuring costumes by Léon Bakst. This theatrical extravaganza fired the imagination of many designers, including couturier Paul Poiret who was a key figure in the emerging modernity of the early twentieth century. Poiret was one of the first designers to realize that fashion could be a potent expression of femininity in a culture in transition, and played out his ideas on the glittering stage of haute couture. In his theatrical outfits women became sensual, exotic beings imbued with worldly desire, transformed, it seemed, almost overnight from staid Edwardian matrons into fleshy odalisques awaiting the attentions of their amour in an overheated Turkish harem.

The opening of Poiret's atelier on Rue Auber, Paris, in 1903, saw a host of historically inspired designs greet

"Diamonds glittered everywhere… it seemed as if the entire wealth of the world were concentrated in the salons of Paris."

Honoré de Balzac

an unsuspecting public. Neoclassical nymphs in empire-line, Directory-inspired tunics were followed by fiery Fauvist orange and shimmering silver kimono gowns in the manner of Diaghilev's Ballet Russes, a production that scandalized Paris in 1908. Poiret's gowns were shocking: they appeared to have no formal structure, no rigorously laced corsets underneath keeping warm flesh at bay; sensuality was in vogue. Wide-brimmed hats gave way to turbans and aigrettes worn with gold-tissue harem pants or the hobble skirt. A language of the aigrette developed: wearing a star marked one out as an intellectual heavyweight; ears of corn denoted a mother; a parrot was worn by the talkative; a butterfly was worn by a flirt.

Chaumet's aigrettes were the most spectacular, taking the form of huge diamond butterflies, crescent moons, ears of corn, or wings; one diamond waterfall aigrette of 1903 has drop diamonds cascading atop the head designed to shimmer among osprey plumes. From 1907 they were sold through Chaumet's flagship boutique at 12 Place Vendôme, designed by François-Joseph Bélanger, an architect who was given carte blanche to design premises of unparalleled luxury opposite the Ritz Hotel. The grand reception room was where the composer Chopin wrote his last Mazurka, *Opus 68 No. 4*, and now houses the Chaumet Museum.

In 1928 a new era for the house began when Marcel Chaumet took control and the Art Deco style began to dominate the design output. The Chaumet look became geometric and spectacular, with innovative designs using cushion-cut diamonds and diamond spacers; streamlined, articulated, pavé diamond-studded plaques that fitted flat to the wrist; and an onyx and diamond bandeau of monochromatic simplicity for the artist Romaine Brooks. Diamonds were set against rubies to create dramatic chromatic effects, and after Lord Carnarvon and Howard Carter's discovery of Tutankhamun's tomb in 1922, Egyptian symbols entered the visual language of Chaumet's wares. Diamond bandeaux were worn low on the brow, complementing the severe lines of the new bob haircut being snipped in the modernist salon of Antoine de Paris. Chaumet also looked to the Far East, India, and Persia for inspiration, using carved precious and semi-precious gems including emeralds, rubies, and sapphires.

Left: Chaumet was one of the first French haute joaillerie ateliers to pioneer Art Deco design such as this enamel, cultured pearl, diamond, and platinum brooch.

Below left: A Chaumet ring in black ceramic, white gold, and diamonds in a stunning modernist design. **Below:** The Chaumet headquarters houses the design studio, workshop, boutique, the Salon des Diadèmes, and the eighteenth-century Grand Salon, now an historic monument.

At the end of the decade, in 1929, Marcel Chaumet took over the business and it continued to thrive through the 1930s when naturalistic designs began to enter jewelry fashion. Tiaras were worn higher on the head akin to halos; Marina tiaras were de rigeur, named after the model worn by Princess Marina of Greece on her marriage to the Duke of Kent at Westminster Abbey in 1934, with its upstanding points like the rays of the sun. After World War II, the house continued its reputation as a pioneer of deluxe designs, and in 1976 Chaumet acquired the French jewelry house of Pierre Sterlé. Sterlé had been in business since 1934 in a workshop on Rue Sainte-Anne, and in 1945 moved to 43 Avenue de l'Opéra near the Place Vendôme. His refusal to display any jewels in the ground floor window gave his label the reputation of exclusivity, and Sterlé's baroque-inspired bird's wings, feathers, and exotic animals were seen only by a chosen few. After the house closed because of financial difficulties, Chaumet bought Sterlé's stock and he became their technical consultant.

Chaumet also had a successful foray into abstraction and began to experiment with textured surfaces and the creation of abstract pieces; artisanal hammered work appeared with unusual hard stones, such as jasper and crocidolite, set to appear as if they had been impressed into the gold or silver metalwork. The house remained a family firm until 1987 when Jacques and Pierre Chaumet filed for bankruptcy, and it was eventually acquired by LVMH in 1999. Chaumet scored a hit in the same decade with the Anneau ring, fashioned from tubular bands of white, yellow, and pink gold set with pavé stones. More recently, the house has become involved in human rights issues as a member of the Responsible Jewelry Council. Chaumet makes a point of sourcing ethical diamonds and supporting the environment—proceeds from the *Attrape-moi…si tu m'aimes* collection support the campaign for the plight of disappearing bees.

1784

JOHN SMEDLEY

In the late eighteenth century, the tiny village of Cromford in Derbyshire, England, was put on the map when northern industrialist Richard Arkwright realized the power and potential of Bonsall Brook and the local moor sough, or drainage ditch, that kept the nearby lead mines from flooding. In 1771 he built the first ever water-powered cotton-spinning mill, followed by Haarlem Mill in Wirksworth and Masson Mill in Matlock Bath in 1783. Labor was plentiful as a result of the decline in lead mining, and, as Arkwright's mills became more successful, he began enlarging Cromford to accommodate workers from outside the local community. A school, chapel, and hotel were built and soon the village became a thriving industrial town.

Just beyond Cromford Mill stood Lea Mills, a spinning complex built in 1784 on the grounds of a former flour mill that dated back to the twelfth century. Owner Peter Nightingale was Arkwright's former accountant and his great-niece Florence, a.k.a. the Lady with the Lamp, famously nursed soldiers in the Crimean War, and on her return gave welfare advice to the mill workers. Lea Mills was set on a hill next to Lea Bridge spanning a brook that was harnessed to power the machinery that span cotton, calico, and muslin and was also used to wash the cotton yarn. By the nineteenth century the mill specialized in the spinning and knitting of wool, and in 1818, worsted spinner and hosiery manufacturer John Smedley, from nearby Wirksworth, took over the lease after his own business had outgrown its premises. He began spinning and knitting hosiery, and later fine-gauge underwear, but it was not an immediate success as noted in his biography *The Smedleys of Matlock Bank* written by Henry Steer in 1897, because "new styles of goods at lower prices were introduced into the market, and the fame of 'Smedley's Hosiery' began to decline. To recover position, an effort was made to spin fine yarn for the Norwich trade, but the experiment failed, because the machinery proved to be unsuited to the work; and this attempt involved a considerable loss. Notwithstanding unwearied attention, the business continued to decline and in the year 1823 Mr. Smedley found himself in a state of insolvency."

His son—also John—took over in 1827, after the untimely death of his brother, George, led to his father's retirement, and he was determined to change the fortunes of the family. Young John Smedley knew the business well after having served as an apprentice for several years in the mill, and he began to expand by adapting the cotton machinery to manufacture fully fashioned knitted garments made from high-quality merino wool. It was a great success, and by 1840 Smedley had earned more than enough to retire to an estate in Cheltenham, although he still kept a hand in the business. He surprised his friends and family by marrying in 1846 and honeymooned in Switzerland. Unfortunately he became ill with a fever after sitting in a damp church and for some years tried to

Left: In the nineteenth century, John Smedley began to gain praise for its fully fashioned knitted garments made from high-quality merino wool. **Right:** Lea Mills, the home of the brand, is situated in the heart of Derbyshire's Peak District, and the colors of the surrounding countryside are reflected in Smedley's knitwear.

"It is necessary to spin good yarn in fact as
well as fable, and the success of the manufacturer
rests on this knowledge."

John Smedley promotional material, 1934

Below, clockwise from top left:
1. Run-on ribs, ready for transfer.
2. Cones of yarn used to knit garments. 3. A garment is pressed.
4. Dyeing cotton in the Dye House.

5. Setting up the frame for the knitting of fully fashioned garments. **Right:** Marking and cutting.

cure his poor health with traditional medicine but could find no cure. Eventually Smedley was persuaded to try a form of alternative medicine called hydropathy (hydrotherapy) administered by one Ben Rhydding in Yorkshire, a treatment involving hot and cold water plunges and baths that dates back to ancient Egypt and had enjoyed a revival in the nineteenth century.

John Smedley was so impressed by how hydropathy improved his own health that he moved back to Lea Mills and began experimenting with the remedial powers of water in the workplace. Steer describes, how "the ordinary business routine of the mills was, for a time, thrown into confusion. Everything was made to give way to experiments with the dripping sheet, the wet pack, the

douche, and so on; and everybody had to undergo some form of the treatment, whether he were ailing or not. Cattle, as well as human beings were experimented on, with more or less success." On the back of his investigations Smedley established a Free Hospital adjoining the mills with thirty beds where he administered his own brand of hydropathy with great success for twenty years. He became a fervent philanthropist, attempting to improve the health and welfare of his workforce by providing cheap beverages and porridge, mackintosh capes and galoshes for the young women who had to walk the 3 miles (4.8 km) back to Cromford after ten hours standing by the mule or doubling machine, and subsidized bread. He also gave his employees U.S. clocks to brighten

up their homes and keep them punctual. In 1853, Smedley decided to invest in his own hydro in Matlock Bath, and from small beginnings it grew into a huge barrack-like institution with hundreds of stained-glass windows inside and out, carpets so thick they were said to feel like moss under the feet, and an interior paneled in English oak and decorated with pillars of Siena marble. It remained internationally renowned well into the twentieth century as one of the first destination spas, and, at its height, it could accommodate 140 patients at any one time, including Robert Louis Stevenson, author of *Treasure Island* (1883), the essayist and artist Max Beerbohm, and composer Ivor Novello.

After selling up in Cheltenham, Smedley moved back to managing his beloved mill until his death in 1874 when his cousin, John Marsden Smedley, inherited the business, whose son, John Marsden Smedley Jr., took over on his father's death two years later. In 1922 the company began to create and manufacture fine-knit underwear in Sea Island cotton, a form of Egyptian cotton or *gossypium barbadense*, introduced to the West Indies from South America and famed for its silken fibers and high-tensile strength. This unique fiber, although cotton, had the feel of cashmere and the sheen of silk and was the yarn beloved by many members of the British royal family, including Queen Victoria whose handkerchiefs were made of the fabric and the trend-setting Duke of Windsor who was happy to let it be known that he was "a steady wearer of Sea Island cotton."

A fashion element also entered into Smedley's range of Sea Island underwear in response to the revolutionary changes in the fashionable silhouette. The *garçonne* androgyny expressed in the streamlined look of the flapper in the 1920s needed a new form of underwear that was physically free yet form fitting, as opposed to the rigid whale boning of the Edwardian corset. Smedley manufactured tubular fine-knit chemises with spaghetti straps that remained invisible under the sleeveless shifts that had become de rigeur for young women. In the 1930s, the company responded to the leisurewear boom, spurred on by the increasing popularity of sports, exercise, and fitness in the interwar period, by creating the Isis

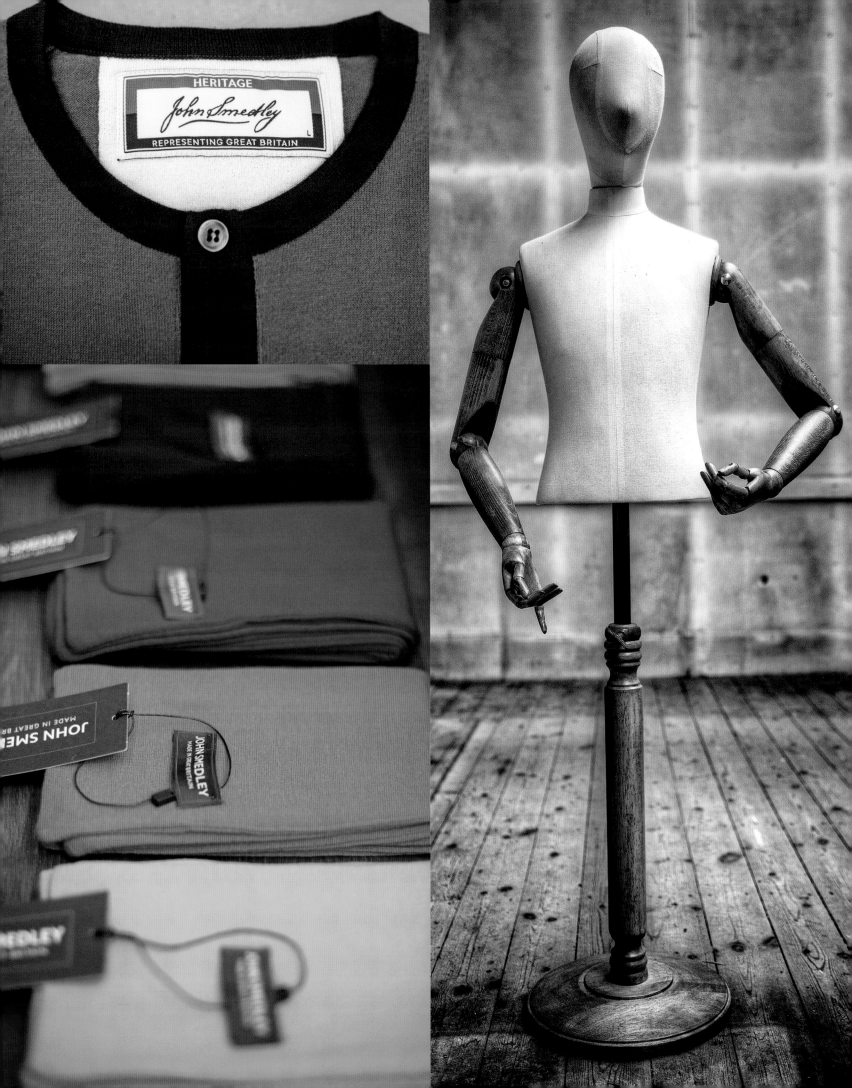

Left: John Smedley revives
knitwear designs from its own
extensive archive but is also a
company of innovation,
experimenting with new yarn and
manufacturing processes today.

JOHN SMEDLEY   41

polo shirt. This iconic item of menswear, again in Smedley's now-signature Sea Island cotton, was launched in 1932 and can be recognized by its unique single-piece knitted construction into which the solid-shaded vestee collar is attached and turned at the bottom to create a flat three-button opening. The Leander, a long-sleeved version of the classic polo, and the Pembroke, a long-sleeved turtleneck pullover, closely followed the Isis polo. The company outlined its philosophy as a commitment to quality as detailed in a document written in 1934, which ran: "It is necessary to spin good yarn in fact as well as fable, and the success of the manufacturer rests on this knowledge. He must not only know the very source of this material but supervise each process it undergoes from the beginning."

The John Smedley twinset dominated women's production in the 1950s; the classic combination of sweater and matching button-through cardigan was the epitome of elegance when worn with a string of pearls. British fashion designer Vivienne Westwood subverted its iconic appeal in 1986 when she commissioned Smedley to knit her own range with her World's End orb motif embroidered on the chest. Derbyshire-born Westwood was well aware of John Smedley's knitwear, an institution in the county, and her love for the company's products corresponded with her awakening of interest in traditional British brands and country clothing as shown in the Harris Tweed collections (Spring/Summer 1985, Fall/Winter 1987–88) which featured twinsets and harlequin leggings by Smedley. Westwood said: "I'm not really trying to be English—you can't avoid it, it's what you've absorbed. I do have fun knowing that I am doing it. I very much enjoy parody and this English sort of lifestyle… and I really am in love with the fabrics." In the same decade, John Smedley also knitted collections for Paul Smith, Comme des Garçons, Nicole Farhi, Margaret Howell, and Katharine Hamnett.

Lea Mills remains in the same picturesque stone Georgian building to this day, manufacturing the John Smedley brand with the factory bell pealing at the end of the worker's lunch break as it would have done more than 100 years ago. Generations of the same families make up the 400-plus workers who produce fine 24-gauge knitted garments up to superfine 30-gauge

of extremely high quality in fine-knit Merino wool imported from the sheep stations of New Zealand's South Island and Sea Island cotton knitted on Italian-made Protti flat bed machines. Every garment goes through rigorous quality control that tests the fastness of the color and any potential pilling. To prevent shrinkage, knits are washed for three one-hour cycles in the Smedley machines that are equal to twenty-seven washes in a domestic machine. The company says: "Washing is a vital part of our production process. We don't waste water or source it from dwindling resources. Instead the water comes from three underground springs that rise from the millstone grit of the Derbyshire Peak District National Park. Its softness and purity help create the luxurious feel of our garments and enhance the shrink resilience. We recognize that for future generations, we must do everything we can to keep the water pure and preserve it as a resource. Some of the water we use is recycled and used again to heat the mill, and strict processes are in place to make sure water that's returned to source is completely clean."

The garments may be knitted by machine but processes are also done by hand; the body panels and sleeves are hand linked then hand finished with a wooden former, steam pressed into shape, and, again with a flat iron before the neck trims, buttons, and labels are applied by hand. In 2011 the company launched the first of a series of capsule collections exclusively for women, comprised of more experimental pieces that challenged traditional knitwear design through the use of whole garment machines. The seamless knits designed in three dimensions were sculpted to mold to the body, pushing the boundaries of the knitting machine with the use of double layers, twisting, asymmetry, and drape in the manner of avant-garde designers such as Yohji Yamamoto and Rei Kawakubo. The result was eight individual seamless garments in black hand-finished merino wool, cashmere, and silk, including a trench coat, shrug, and turtleneck that could be worn individually or together.

In 2013 the Royal Warrant of Appointment was granted to John Smedley, the first in the company's history, by Queen Elizabeth II, who through her household, had been purchasing its fine knitwear for several years. It was a public acknowledgment of the excellence of John Smedley's knitted garments.

Overleaf, clockwise from top
left: 1. A close-up of a John Smedley sweater showing its smooth surface and meticulous weave. 2. The firm's ultra-fine knitwear undergoes a complex process using both hand and machine. 3. Close-up of a knitted New Zealand merino yarn in lime green. 4. Raw wool and cotton at the first stage of production.

Below: A print is made from the original painted design in order to transfer all the original design detail onto the shawl.

Right: A design in gouache on paper, *c.* 1900, shows a typical Pavlovsky Posad combination of a bright floral design on black.

1795
PAVLOVSKY POSAD

The Pavlovsky Posad shawl factory is more than 200 years old and is one of heritage fashion's greatest survivors—the Russian Revolution, two world wars, and Perestroika have not succeeded in closing its doors. The original business was founded in 1795 by farmer Ivan Dmitriev in the town of Pavlovo near Moscow. The choice of town was significant for it had grown from a monastic village to become an important center of silk weaving and many weavers were already settled there; by the 1780s there were fifteen textile mills manufacturing silk products of various kinds in Pavlovo, for it held a strategic position at the junction of the Vokhna and Klyazma rivers.

Dmitriev's concern was for the manufacture of silk shawls "of middle end," or moderate skill, and his enterprise was small-scale, a workshop employing twelve women silk weavers who crafted handmade shawls in very limited quantities. By 1812, the firm passed to Dmitriev's descendant Semen Ivanovich Labzin and through to Labzin's sons Yeremey, Andrey, and Ivan. By the time Dmitriev's son, Yakov Labzin, and his assistant Vasiliy

Gryaznov took over the enterprise in the late 1840s, the workshop had become a mill and the family was the wealthiest in Pavlovo.

The pioneering pair introduced the Jacquard loom into the factory, which mechanized the weaving process and, because it could produce elaborate designs in intricate weaves, made possible a larger output of fine woolen shawls and babushka, or head scarves, in wool, cotton, and silk. The shawls that date from this time tend to be made with a cotton warp and a woolen weft and are decorated with Far Eastern or Turkish carpetlike designs in natural vegetable-dyed tones that were in vogue all over Europe. By 1861, the business employed printers, engravers, three colorists, and three artists, Ivan Ivanov (Ivanov), Michaila Ilyin Sudyin, and Ivan Vasilievich Sorokin. Their work began to win awards at international fairs, and in 1861 Yakov Labzin was appointed as supplier to the Grand Duchess Alexandra Petrovna. Vasiliy Gryaznov was also a true philanthropist and saw the factory not only as a place of employment but also as a means of helping the poor; to this end, the factory complex housed a hospital and an almshouse for sixty people, and funded several local schools.

By the 1870s, Eastern motifs began to combine with more naturalistic forms, and flowers began to dominate the pattern design. The designs were printed manually onto the fabric of the shawls, a laborious process that involved crafting blocks from maple, lime, or pear wood and carving the required pattern in relief on one side; the pattern was covered with dye and pressed or block-printed onto the fabric. The *manera* printed the outline and the *tsvetkas* contributed the colored infill; each color needed a separate block and up to 400 applications of color had to be made. The shawl was then sent to the

zrelnya, a humid room that fixed the colors, followed by the *zaparnya* or steam room, and it was then trimmed and fringed. Fringed shawls were an indispensable fashion item in Russia worn by rich and poor alike by day and night, even in the ballroom, and they were originally imported from the Far East. The Dmitriev factory's distinctive large black shawls with a lush perimeter design of luminously bright flowers printed with dyes created in secret by Nikolay Andreyevich Andreyev became popular, and the late nineteenth century was a successful period for the company. The mill became the largest manufacturer of shawls in Russia and by the early 1900s employed 2,000 workers.

From 1918 to 1919, all the factories in Pavlovo were nationalized, including Gryaznov's mill, and due to the shortage of raw materials the main products were made of cotton while woolen shawls were made of old pre-

Below: Boris Mikhailovich Kustodiev (1878–1927) shows how the shawl became an indicator of status in Russia in his painting of a provincial merchant's wife.

Right: Four Pavlovsky Posad shawl designs display how the use of ornate botanical motifs saturate the surface of the wool, allowing little of the ground color to show through.

"We are moving ahead with the times, but some key decorative elements remain unchanged, like our trademark rose."
Elena Zhukhova

revolutionary yarn, until the supply ran out in the 1920s. Socialist Realism began to have its effect, and sheaves of wheat, sickles, and tractors appeared in the prints as propaganda for the Russian people. Despite the traditional flower ornament being decried as a bourgeois conceit, the mill kept the botanical designs in production including designs by N. S. Postigov, N. I. Chudin, and K. Ye. Abolikhin. Stylized animals appeared in the 1930s designs; one unusual design of 1937 has a repeated motif of a leopard's head and paws radiating from its center.

During World War II, the factory was turned over to the manufacture of fabrics for the uniforms of the Red Army, but was back to producing wool shawls by the early 1950s, designed by Yevgeniy Ivanovich Shtykhin and Yekaterina Petrovna Regunova. New color variants were introduced in the 1960s, including brightly colored grounds of crimson, claret, green, and turquoise. In the 1970s, subjects were taken from Georgian chasing and the brightly colored ornaments on pottery from the Carpathians. Screen printing was introduced, which although still done by hand, obviated the need for the carved wooden blocks and was less time-consuming and expensive. At the end of the 1960s, Buzer printing machines were imported from Switzerland allowing more ornate compositions and innovative designs, and a new spirit entered the vocabulary of design; bold, dynamic patterns were devised by artists such as Z. A. Olshevskaya and E. P. Regunova, whose goal was to create a shawl whose design was "not tedious… and look(ed) like a Persian carpet, at which one is looking and is always finding something new, and a kerchief must leave the impression similar to the sight of the sea, which never makes one feel tired."

Today the work created at Pavlovsky Posad is regarded as important folk art in Russia. Every year, designs are created by artists from the Pavlovo Posad school of shawl

design, who use a combination of traditional designs and new compositions in gouache, which are vetted by a panel represented by the Ministry of Culture and the Council of Folk Crafts for the Moscow region. Once a design is affirmed, colorists make up recipes for the dyes that exactly replicate the tones used in the design. The dyes have to be applied to the fabric, then fixed with steam, and washed to make sure that the colors are identical to the design. Lyubov Pylnova, a master at the factory's printing workshop explains, "For each design that is going to be printed on a shawl, we make a set of stencils. The colors are printed onto the fabric separately, one by one. Up to twenty different colors are usually used for a single shawl, so it's quite a complicated process." The design is printed onto natural fabric that has been woven in the mill either

manually or with a series of automatic printing carriages on print tables. The knotted fringing remains hand-crafted by the new generation of weavers. Nadezhda Totoshkina, who has been working at the factory for more than twenty years says, "Machines can't do everything. It takes a lot of practice, but for me it was easy because both my grandparents and my parents worked here. We even had special weaving and knitting lessons at school to learn the trade."

The factory is unique in that it follows a complete production cycle and 80 percent of its sales are still to Russian people. Painter Elena Zhukhova says, "When we create new designs, inspiration is important but knowledge and experience are even more so—because these shawls are all about traditions that we have to respect."

NINETEENTH CENTURY

At the end of the eighteenth century, Anglomania invaded Europe after the French Revolution marked an end to the ostentatious fashions of the Versailles court. The great English sartorial tradition was consolidated during this period by tailors such as Jonathan Meyer, Gyula Schultz, and John Weston emphasizing the importance of cut, the bucolic sporting tradition influencing dress, and the celebrated figure of George "Beau" Brummell establishing an etiquette for menswear. During this period, key names emerged situated around specific city areas known for the best bespoke, including the Place Vendôme in Paris and Savile Row and St. James's Street in London.

Left: A nineteenth-century Louis-heeled shoe by John Lobb.

Left, clockwise from top left:
1. A *schusterei* or cobbler working
at Scheer's street-level atelier and
workshop. 2. The sewing of the
upper. 3. A collection of vintage

Scheer lasts. 4. The welt
is meticulously hand-sewn.
Below: A high-collared, tasseled
slip-on shoe with a hand-stitched
inset of thin black calf leather.

51

1816
RUDOLF SCHEER & SÖHNE

Vienna remains a city of magical bespoke ateliers that have survived the most cataclysmic events in European history. From Knize's impeccable tailoring, which has been rivaling the best of London's Savile Row since 1858, through to Mühlbauer, a milliner that has been in existence since 1903, this stimulating city, like Paris, New York, and Milan, has always catered to a population of sophisticates, which over the past 200 years has included composers Mozart and Mahler, artists Egon Schiele and Gustav Klimt, and the father of psychoanalysis Sigmund Freud. Although style has become homogenized in most global cities, indigenous brands still survive in Vienna, a city close to the former Iron Curtain, and its relative isolation until the 1990s may have allowed vernacular fashion to flourish.

Rudolf Scheer & Söhne is a heritage Viennese firm steeped in tradition and it has been making shoes since 1816. Markus Scheer is the seventh generation of the family to run the business, and, as he puts it: "Whatever happened, world wars, whatever… the one thing we always thought of was shoes." Scheer's bespoke shoe shop resides in a grand red ocher *Gründerzeit,* or mid-nineteenth century house, on the Bräunerstraße in the center of Vienna, identifiable by its gilt lettering and window full of wooden lasts. It inspires reverence on entry with its thick carpeting, eighteenth-century frescoes, and hushed tones, for Scheer is a name only for those in the know, understandable because the firm only produce 300 pairs of bespoke shoes per year and has a long and illustrious history with both kaisers and kings buying their calf leather shoes.

The original founder, Johann Scheer, came from a family of Viennese wine growers; since the twelfth century, each district of the city worked its own vineyards, and by the sixteenth century they were supplying the popular *Heurigen,* or wine taverns. An imperial edict allowed growers to serve food with their wine but as the city expanded, many of the vineyards were lost to development. Johann saw no future in the family vineyard and retrained as a shoemaker, setting himself up in business in 1816 in the 3rd district of the city, now known as the Landstraße. In 1837, the business was taken over by his son, Matthias Scheer, and in 1840 relocated to Praterstraße in the 2nd district, the street where Johann Strauss lived and wrote *The Blue Danube* (1866). After studying in Paris, Johann's grandson Rudolf Scheer joined the firm in a newly erected building in 1866 in its present location on Bräunerstraße.

Rudolf Scheer began crafting bespoke shoes at a time when the asymmetric last had revolutionized the trade at the beginning of the nineteenth century. During the Age

of Enlightenment, philosophers such as Jean-Jacques
Rousseau advocated the notion of the "noble savage,"
the primitive state of man before he was fettered by
civilization. He began to advocate the reform of dress,
deriding, in particular, the physically restricting practice
of tight-lacing. The cult of the "natural" was applied
to the foot, and shoemakers began to study the foot's
anatomy rather than using standardized wooden lasts
that approximated the dimensions of the foot, with
no distinction being made between right and left.
The asymmetric last took into consideration the actual
measurements of both feet and was the route to the
custom-fit bespoke shoe.

In 1873, Scheer won the Gold Medal at the World's
Fair in Vienna, followed by the same prestigious award in
1880; he began to make bespoke footwear for Viennese
aristocrats and his shoes appeared in the royal houses of
Germany, Greece, Serbia, and Romania. Scheer's best-
known customer was Emperor Franz Joseph I, who
remained on the Hapsburg throne for sixty-eight years.
He was a traditionalist who loved to hunt but refused to
use telephones or elevators, and also had a well-known
fondness for well-polished shoes. In 1878, after both
Franz Josef and the German Kaiser Wilhelm patronized
Scheer, Rudolf was made imperial and royal shoemaker
to the Austro-Hungarian Imperial Court and supplied
the chestnut-brown leather boots for the officers of the
imperial army. Today, the Viennese firms that were
picked to provide for the court because of the quality of
their goods have *K.U.K Hoflieferant*, or Royal Warrant of
Appointment, emblazoned on their shop fronts; before
the empire collapsed after World War I there were more

than 500 official purveyors to the royal court in Vienna.
Today only a few, including Scheer, survive.

In 1899, Rudolf Scheer's sons, Karl and Edmund,
became involved in the running of the company, and it
underwent a name change to Rudolf Scheer & Söhne.
The company survived World War II by specializing in
orthopaedic products and it continues to prosper. Today,
prospective customers climb a wooden staircase to the first
floor where Markus Scheer is on hand to personally take
the measurements of the client's foot before making the
first rough cast of the last; the bespoke shoe is then
assembled by hand from more than 200 component
pieces. Every pair requires three fitting sessions and takes
sixty hours to create, with all processes carried out by
hand down to the ritual fifteen bouts of buffing with
crème applied to the finished shoe. All Scheer's shoes are
made on location in central Vienna and the limited output
is a purposeful strategy to ensure that their stratospheric
standards are kept. Customers from all over the world can
also send their shoes through the post to be polished. The
choice of leather is extraordinary, including antique calf
and crocodile skins that are more than 100 years old, and
recent commissions include a pair of zebra-skin loafers.

The elegant premises that housed the earlier generations
of the family who lunched on the table where the shoes
are now polished recently opened their doors to another
audience. In 2012, Markus Scheer revived the house's
reputation for hospitality by extending and renovating
the ground floor and launched Scheer Wining & Dining,
with chefs Otto Bayer and Bojan Brbre blending the rich
aromas of leather and fine food, and guests' conversations
punctuated by the sound of the artisans' hammers.

"Whatever happened, world wars, whatever... the one thing we always thought of was shoes."

Markus Scheer

1818
BROOKS BROTHERS

The year 1818 was a significant moment in U.S. history: four years earlier, during a sweltering summer, the British army had made its way into Washington from Chesapeake Bay. The invasion was strategic; by burning and looting the president's city, the British thought they would quash the spirit of an upstart colony. Having arrived at Capitol Hill, the army began to target any of Washington's public buildings that had a connection with the government, and as the flames of destruction lit up the sky they marched on the White House, looting its contents and gutting the interior. When the refurbished White House opened its doors four years later, it was a symbolic step toward U.S. independence. The country was shaking itself free of colonial restraint and inventing its own traditions, including the sartorial—for this was the year of the founding of Brooks Brothers, the United States' oldest clothing retailer. The original business was set up on the northwest corner of Catharine and Cherry Street in New York on the site of the former residence of Dr. David Brooks, born in Stratford, Connecticut, in 1747. After he

died of yellow fever, his son, Henry Sands Brooks, opened the first clothing store, H. & D. Brooks & Co., with the slogan, "Makers and Merchants in One."

Brooks believed that by making and retailing products in one business he could ensure the highest quality, and by 1833 the concept had taken off to such an extent that he asked for the assistance of his sons to help run the business. After Henry's death in the same year, his eldest son, Henry Jr., took charge and remained so until 1850, when his younger brothers, Daniel, John, Elisha, and Edward, assumed control and changed the name to Brooks Brothers. A company logo was developed in the form of a golden fleece hanging with a ribbon around its stomach, taken from a medieval chivalric order and dating back to the ancient Greek myth of Jason and the Argonauts who won the original fleece from Phrixus. In 1430, Philip III of Burgundy founded the Order of the Golden Fleece to celebrate his marriage to Infanta Isabella of Portugal, and knights wore a regal chain from which hung a sheep, a logo that indicated Philip's erudition and

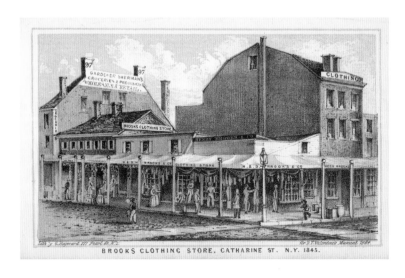

BROOKS CLOTHING STORE, CATHARINE ST. N.Y. 1845.

Left: This illustration from 1845 depicts the original H. & D. Brooks & Co. clothing store on the corner of Catharine and Cherry Street, New York. **Above, from left to right:** Daniel, John, Elisha, and Edward Brooks—the original Brooks brothers, who developed their father's brand from 1850. **Right:** A classic Brooks Brothers jacket, shirt, and tie combination.

ESTABLISHED 1818

Top: The Brooks Brothers flagship store opened on Madison Avenue, New York, in 1915. **Above:** The emphasis is on quality control in a photograph taken in a Brooks Brothers tie workshop in the 1940s.

Right: Brooks Brothers created 500 1920s-inspired looks for *The Great Gatsby* (2013), based on its archives. In this movie still, Leonardo DiCaprio wears the ivory linen jacket and pants.

vast wealth from trading in wool. It became the tradition for English traders in wool to hang the same icon outside their shops or to have it stamped into tokens as a symbol of their trade. The Brooks family understandably enjoyed the ancient regal and sartorial connotations of the fleece, for U.S. menswear was taking many of its cues from English style, and it would be an astute business decision to associate its firm with such fine traditions. The symbol of the golden fleece also expressed the Brooks' commitment to sourcing the best of European and colonial products, including Saxony, flannel, and worsted cloth; Isle of Harris tweed in 1900; fine cotton check or Madras from India in 1902; the Shetland sweater in 1904; and crinkled Indian seersucker in the 1920s.

In 1849, Brooks Brothers led the way in what was to be a revolution in menswear: the ready-made suit, made for businessmen too busy to wait for bespoke, which was sold through the original New York store and a large premises that opened on Broadway in 1859. The editors of *Carroll's New York City Directory* publicly recognized the ready-made and how the family firm was "the first to embark on that which is now a leading commercial pursuit." In the same year a Brooks Brothers advertisement ran, "At either of these establishments the above firm keep always on hand a large and carefully selected stock of Ready-Made clothing, together with a great variety of furnishing goods, including every requisite for a Gentleman's wardrobe… Citizens and strangers will find here an attractive and convenient place to purchase clothing."

The advert also specified that Brooks Brothers made army uniforms, at the time a profitable business opportunity, and patrons included Generals Grant and Sherman. However, in 1863 it was to prove a problem after Congress passed a bill to draft men to fight in the American Civil War. This directly affected working men rather than wealthy men, who were allowed to pay a commutation fee of $300 to exempt themselves from military service by hiring another man as a substitute. The workers of New York felt betrayed, and the city became the focus of one of the United States' largest civil insurrections, which lasted from July 13 to July 16, with angry mobs ransacking public buildings and any businesses connected with the war. Brooks Brothers was targeted as it was known to supply Union uniforms, and, according to *Harper's Weekly*, "a large number of marauders paid a visit to the extensive clothing store of Messrs. Brooks Brothers, at the corner of Catharine and Cherry Streets. Here they helped themselves to such articles as they wanted, after which they might be seen dispersing in all directions." The next night there was concern that the same fate would befall the Broadway store, but guarded by a twelve-year old boy named Francis G. Lloyd, among others, it remained intact. Forty years later, Lloyd would be admirably rewarded by becoming the first person outside of the family to lead the firm. The American Civil War came to an end on April 14, 1865, when John Wilkes Booth, an actor and Confederate sympathizer, fatally shot President Abraham Lincoln at Ford's Theater in Washington, D.C., five days after the Confederate General Robert E. Lee surrendered his army. Lincoln was wearing a Brooks Brothers greatcoat with a hand-embroidered lining depicting an eagle and the inscription, "One country, one destiny."

In 1884, the company moved into new premises on the southeast corner of Broadway and 22nd Street, incorporating the old Catharine and Cherry Street business, and all of Brooks Brothers merchandising was consolidated under one roof. Brooks Brothers was run as a copartnership with members of the family on the board of directors, and sales offices opened in Newport, Rhode Island, and Boston. In 1915, the flagship store opened on Madison Avenue and began selling lines of garments that have now become iconic pieces of U.S. menswear, including the button-down shirt, discovered, as the story goes, when John E. Brooks, grandson of the founder, attended a polo match in England in 1896. The sport of polo was an elite activity with elegant gear to match, and the slimline silhouette that developed apparently included a collar with button-down ends to prevent the player being distracted when galloping full pelt. John Brooks saw its neat appeal and applied the collar to a standard shirt, creating a garment that ushered in the end of separate shirts and collars and has sold in its millions. However, as the English polo shirt typically does not have a button-down collar, it has been suggested that English tailors put out this story to discredit the all-American invention. Dancer Fred Astaire wore the 346 model of

button-down shirt by Brooks Brothers under his bespoke Anderson & Sheppard suits, creating a cool transatlantic style, and he continued his own fashionable improvisation by wearing a collar pin across the wings. When Andy Warhol received his first paycheck in 1955 for a series of illustrations he had created for shoe retailer I. Magnin, he spent it on 100 identical white Brooks Brothers shirts.

In 1901 the Number One, or Sack suit, entered Brooks Brothers' repertoire following a trend among college students to press back the lapels of their single-breasted, three-button jackets to ape the line of the two-button and to show off their neckties. The Number One jacket had a natural unpadded shoulder line with loosely fitted armholes, no vertical seams to give a fitted waist (hence the term "sack"), one vent at the back, and a third button that had no functional purpose. The accepted practice was to only close the center button of the jacket; today this vestige appears in authentic Sack jackets as the top button is pressed into the lapel so it cannot be buttoned up. The pants sat high on the hips, worn shorter than their European counterparts, and could be ordered with or without pleats.

The repp, or tightly woven ribbed silk tie, was also given a makeover by the firm in 1902; this conservative, clubby tie hung around the necks of the English gentry

"Many grown men would feel uncouth if they ever had to appear in public without their Brooks Brothers suit."

Vance Packard in *The Status Seekers*

Left: Brooks Brothers garments are made with the highest standards of craftmanship and materials. Their Golden Fleece suits have full canvas construction, linen under collars, horn buttons, and hand-sewn buttonholes. **Below left:** Brooks Brothers Fall 2012 display at the Madison Avenue store.

with pride and proclaimed the membership of military battalions, public schools, and gentlemen's clubs. The stripes ran on a high diagonal at left to low on the right, or "heart to sword"; Brooks Brothers democratized the look and thumbed its nose at English etiquette by reversing the direction of the stripes, although Robert Gieves at Gieves & Hawkes thinks the reason behind this change is more prosaic: "European tie makers cut the material with the surface uppermost, while Americans cut on the back." The repp tie became a staple of the Ivy League wardrobe and was followed by the block-printed silk foulard in 1908 and the polo coat in 1910. In the 1920s, Brooks Brothers became the first U.S. retailer to manufacture argyle socks for men; by the early 1930s the first lightweight summer suits made of cotton corduroy and seersucker were introduced. In 1953, wash-and-wear shirts made from a blend of Dacron, polyester, and cotton were launched under the brand name Brooksweave, and the Brooks Brothers look epitomized the U.S. businessman so much so that sociologist Vance Packard wrote in *The Status Seekers* (1959), "Many grown men would feel uncouth if they ever had to appear in public without their Brooks Brothers suit." When the television series *Mad Men,* set in an early 1960s advertising agency on Madison Avenue, premiered in 2007, Brooks Brothers supplied bespoke suits for the character of Don Draper and created its own *Mad Men* Edition slim-cut medium gray sharkskin suit with side vents in collaboration with the show's costume designer, Janie Bryant.

The Ivy League look as exemplified by Brooks Brothers became a popular trend in Europe in the 1960s, known as the "Kennedy look" in France, and became a source of inspiration for the mod subculture in Britain. Hallmarks of the European take on Ivy League included the Brooks Brothers button-down shirt, three-button seersucker jacket, and Bass Weejun penny loafers.

Abraham Lincoln was not the only great U.S. figure to be clothed by the company: in the 1920s F. Scott Fitzgerald wore its button-down shirts; aviator Charles Lindbergh touched down in France after crossing the Atlantic wearing a Brooks Brothers suit loaned to him by the U.S. ambassador; cinematic idol Clark Gable bought many a loosely woven cotton or Oxford shirt with a split yoke to fit his 44-inch chest; and in 1953, John F. Kennedy married Jacqueline Lee Bouvier in a Brooks

Brothers suit. In 1949, a woman's shirt in pink was launched as the company realized how many female Ivy League students were wearing items of men's clothing. Pink was not a color unknown to the company—a male shirt of the same hue had been introduced in 1900 but went largely unnoticed until women adopted it—and by 1955, men had begun to wear pink Brooks Brothers shirts, too, as a contrast to their charcoal gray Sack suits. Women could also now shop in Brooks Brothers at a counter discreetly set at the rear of the male floor and, wrote *Time* in 1955, "given this opening, more and more women have encroached upon the whole store, greedily discovering other items of male apparel that they can take over for themselves," including polo coats, silk dressing gowns, and mufflers.

The first international Brooks Brothers store opened in Aoyama, Tokyo, in 1979 and the firm continued to retain its old-school Ivy League reputation. In 2001, Brooks Brothers was purchased by long-term customer Claudio Del Vecchio of Retail Brand Alliance, and began looking into its back catalog and mixing U.S. heritage with an Italian fashion sensibility that included the launch of the Regent in 2006, a suit with a slimmer silhouette and narrower lapel; the Black Fleece collections designed in collaboration with Thom Browne; and the Fitzgerald, named after John Fitzgerald Kennedy, in 2008. In the same year, another iconic moment for the firm occurred when President Barack Obama wore a Brooks Brothers black cashmere topcoat, black leather gloves, and a burgundy cashmere scarf at his swearing-in, making him the thirty-ninth of forty-four sitting presidents to wear the company's clothes. Much of the firm's production is still in the United States in Haverhill, Massachusetts, with the silk for its popular repp ties imported from England or Italy and cut and piled in Long Island, New York; many of its shirts are manufactured at the Brooks Brothers shirt factory in Garland, North Carolina, and it has a higher-end label in the Golden Fleece line, featuring suits that are hand-tailored in the United States. The no-iron made-to-measure dress shirt was recently put to a test by the executive editor of *Best Life* magazine, "during a workday that included two hour-long commutes, a handful of meetings, and a rather unfortunate sprint through a rainstorm. After twelve hours, it had nary a wrinkle."

1830
JAMES SMITH & SONS

The following two lines from Jonathan Swift's evocative poem of 1710, "A Description of a City Shower," are significant because they are one of the earliest descriptions of a British umbrella:

"The tuck'd up seamstress walks with hasty strides,
While streams run down her oiled umbrella's sides."

The early umbrella would have been an unwieldy object with a canopy constructed from oiled silk set with baleen or whalebone ribs that habitually lost their flexibility and cracked when drying. It was also a weighty affair, difficult to lug around because of its thick wooden shaft and handle, and owners were deemed of low status, too poor to pay for a hansom cab in a downpour. All in all, the umbrella was regarded as a useless and rather frivolous woman's accessory, since "real" men could cope with a spot of rain.

Such strong associations with class and femininity are perhaps why the first men to carry umbrellas in public

Left: Staff in the doorway of James Smith & Sons' Victorian premises, photographed in 1976. **Right:** In 1857, James Smith opened premises on New Oxford Street, London, where it remains today with the original nineteenth-century frontage.

were exposed to much ridicule on the streets. The English explorer and philanthropist Jonas Hanway, whose portrait hangs on the wall in James Smith & Sons because of the important role he played in popularizing the umbrella, was openly jeered at in London around 1760 after copying the men of Persia whom he had seen using umbrellas while on his travels. Despite this, Hanway continued to use one for thirty years. In 1770, a footman, John Macdonald, appeared with a fine oiled silk umbrella that he had bought from Spain and was accosted with the cry, "Frenchman, why don't you get a coach?", suggesting that his accessory was foppish, cheap, and unmanly. However, in the aftermath of the French Revolution, when the trappings of aristocracy were decried as having been achieved at the expense of the poor, the umbrella became a symbol of masculine republicanism—here was a man who walked the city streets rather than speeding by the hoi polloi in the shelter of his carriage, and the cultural meaning of the umbrella subtly shifted to that of a visible symbol of middle-class respectability carried by a new class of businessman. In 1855, William Sangster wrote a paean to just such an umbrella owner, *Umbrellas and Their History,* in which he exalted the umbrella carrier as an upstanding man of impeccable character: "There is something about the umbrella which stamps its wearer with a peculiar, and surely may we call it, exalted character; such men, we feel certain at the first glance, are not addicted to dissipation, nor do they yield to the seductions of the casino: they are essentially family men; and just as the baton is the symbol of the field-marshal, the truncheon of our police, so is the umbrella the distinguishing mark of the respectable paterfamilias."

Umbrellas were originally known as "Robinsons" after Daniel Defoe's account of the shipwreck survivor, *Robinson*

Crusoe, was published in 1719, in which a primitive umbrella is fashioned by Crusoe from goatskin with the hair set outward for waterproofing, "so that it cast off the rain like a penthouse"; by the end of the eighteenth century the term "umbrella" was the more popular desriptor after the Latin *umbra,* meaning shade or shadow. The use of gingham and lighter silks made umbrellas easier to carry, and the extensive British colonies supplied the necessary materials, including whalebone, horn ivory, and bamboo cane. As umbrellas became more widespread, it was felt that owners also needed a little push when it came to etiquette. In 1809, John Shute Duncan categorized the worst offenders in *Hints to the Bearers of Walking-Sticks and Umbrellas* as fencers, twirlers, arguers, and unicorns who hold their sticks out to poke people from the front. He was also prepared to make himself

available at the Lyceum in the Strand, London, "for the purpose of drilling ladies and gentlemen in the approved method of handling walking-sticks and umbrellas with a view to individual grace and general convenience."

In the nineteenth century, the construction of the umbrella vastly improved as a result of the introduction of the steel Fox frame invented by Samuel Fox in 1848 in the village of Stocksbridge near Sheffield, the center of the world's steel industry. Fox was a skilled drawer of wire, a worker who could pull the most slender filament for needles and fish hooks, and he hit upon the idea of manufacturing steel ribs for umbrellas. The Fox steel frame took over from whalebone and the lightweight yet durable umbrella was born; the inventor continued finessing his product up to 1913 when his son, William Henry Fox, joined him under the Paragon brand. William

Left: Umbrella handles are fashioned from the traditional wood and antiqued silver, or can be surmounted with a carved figural or molded-resin head.

Below left: The interior of James Smith & Sons with canes, sticks, and umbrellas displayed in the original Victorian mahogany shop fittings.

JAMES SMITH & SONS   63

Sangster responded enthusiastically to this new invention, writing, "At present it is generally allowed that a good steel-rib umbrella can be as easily procured as a carefully tempered razor or sword. Mr. Fox's Paragon frame, simple in its construction, half the weight of whalebone, but equally strong, is admitted to be the greatest improvement yet introduced in the manufacture of an umbrella. The ribs are made in the form of a trough with flat sides, by which shape the greatest amount of strength is obtained. The same principle, as is well known, has been successfully applied in the construction of the Great Tubular Bridge over the Menai Straits, from which Mr. Fox took the idea."

The first umbrella manufacturer to use the Fox frame was the esteemed establishment of James Smith & Sons, which opened in Foubert Place in London's West End in 1830. Under the aegis of the first James Smith, umbrellas were manufactured at the back of the shop and sold to customers at the front. After a few years, his son and heir, James Smith Jr., emigrated to Tasmania with two of his sons to become a farmer, leaving the rest of his family, including six sons and a daughter, to run the business. In 1857, the shop moved to premises in New Oxford Street, after the Fox frame was added to the production process. A smaller premises opened near Savile Row, catering to a respectable clientele including Prime Ministers William Gladstone and Andrew Bonar Law, and Lord Curzon Viceroy of India, and in 1930, the great grandson of the original founder moved back from Tasmania to take over the running of the business. After a road-building program forced a change of venue to New Burlington Street, the second James Smith & Sons establishment remained open until being bombed during the Blitz. The New Oxford Street shop continued selling umbrellas throughout the twentieth century, in addition to gentlemen's canes, maces, and swagger sticks, a short cane originally used by officers to direct military drills developed into a symbol of military authority and had a silver top engraved with the regimental insignia. In the 1950s, silk, alpaca, and oiled cotton canvas canopies were replaced by nylon, and this lightweight yet strong material was an immediate success. It led to an end of the mildew that crept up on umbrellas that were furled up when still damp, and had a surface that could be printed on, paving the way for the huge and multihued golf umbrella.

Today New Oxford Street itself may have moved on from its Victorian cobbles and horse-drawn carriages, but the nineteenth-century exterior and original shop fittings of James Smith & Sons remain untouched, with walking sticks stowed away in wicker baskets and umbrellas with carved resin animal-head handles kept upright in solid oak stands. In the basement of the same premises, umbrellas are handmade and, if required, fitted with bespoke frames measured to suit the height of the customer, and there is also a repair service for those that return. Handles are fashioned from an array of materials, including the traditional wood, porcelain, and antiqued silver that can be engraved with the customer's personal monogram, or they can even be surmounted with a carved duck, cat, parrot head, or silver skull. Finishings other than the usual ferrule include engraved silver collars and tassels for the more adventurous. Walking sticks in the traditional shepherd's crook or hooked Derby style can be cut to length on site, and made-to-order styles include a drinking stick that houses two glasses and a flask or a briarwood pipe. There is a successful overseas market for James Smith & Sons's wares too, particularly for ceremonial umbrellas in West Africa that have made up the king's regalia since the eighteenth century; Victorian photographs show the kings of the states of Ashanti, Benin, Sokoto, and Dahomey conducting royal business from beneath a large umbrella. This specialist market notwithstanding, the best seller at the shop remains the classic black city eight-rib umbrella with its strong steel frame, slim shaft, whangee cane handle, and metal ferrule. This classic British item from such a prestigious address as James Smith & Sons is much sought after, and these days, as the assistant points out, "it is inadvisable to lend your James Smith umbrella to even your closest friend. Give them our address instead."

"The tuck'd up seamstress walks with hasty strides, While streams run down her oiled umbrella's sides."
Jonathan Swift in "A Description of a City Shower"

1836
MAZARIN GRAND FAISEUR

The word "sock" is derived from the Latin *soccus*, or light shoe, and is one of the earliest known items of dress, dating back to AD 300. The first socks were fashioned from animal skins tied around the ankles for protection and warmth; Romans used felted skin and woven cloth cut on the bias so as to wrap around the lower leg. Hand-knitted socks were found in Egypt as far back as the twelfth century, and the process of construction speeded up with the invention of the first knitting machine in 1589. Socks were made from wool, cotton, and silk, and, from 1938 onward, blended nylon. The changes in sock style occurred in the early twentieth century when a distinction began to be made between the casual and formal sock; black silk was considered appropriate for evening, and by day casual patterned,

striped, or spotted socks were worn. The fashion for knickerbockers as started by Albert Edward, Prince of Wales, a.k.a. "Bertie" at the turn of the century, displayed a degree of male calf and by the 1920s argyle had become the most popular sock pattern.

Today there is definitive sock etiquette; any man who wants to get on in the world should sport the "executive-length" sock, one that covers the calf rather than merely the ankle and prevents a display of hairy leg when the knees are crossed. John Bridges in *A Gentleman Gets Dressed Up* (2012) advises on the finishing touch of the sock, writing: "A gentleman is not just a man of broad gestures. He is also a man of detail. His appearance is not meant to hold the limelight with his witty conversation and trenchant analysis of recent politics, the most seemingly insignificant of his accessories may steal away a listener's attention."

The connoisseur of socks will know the name Mazarin Grand Faiseur, a French brand launched by Paris-born Alain Stark, owner of the bespoke tailor Stark & Sons founded in 1910. Bertie, Prince of Wales, was one of its best-known customers and gave permission for Stark to display the royal warrant. This bespoke establishment holds an important role in French culture—the tailoring of the uniform, or *L'habit vert,* worn by members of Académie Française, a body comprised of forty *immortels* named after their motto, "*À l'immortalité,*" set up in 1635 by Cardinal Richelieu "to work with all possible care and diligence to give strict rules to our language and to make it pure, eloquent, and capable of dealing with the arts and sciences." Thus the academicians were a type of linguistic jury acting as officials and regulators of the national language. Richlieu commanded that they compose a dictionary, and Louis XIV gave them an apartment in the Louvre and forty goose quills to be whittled into pens to

Below: Mazarin's socks come in a rainbow of colors and are hand-linked, creating almost invisible seams.

Right: The Mazarin brand is owned by Stark & Sons, an elegant firm of French tailors established in 1910.

write it. *L'habit vert* was created during Napoleon Bonaparte's reign in 1803, made up of a long black swallowtail coat, with the large lapels and edges covered in lavish hand-embroidered olives and olive leaves, and an ostrich-plumed bicorne hat. Today each bespoke uniform takes six months to make and personal touches can be incorporated into the embroidery; Lebanese novelist Amin Maalouf had the Lebanese symbol of the cedar tree worked into the center of the back, and when French lawyer and politician Simone Veil was inducted into the academy as one of only six women academicians in its history, she chose to wear a Chanel couture version of the uniform in black crepe, designed by Karl Lagerfeld, with the leaf embroidery stitched by the House of Lesage.

Over the years the academicians found it difficult to source matching socks, so Stark set up a subsidiary company, Mazarin Grand Faiseur, to manufacture olive green over-the-calf socks. A cylindrical 240-needle machine, with the needles arranged in a circle knits the socks; as the sock leaves the cylinder it has an open toe.

The skilled hand linker takes the edges of the sock toe and links them together by matching the two edges by hand using the same thread that makes up the sock and slowly feeds them onto a serrated wheel that picks up the edges thread by thread. A hand-stitched or linked toe has an almost invisible seam, giving a flatter and consequently more comfortable finish that cannot be felt when wearing, as opposed to cheaper machine-linked socks that are commonly closed with nylon thread. All top-quality hosiery such as Mazarin; Pantherella, an English company founded by Louis Goldschmidt in 1937; and Bresciani, established in 1970 in Italy, is hand linked.

Mazarin's color palette is extensive and covers a veritable spectrum from the classic black and navy blue through vibrant yellow, orange, and pink in mercerized Egyptian or Sea Island cotton, and despite the company being based in Paris, the socks are manufactured on traditional looms on the outskirts of Rome. Customers include Bill Clinton and Vladimir Putin, and several French presidents, such as Charles de Gaulle and Jacques Chirac.

1836
ANTIGUA CASA CRESPO

In the Malasaña district of Madrid lies Antigua Casa Crespo, a manufactury and shop established in 1836 by Gregorio Crespo. For over 175 years, it has specialized in the traditional *alpargata* or more popularly known espadrille, a name derived from *esparto* after the robust Mediterranean grass used in its production. The alpargatero was a medieval shoemaker who specialized in making this typically paysan sandal by singeing the strands of esparto over an open fire and then braiding them together to create the ropelike sole that was then covered in pitch for protection. The uppers were woven from flax and hand-sewn by the women of Catalonia who seamed them to the sole at the sides and added a braided back strap. The result was a shoe that was cheap, light, flexible, and incredibly comfortable, since the natural rope sole molded to the shape of the wearer's foot over time.

The alpargata is said to have originated over 4,000 years ago in Albuñol, in the Granada province of Spain, and became the humble shoe of the *paisano,* an agrarian worker who lived and worked on the land. The colors of the original shoe were simple, unlike the rainbow hues available in Antigua Casa Crespo today—black was the traditional shade worn for the *paisano*'s working week and the undyed canvas was left in its natural color for Sunday best. By the nineteenth century the trades associated with the production of the *alpargata* had a considerable presence in Spain; in the city of Castellon, for instance, 600 people were employed spinning and weaving the *esparto* grass, many working from home with their families and others in small-scale workshops.

The Crespo *alpargata* is the same unassuming shoe that has been manufactured in small-scale cottage industries in Spain for centuries. It has had its fashion moments; the

Far left: Gregorio Crespo with his wife and son in a studio portrait from the mid-nineteenth century.
Left: In the 1970s Martin Garbayo introduced the colored espadrille to complement the traditional black and white—a tremendous success that led to queues forming outside the shop and around the block.
Right, clockwise from top left:
1. The interior of Antigua Casa Crespo showing the shelves stacked with traditional espadrilles.
2. Antigua Casa Crespo is a manufacturer and shop established in 1836 by Gregorio Crespo in the Malasaña district of Madrid.
3. A selection of modern styles of espadrille.

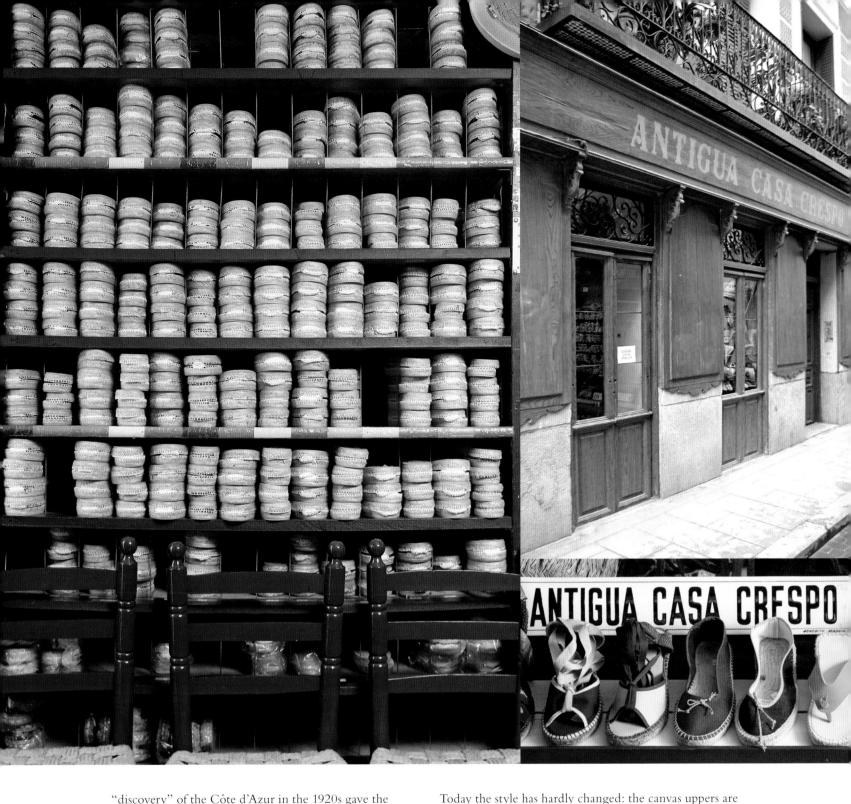

"discovery" of the Côte d'Azur in the 1920s gave the shoe celebrity cachet when it was seen on the feet of Coco Chanel, Spanish obsessive Ernest Hemingway, and, in 1938, John F. Kennedy. Hollywood stars continued to flaunt their French Mediterranean tans in the 1950s, and *alpargata* became the last word in elegance when worn by Cary Grant and Grace Kelly. Sophia Loren wore a pair with ribbon ties (the Pamplonas version can be bought at Antigua Casa Crespo today) and maverick Surrealist artist Salvador Dalí wore them under a formal evening suit.

Today the style has hardly changed: the canvas uppers are hand-stitched by the region's seamstresses, and the twines of the jute are braided by machine and then formed into the shape of the sole by hand in Spain's La Rioja region. The sole is heat pressed and vertically hand-stitched into place and vulcanized underneath to give a waterproof finish. There may be many designer labels that create modern versions of the artisanal *alpargata* but, at Antigua Casa Crespo, shop owner Maxi Garbayo says, "The classic version is just as my ancestors made them over 100 years ago."

1837
HERMÈS

Thierry Hermès was born in Krefeld, a German town today but officially under Prussian rule in the early nineteenth century. Krefeld was famed for its silk weavers and known as the *Stadt wie Samt und Seide*, or city of velvet and silk. Thierry's father, Dietrich, was an *aubergiste*, or innkeeper, but tragically Thierry was orphaned by the age of thirteen after the Hermès family, including his four siblings, was wiped out by disease. Two years later in 1821, he set off to find employment by walking to Paris; he journeyed to Normandy to be schooled in the techniques of harness making, and returned to Paris in 1837 to set up his own business near the Madeleine Church, moving to Boulevard des Capucines in 1842. The new location was on one of the "grands boulevards," its department stores and hotels later immortalized on canvas by the Impressionist painter Claude Monet in 1873. Here, the company specialized in finely wrought bridles and harnesses for the carriage trade—as chairman Jean-Louis Dumas, the great-great-grandson of Thierry said, "The first customer was a horse. The first design, a harness." In 1849 the founder retired to Normandy, and after his son, Charles-Émile,

took the helm, Hermès began winning awards, including a first prize at the Paris Exposition in 1855. By the 1870s the company was supplying all the royal courts of Europe from premises on Rue du Faubourg Saint-Honoré, the home of the Hermès museum today. As the century progressed and the horse began to be overtaken by more modern forms of transportation, such as the railway and the automobile, the Hermès family realized that the company had to adapt in order to survive. The techniques used for hand-crafting utilitarian saddle-stitched nosebags and saddlebags were used to make trunks, bags, wallets, and overnight cases that consolidated the company's reputation, including the saddlebag, or *haut à courroies*, inspired by the leather satchels that Argentinian gauchos used to transport their belongings when on horseback.

Hermès transitioned to creating stylish handbags for the new female consumer using the most exquisite leathers, such as alligator, ostrich, and crocodile, while retaining attention to detail and durability. With the increased possibilities for travel, women needed a larger handbag to carry their personal items for daily use. Bags changed from dainty Edwardian reticules into more sturdy, substantial shapes, and, as shopping became more of a social event, they became a necessity for women who were staying out for longer periods during the day. Hermès created a whole series of saddle-stitched bags with elegant, minimalist lines, such as the valise of 1923 and the *sac pour l'auto,* or Bugatti, in 1925, a large handbag designed for women who rode in automobiles (it was later renamed the Bolide for legal reasons). Significantly, the Bolide also had a zipper running across the top for ease of closure; Hermès was the first firm to use the toothed zipper in its designs. The "alligator of ecstasy," as writer Tom Robbins later dubbed this modern mechanism of daily life, was

Left: The founder of the global luxury brand, Prussian harness maker Thierry Hermès. **Above right**: Prince Rainier helps his wife use the Hermès Kelly bag, designed in 1935 by Robert Dumas, to deflect attention from her pregnancy in 1956. **Right**: A rose ostrich-skin version of the Kelly bag, which became a hit in the late 1950s.

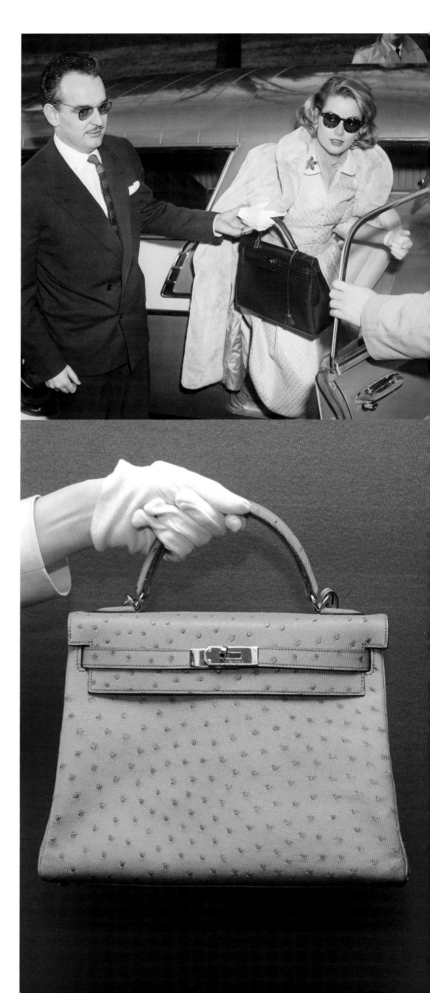

invented in 1893 by U.S. engineer L. Judson as a device for fastening shoes; the zipper was soon fitted in gloves, corsets, tobacco pouches, and mailbags, or, as Judson's Universal Fastener Company advertised, "whenever it is desired to detachably connect a pair of adjacent flexible parts." Émile-Maurice Hermès had come across the zipper when traveling in the United States and astutely secured the European patent from 1922 to 1924. Women were very receptive to the zipper because it had a fashionable modernity that suited the stream-lined aesthetic of the decade; it also developed erotic connotations because it eased access to the body. After Hermès made the zipper a feature, it became known as the "fermature Hermès," and with the Bolide, the luxury branded handbag as we know it today was born.

During the 1920s, the company expanded into what Emile-Maurice Hermès described as, "leather, sport, and a tradition of refined elegance," launching a whole series of luxury items to appeal to the fashionable motoring set, including a range that catered to the latest trend of picnicking. The practice of eating in the open air had formerly been associated with the laboring man but with the advent of the automobile it became fashionable to drive to a beautiful spot and eat *en plein air.* Motorist Marius Carle, for example, wrote of cruising through the Alps and recommended always having a supply of food in one's car so as to stop at a beautiful vista, eat lunch, and enjoy the view. In 1925, Hermès began selling a *malette à pique-nique,* or luxury picnic chest, containing beautifully crafted Thermos flasks, a platter, goblets, cups, and folding tableware.

The company also began making ready-made clothes from buckskin, Paris's earliest items of ready-to-wear, as well as bespoke that could be bought at boutiques in the

"The first customer was a horse.
The first design, a harness."
Jean-Louis Dumas

voguish resorts of Biarritz, Deauville, and Cannes. One of the first pieces was a zippered leather golfing jacket for the Prince of Wales, and modernist writer Gertrude Stein wrote of how she spent the profits from her successful autobiography in 1933: "I bought myself a new eight-cylinder Ford car and the most expensive coat made to order by Hermès and fitted by the man who makes horse covers for race horses." In 1934, the Cannes boutique was name checked in F. Scott Fitzgerald's novel *Tender Is the Night,* when his female lead, Nicole Diver, based on his wife Zelda, "buys two chamois leather jackets of kingfisher blue and burning bush from Hermès." The company also capitalized on the fashion for sunbathing and swimming off the beaches of the Côte d'Azur by introducing swimwear collections, Hermès de Bains, from the early 1930s, which included knitted bathing suits and matching robes, striped canvas bags, and coordinating parasols.

The *sac à dépêches,* later named the Kelly bag, was introduced in 1935, and well-known owners at the time included screen legends Marlene Dietrich and Ingrid Bergman. Today the Kelly remains entirely handmade and hand-crafted to order in Pantin, a suburb of Paris. Materials include canvas, hide, ostrich, crocodile, and alligator. The skin is laid out and thoroughly inspected for any flaws by the cutter; after being cut with a toothed griffe, the goatskin lining is the first section of the bag to be sewn. As there are 2,600 stitches in each bag, the experienced artisan wears double-magnifying glasses to make sure the tiny stitches are perfectly even. An awl is used to make the puncture point for the bees-waxed linen thread to pass through, and the base of the bag is double saddle-stitched to the front and the back of the lining. The handle is shaped by hand and, according to Hermès artisan Pierre Grosperrin, "is the most difficult part of the bag to make; it takes four hours to craft." After construction, the layers of stitched leather are smoothed with sandpaper and dyed to match the color of the handbag and then painted with hot wax to protect the handle from moisture. The front flap is added to the body of the bag and the hand-riveted hardware added, including the signature flap closure, engraved gold buckle, and four tiny gold feet on which the bag stands in order to prevent the three layers of skin that make up the base from wear.

The bag is ironed to smooth out the wrinkles in the skin and stamped with the gold lettering, "Hermès Paris."

This luxurious leather handbag was just another member of the Hermès stable until its reputation went sky-high in 1956. Movie star Grace Kelly had given up her successful career in Hollywood when she married Prince Rainier of Monaco in that year, a union some said was predicated on economic necessity rather than love, as Rainier had decided that the publicity attached to marrying a famous blonde would attract tourists to his tiny cash-strapped principality. His first choice of bride, Marilyn Monroe, turned him down but Kelly agreed—despite the fact that Rainier insisted on her family paying him a $2 million dowry. She became pregnant by Rainier in the same year as the wedding and was famously photographed for the cover of *Time* magazine shielding her stomach with a classic Hermès bag—thereafter known as the Kelly and still a bestseller today. The Hermès Kelly, now considered the Rolls Royce of handbags, is instantly recognizable and incredibly covetable. The 2004 movie *Le Divorce* played on its expensive allure; in this romantic tale set in Paris, Kate Hudson begins an illicit affair with a much older married French aristocrat who seals the deal with an Hermès Kelly in red, a gift he offers every lover at the start of an affair (only sixty Kelly bags are created each season).

The 1930s continued to be a fruitful decade for the company; Hermès launched its first timepieces after employing Swiss watchmaker Universal Genève, which designed a range of men's wrist chronographs manufactured in eighteen-karat gold or stainless steel, and cuff watches in the popular Art Deco style in gold, steel, or platinum for women. In 1937, the Hermès *carré,* or square, silk twill scarf was introduced by Émile-Maurice's son-in-law, Robert Dumas, who became the director of the company in 1951, after being inspired by the silk used for the riding colors of the Longchamps jockey. The first print, "Le Jeu des Omnibus et Dames Blanches" by Hugo Grygkar, was based on a woodcut of a popular French parlor game, and the designer went on to provide images for the company until 1959. Since 1937, more than 2,000 designs have been created for the *carré* by artists including Philippe Ledoux, Pierre Péron, Françoise de la Perrière, and African-American postman and artist Kermit Oliver, whose "Les Danses des Indiens" and "Les Cheyennes"

evoke the spirit of Native American culture. Madame La Torre's evocative "Vieille Chine" design of 1963 was based on the patterns found in nineteenth-century *chinoiserie* wallpaper and was one of many Asian-inspired designs created for Hermès by this talented artist.

Today Hermès has its own silk farm in Brazil rather than importing silk from China, and it takes 300 individual cocoons of the mori moth to make the silk thread needed to weave one Hermès *carré*. The silk thread is imported to the Hermès facility in Lyon, the ancient home of the French silk industry. Here it is woven into a silk twice as thick and heavy as is the norm in high-end scarf production and the artwork is studied to work out how many colors will be needed for the final print. The colors are transferred one by one onto clear film, a process that takes hundreds of hours of labor, and photo-transferred onto a polyester mesh screen. Both sides of the screen are coated with photo-sensitive gelatin and it is from this that the scarves are printed with vegetable dyes. This is a laborious process, because after one color is printed, it is dried for one month before the next is applied. The printed silk is set with steam and the scarves are washed with a special oil-based Provençal soap that removes any excess color or gelatin. The printed silk is then cut into the *carrè*, which is meticulously hand rolled and the hems hand stitched.

In 1938, the *Chaîne d'Ancre* chain-link bracelet was introduced, followed by the first Hermès silk tie in 1949, and the fragrance, Eau d'Hermès, in the same year.

The war and subsequent occupation of Paris by the Nazi forces halted much of Hermès's production, and the family removed themselves to Cannes. Packaging was scarce and at one point only orange card was available. It was adopted by the company as its signature color, and from 1945 was printed with the equine logo, a *calèche*, or horse-drawn carriage, based on a drawing by Alfred de Dreux, a nineteenth-century equestrian painter. The company continued its expansion, introducing new items including porcelain, crystal, and fragrances, and it benefited from the logo mania and power dressing of the 1970s and 1980s. In 1984 the Hermès Birkin was launched, a stratospherically successful bag introduced after Jean-Louis Dumas, who had taken over the leadership of the company in 1978, found himself sitting next to actress Jane Birkin on an airplane flight. She had a beaten-up straw bag overflowing with her possessions and complained to Dumas about how handbags were not large enough to cater for the demands of a busy working woman, and the problem with having a more sizable travel or weekend bag was that when it was full it became much too heavy. Dumas asked her to describe her ideal bag and she came up with a leather bag with a large opening, essentially a form of expensive tote. Dumas modified the *haut à courries*, and it was renamed the Birkin in her honor.

Dumas had a respect for craft that never faltered, famously saying, "The world is divided into two; those who know how to use tools and those who do not." During his tenure, Dumas took his artisans traveling around the world to meet craft workers in traditional cultures including goldsmiths in Mali and Tuareg silversmiths in Niger. He was also a realist; the company needed to attract a younger clientele without compromising on its quality, so he relaunched the ostrich-skin Kelly in an array of bright colors, creating a globally revered it bag while buying into a range of heritage bespoke companies, including the shoe label John Lobb (see page 118), before retiring in 2006.

Today a person can be dressed literally from head to toe in Hermès's products if desired, yet despite its domination in the world of luxury goods, the company remains dedicated to family ownership, artisanal craftsmanship, and attention to detail, and it still refuses to license its goods, thereby ensuring the quality of its output.

"White doesn't lie; it is the truest expression of the fabric."

Jean-Claude Colban

Left, clockwise from top left:
1. Charvet is renowned for its beautifully constructed men's shirts, ties, and pocket squares.
2. A selection of fine shirt fabrics.
3. The elegant exterior of Charvet

at 28 Place Vendôme in Paris.
Below: By the outbreak of World War I, Charvet had become a French institution with its fine shirts worn by the best-dressed Parisian gentleman.

75

1838
CHARVET

"Sebastian entered—dove-grey flannel, white crêpe-de-Chine shirt, a Charvet tie, my tie as it happened, a pattern of postage stamps," so Evelyn Waugh introduces Lord Sebastian Flyte in his novel *Brideshead Revisited* (1945) illustrating his and the narrator's exquisite urbanity by name checking a French institution, the men's outfitters Charvet. Entering this grand establishment on the Place Vendôme in Paris today is to discover menswear's most sumptuous materials: fine French silk and Irish linen; Sea Island and Nile cotton broadcloths and woven pinpoint oxfords; gabardines and feather-light voiles; opaque batistes and brightly hued chambrays. On being asked just how many fabrics Charvet stocks from which a bespoke shirt can be created, director Jean-Claude Colban says, "Well, it's not easy to say exactly—the numbers keep changing. New fabrics are always being added and others dropped, but I should say certainly more than 3,000."

This bespoke shirtmakers, or *chemisier*, was founded by Josephe-Christophe Charvet in 1838 and became the destination of choice for royalty and heads of state. The company's ties, in particular, were of such unqualified success that today the word Charvet is used as an adjective to describe a particular kind of woven ribbed silk, popular in the nineteenth century for creating subtle stripe effects and identified by its glossy surface, soft feel, and superb drape. Today the third floor of the historic store remains a temple of bespoke; customers have the opportunity to choose from full bolts of Charvet-designed fabrics instead of the nominal swatch and can survey the mind-boggling *Mur des Blancs*, or "wall of whites," 400 fabrics in more than 100 different shades of white. Jean-Claude Colban who co-owns Charvet with his sister, Anne-Marie, says, "White doesn't lie; it is the truest expression of the fabric so even in sheer broadcloth, minute changes of quality in

the yarn and construction in number of threads and so on all show and give new shades of color," and thus determines the skill of the bespoke shirtmaker.

The first fitting of a Charvet shirt famously involves the transcribing of twenty-six detailed measurements from which a paper pattern is drawn up; a Charvet shirt will fit like no other because it takes into consideration the fact that each customer's arm is slightly different in length, no body is entirely symmetrical, and posture affects the fit of the shirt. The measurements are so precise that even the thickness of the watch is taken into consideration because it will determine the fit of the cuff. The customer can now customize the shirt to his satisfaction; he has the luxury of choice from a plethora of different fabrics to eighty different collar styles and the opportunity to add a personal monogram to the chest or cuff. The paper pattern is used to create the first fit, a shirt made from white cotton that is adjusted to the customer's body before being made up in the chosen fabric by hand by one artisan only, a process that usually takes three weeks. Bespoke shirting material is pre-shrunk using the *décatissage* method in which it is washed with rapid changes in temperature so

Top: Bespoke shirting material is pre-shrunk so the shape will remain unchanged after being laundered. **Above**: A bolt of cloth is taken to the window to be examined in natural light. **Right**: Customers have the opportunity to choose from full bolts of Charvet-designed fabrics instead of the nominal swatch.

that the shape will remain unchanged after being laundered, and if the shirt is striped it is painstakingly matched up so that it looks as if it has been constructed from one piece of material. All Charvet buttons are Australian mother-of-pearl cut from the surface of the oyster's shell as this area is strong and clearer in color.

The Charvet family had strong links with nobility from the outset; Josephe-Christophe's father, Jean-Pierre, had been assistant to Napoleon's wardrobe master and his first cousin, Louise, made the imperial shirts. Shirtmakers existed before Charvet, but they worked at the behest of the customer who had previously sourced the fabric from a linen supplier, and as the garment was almost hidden by other clothes, its shape was a simple square that bore little relationship to the body underneath. Charvet consolidated all the processes of shirt making on site and, most significantly, paid attention to the customer's proportions so as to create a fitted tailored shape. Charvet also created the concept of a folded, detachable collar and, for U.S. dandy Evander Berry Wall, a signature spread-eagle collar and bespoke cravat. Wall, who lived with his wife at the Hotel Meurice near the shop, also had matching cravats and dog collars hand-made by Charvet for his chow, Chi Chi.

French lions or dandies flocked to the store, including the celebrated French poet and dandy Robert de Montesquiou, who was the inspiration behind Marcel Proust's character Baron de Charlus and declared, "Charvet is the greatest artist in creation." Aesthete and author Proust was a well-known aficionado of Charvet; an early biographer described him as "a cross between a refined dandy and an untidy medieval philosopher. He wore poorly knitted cravats under a turned-down collar, or large silk shirt-fronts from Charvet in creamy pink whose exact tint he spent a long time tracking down." In the first volume of his elegiac *Remembrance of Things Past* (1913), the character, Marcel tightens "every few minutes the knot of a gorgeous necktie from Charvet's," and Charles Swann is a member of the renowned Jockey Club, in reality a group of 250 fashionable boulevardiers for whom Charvet was official shirtmaker. The Jockey Club de Paris opened in 1834 and became the meeting place for the social elite during the Belle Époque, situated above the Grand Café of the Scribe Hotel near the Longchamp racetrack. The character of Swann was said to be based

on art collector and critic Charles Haas—Haas was actually admitted to the club in 1871.

When Charvet exhibited bespoke shirts at the World's Fair in Paris in 1867 they were spied by the Prince of Wales, later Edward VII, and he was so impressed by the quality that he became one of its most loyal customers. Charvet designed a stand-up fold-down collar named the HRH in 1898 especially for the prince, and by the end of the century Charvet was an important location for tourists in search of the same *fin de siècle* elegance. Its window displays were legendary: one journalist compared their beauty to the performances of Loie Fuller, and another journalist visiting from Chicago in 1909 described "shirts of every variety and almost every color… each and every one most beautifully made" and "scarf pins that match in color any scarf that may be bought and some have the same designs carried out in them done in enamel. There are also waistcoat buttons to be worn with certain ties and there are sets of these, cufflinks, and pins, all of which exactly match." Charvet commissioned artist Raoul Dufy to design silk fabric for its products; it was woven by Bianchini-Férier and made up into silk squares, shirts, and dressing gowns. By the 1920s the cravats were legendary and came in a series of Art Deco, Cubist-inspired designs that could come in matching sets of pajamas and dressing gowns. Filmmaker Jean Cocteau called such wares "magic" and "where the rainbow finds ideas." A hint of

Parisian decadence could be found in Charvet's pure silk bed sheets in shades of purple, green, and violet, and their signature silk *passementerie* knot cufflinks.

In 1965 the family-run company was bought by one of its main suppliers, Denis Colban, an importer of English shirt fabrics. Son Jean-Claude says, "At the time, he rarely visited the old Charvet shop on 8 Place Vendôme. That was because there was a rule that all suppliers had to use the back door. It was rather nice that on the day he purchased the brand, he finally walked in through the front door." Colban invested more heavily in ready-to-wear to expand the firm's business overseas but retained the celebrated bespoke heart of the business. An important innovation was introduced into the tie design, a unique form of interlining that remains Charvet's secret, in which silk ties keep their spring after being pulled to create the knot without being stretched out of shape or conversely being too rigid so that the tie is too hard to knot.

The business remains in the same family today and in an elegant three-story building with a Jules Hardouin-Mansart-designed façade on the Place Vendôme, and it is still frequented by any gentleman with a modicum of style. As Anne-Marie Colban points out, "Men come here alone and get lost for hours. It's a candy store for grown men. We love it when men come here and spend almost an hour just creating one shirt. We understand that this is the pleasure—almost a type of therapy."

1839
CORDINGS

The Strand, one of the grand thoroughfares of Victorian London, was once a muddy track running east along the River Thames; King Henry VIII pronounced it as "full of pits and sloughs, very perilous and noisome." During the reign of Queen Elizabeth I, the route was improved, so much so that members of the nobility such as the Dukes of Buckingham and Northumberland began to build their grand mansions on both sides of the unpaved road. In 1762 the Paving Act was passed in Parliament and the disposal of rubbish was regulated; the *London Chronicle* wrote, "All sorts of dirt and ashes, oyster-shells, the offals of fish, poultry, and other kinds of meat will now no longer be suffered to be thrown loose into the streets… nor will the annoyances erected by coach-makers be permitted; and when a house is pulled down the rubbish must be carried to the proper place, and not left on the footway."

The Strand connected Britain's two most powerful institutions, the government at Whitehall and the City of London. By the end of the nineteenth century, it had become a meeting place for gentlemen to discuss the affairs of the day over roast beef at Simpsons or a drink at the Savoy. It was thus the perfect location for a gentlemen's outfitters and accordingly in 1839 Cordings opened at No. 231. The owner was John Charles Cording, who had been working from home for many years in a family concern with his mother, Mary, and sister, Ellen. At the age of thirty-five he had decided to set up on his own as a specialist in waterproofed outerwear, such as oiled or rubberized coats and boots that could be bought by gentlemen working in the City to take to their country piles at the weekends or on journeys abroad. From 1849 through the 1850s Cordings advertised many such items

Left: The exterior of Cordings at 19 Piccadilly, London, only half a minute away from the iconic statue of Eros. **Right**: The interior of Cordings where Sir Henry Moreton Stanley was kitted out in 1871 before venturing on his search for Dr. Livingstone. As the Duke of Wellington put it, "Without question, Cordings is the complete outfitter, you have everything under one roof."

for both men and women; in 1851, a promotion described
their Dreadnought waterproof coats and capes as "the best
articles ever made up for sportsmen, sailors, and travelers.
They will resist the heaviest rain and greatest tropical
heat for any length of time, and their durability is equal to
their waterproof qualities. Officers and others proceeding
to the colonies will find these articles invaluable."
Dreadnought was heavyweight wool used to make winter
hats and box coats worn by men who worked outside,
such as coach drivers, or by gentlemen when in extremely
inclement weather or at sea. There was an etiquette
concerning when it was worn; the *London Magazine* of
1823 published a story of the misfortune that befalls a
man wearing a Dreadnought to the theater during a
particularly hot August; this is such a severe sartorial
faux pas it causes him to be heckled from the stalls and he
ends up throwing the Dreadnought out of the window.

The waterproofed Dreadnought was the predecessor
to the Cordings rubberized Macintosh, which became an
essential piece of kit for hunting and was adopted by the
first motorists to be worn in their open-top cars. Other
items included Sheet India rubber fishing boots, precursors
to the rubber Wellington that were "impervious to water
and required no dressing to keep them in condition" as
well as sou'westers, ladies' riding capes, hoods, and petticoats.
Business was brisk, and, in 1857 with no direct heirs of
his own, John Cording employed his cousin, Henry Wilson,
who eventually inherited the company. In 1860, Cordings
was offering a full tailoring and bootmaking service, and
customers included the Duke of Connaught and most
significantly, in 1871, journalist Henry Morton Stanley
who called in to buy the tropical gear for his expedition
to Africa to find missing missionary Dr. Livingstone.

In 1877 Cordings moved to 19 Piccadilly, an area that
was regarded as the playground of the English gentleman
especially after the construction of the Ritz Hotel in
1906. Additional premises were acquired at 24 Jermyn
Street and 35 St. James's Street, in a building that today
is known as Cording House. In the early 1900s, Cordings
was granted a royal warrant for providing waterproofs
for the Prince of Wales, later King George V, followed
in 1922 by his son, the Duke of Windsor. The firm
also made water-resistant canvas and leather Newmarket
riding boots for both him and his consort, Mrs. Simpson,

that were patented in 1920. Cordings became the place to buy country clothing, in particular the outfits needed for hunting, shooting, and fishing; it moved into off-the-peg tweed suits and introduced the iconic Covert top coat with a straight cut and short length designed to be worn when riding. The name "Covert" was derived from the thicket or cover for game where riders would congregate before the day's hunt; the coats displayed their bucolic origins as they were originally constructed of a tightly woven tweed to protect the rider from brambles when jumping and a green to brown color so that the splatters of mud from a hack would be camouflaged after the hunt. The Cordings Covert was single breasted with notched lapels, a fly front, and two flap pockets, and it had two distinctive details; four lines of stitching on the cuffs and a velvet collar. The woolen cloth was originally woven by Fox Brothers & Company of Somerset, a mill established in 1772 to supply the Savile Row tailors; the same mill continues to supply the same cloth more than 100 years later. The Covert coat remains a staple of Cordings; London tailor Mark Powell says, "Cordings make the best Covert coats. When I need a Covert coat I get it from Cordings rather than make one myself and I'm a tailor so I should know! Cordings are without doubt the best at what they do; they produce a quality which surpasses any other company of its kind in Britain."

Cordings is also associated with the development of the Tattersall shirt, a woven checked flannel shirt that takes its name from Tattersall's, an eighteenth-century horse market in which the thoroughbred horses were covered with checked blankets. The checks are formed of simple lines that stand out against the colored ground of the shirt. Today Cordings remains the destination address for traditional British country clothing and sells fitted heavy tweed suits with three-button, single-vent jackets; tweed field and Covert coats; rubberized Macintoshes; shooting pants in needle cord, a corduroy fabric with narrow ribs or moleskin, a soft cotton cloth in a satin weave; and double twill weave worsted or cavalry twill pants, a woven fabric with a diagonal raised cord or double wale line that takes the form of a pronounced groove in the fabric. This form of twill was originally used for the khaki breeches of cavalry officers during the World War I but today is more usually worn in a fawn or buff color.

Shooting attire also includes traditional plus fours, named after the four additional inches of cloth required to create the overhang at the knee and popularized by Edward, Prince of Wales, in the 1920s for golfing. The prince was a self-conscious style leader who, by wearing plus fours outside of the grouse shoot, was trying to shake off the stuffy conservative dress of his royal forebears. The prince claimed to wear "plus twenty-fours" because of their voluminous bagginess and after he was photographed wearing a pair in the United States in 1924, plus fours became an interwar transatlantic fashion. This was not the first time that young American men had worn this fashion, however; from the late nineteenth century, plus fours were seen as so impeccably English that they were adopted by Rhodes scholars, Americans who were studying at Oxford University.

In 2004 Cordings hit the headlines when rock guitarist Eric Clapton bought a 50 percent share in the business, together with managing director Noll Uloth, after it experienced financial difficulties. He had been a huge fan of the firm since a teenager when he had regularly passed by the Piccadilly shop. As Clapton put it, "Just walking the West End it stuck in my mind as a place of tradition, something to do with the heritage of England. I saw this suit; it was in a moss green herringbone tweed. It had the most exquisitely cut jacket. It was like entering a gentlemen's club; I came in, very shyly tried it on and it was immaculate and stormproof. Now I feel like I've come to a kind of home in terms of what I need in the country. It's not for our everyday high street shopper, thank God."

Below: Many of the blocks for Cordings English suits have not been changed for fifty years.

Right: A selection of printed silk ties including, on the top left, the 36 oz Silent Hunter design in a distinctive bright orange.

"Cordings are without doubt the best at what they do; they produce a quality which surpasses any other company of its kind in Britain."

Mark Powell, London tailor

1845
LADAGE & OELKE

The great port of Hamburg in Germany was an international center of trade throughout the nineteenth century until disaster struck on May 7, 1842. A huge fire broke out in the city and burned for four days, the flames fueled by the half-timbered buildings crowded in narrow alleyways; 70,000 inhabitants fled from the conflagration and more than a quarter of the city was destroyed. Hamburg was reconstructed during the next forty years with help from the crowned heads of Europe who held the historic city in high esteem. It was modernized according to the new principles of urban planning, which included the construction of the Alsterarkaden, an Italianate-inspired colonnaded walkway from which the Mellin Passage branches off, an arcade renowned for its Art Nouveau painted ceilings. Here lies Ladage & Oelke

with its distinctive nineteenth-century frontage, and a cursory glance in the windows will tell any prospective customer that this is an old-school institution devoted to all that is best in classic European fashion—in fact, menswear expert Alan Flusser describes it as "so fuddy-duddy it's charming." Ladage & Oelke's own-label Argyle socks, Duffel coats, and tweed knickerbockers sit alongside Burberry trench coats and Barbour waxed jackets, and the stunning shoe salon, Crossford's Number One, displays handmade shoes from Edward Green, Aigle, and Crockett & Jones. Eighty percent of the clothing is made under the shop's own label using top-quality materials such as Harris, Saxony, and Donegal tweed, Scottish tartan, and leather from Italian tanneries, with finished goods stacked so high on shelves that they reach the stucco ceiling.

Left: Ladage & Oelke opened in 1845 as a draper selling cloth that was made up into garments using bespoke tailoring skills. **Right, clockwise from top left**: 1. Ladage & Oelke sells made-to-measure and ready-to-wear European clothes including high-quality menswear. 2. The elegant interior of Ladage & Oelke, the first shop to sell "English style" in Germany. 3. Much of the Hamburg-based shop's original nineteenth-century interior remains intact.

"This is an old-school institution devoted to all that is best in classic European fashion."

When Ladage & Oelke opened in 1845, the gentlemen of Europe were obsessed with the concept of English style, encapsulated in London's Savile Row and, later in the century, the figure of "Bertie," a.k.a. Edward, Prince of Wales, who succeeded Queen Victoria in 1901 as King Edward VII. He was a bon viveur, frequenting the nightclubs, hotels, and spas of Europe's major capitals, including Marienbad in the Czech Republic where, according to popular mythology, tailors would surreptitiously gather to sketch his clothes.

Ladage & Oelke was the first company to sell the "English style" in Germany after master tailors Georg Wilhelm Carl Ladage and Johann Diedrich Wilhelm Oelke set up shop in 1845. The shop was originally a drapers selling cloth that was made up into garments using bespoke tailoring skills; by the 1870s the duo had established a staggering 100-plus branches, including in Bremen and farther afield in Hong Kong, Shanghai, and Yokohama, Japan. Ladage retired in 1866 and the international outlets were closed in the 1870s; the last in Yokohama shut its doors in 1875. Subsequently the sudden death of Oelke led to his widow selling the business to her brother, Julius Franck, in 1912. The company remained Anglophile, not only importing English labels but also creating their own Teutonic version of the hunting, shooting, and fishing look by incorporating Bavarian feathered hats as popularized in England by Edward VIII, Austrian shooting coats with game pockets, and the classic green Tyrolean Loden coat. Loden from the German "lode," or coarse cloth, is a thick short-pile felted wool woven from the oily coat of the Austrian mountain sheep and is thus relatively water repellent. Loden cloth is worn throughout the Alpine regions as it keeps the body warm when exposed to high winds and is thick enough to be thorn-proof.

The Loden Janker jacket and Loden coat are key examples of traditional country garments transforming into fashionable city wear; the coat can be recognized by its turn-down collar, exaggerated width and length, and a distinctive vertical box pleat at the rear; the traditional Loden Janker, or Schalk, is a rural hip-length jacket that dates back to the eighteenth century. It is manufactured in gray, green, and red with a coordinating color at the edges, including the front pockets, and has metal or horn buttons. After celebrated couturière Coco Chanel saw the jacket being worn while traveling in Switzerland, it became the inspiration for her classic tweed suit with its collarless central button jacket, and when worn with a string of pearls, which became the ultimate in petit-bourgeois fashion. The Loden cape is a derivative of the coat and takes the form of a buttoned sleeveless poncho that allows great freedom of movement and can accommodate a game bag underneath while protecting the wearer from inclement weather.

Today Julius Franck's grandson, Heinrich, runs the business with his wife, Elke; Ladage & Oelke no longer does bespoke but concentrates on the best made-to-measure and ready-to-wear European clothes, including traditional menswear and womenswear, clothes for children, and leather accessories, with a variety of finishes and materials available according to the customer's specifications. Outerwear is one of the shop's specialties produced in a location close to the North Sea, and it includes its celebrated hand-tailored Duffel coat. The hooded Duffel coat is a nineteenth-century invention, named after the heavy Duffel wool woven in the Belgian town of Duffel from the fifteenth century. In 1887, the English sports outfitters John Partridge manufactured a coat with a wooden toggle closure that was later put into production in boiled woolen cloth with a boxier cut, square shoulder yoke, and large patch pockets by the British Navy and popularized by Field Marshal Montgomery during World War II. Ladage & Oelke stocks expertly made, traditional Duffels, considered the best around by those in the know, and the firm maintains its standards by being in the Seal of Good Addresses, an organization set up within the Hanseatic city community for the suppliers of the most premium of specialist products; it includes Lenffer tableware and Wolkenstürmer kites. Ladage & Oelke remains determined, as the owners put it, to be "an oasis of style in a modern world."

Left, clockwise from top left: 1. Clothing is made under the shop's own label using top-quality materials such as Harris, Saxony, and Donegal tweed. 2. The in-store shoe salon, Crossford's Number One displays handmade shoes from Edward Green, Aigle, and Crockett. 3. Ladage & Oelke remains determined, as the owners put it, to be "an oasis of style in a modern world."

1847
CARTIER

Above: Louis François Cartier, who established the Cartier empire in Paris in 1847.

Above right: The Cartier jewelry team in the firm's workshop pose for a photograph taken in the early twentieth century.

Traditionally, the most impressive pieces of jewelry belonged to aristocratic dynasties who passed the "family jewels" down from generation to generation, having the stones reset or recut according to changes in taste and fashion. In the nineteenth century, however, the rise of the new haute bourgeoisie created a class with a taste for the trappings of status, and jewelry became desirous, not only for the stones in the settings, but also the status of the maker's name. One such maker was Cartier, a jewelry house that had its origins in a business established by Louis-François Cartier in 1847 to sell high-end jewelry and luxury goods, including the most magnificent of historical pieces. Customers soon included the wealthiest scions of aristocratic Europe, such as the Empress Eugénie, renowned worldwide for her spectacular fashion sense in gowns designed by the great nineteenth-century couturier Charles Frederick Worth. The subsequent revenue generated by the firm, and the increased confidence inspired by the name, led to Cartier creating its own pieces in-house by the late 1880s, after Louis-François was succeeded by his son, Alfred, in 1874.

It was during this period that Paris became notorious as a glittering city of Belle Époque decadence and the backdrop to the international celebrities and queens of the demimonde Carolina "La Belle" Otero, Liane de Pougy, and Émilienne d'Alençon, women collectively known as the *grandes horizontales*, who used their wit and guile to amass huge fortunes from a series of wealthy suitors. Spanish dancer Carolina Otero was a talented performer renowned for a salacious fandango, habitually performed after leaping onto a table at the notorious restaurant Maxim's. She had a list of lovers that included Edward, Prince of Wales, and Nicholas, Czar of Russia, who showered her with a collection of jewelry that was world renowned. As Otero put it, "No man who has an account at Cartier's can be regarded as ugly," and she was duly

welcomed at 13 Rue de la Paix where the elegant and discreetly luxurious premises of Cartier were situated, by that time one of the most prestigious names in the history of jewelry. Cartier created the most extraordinary breast ornament for Otero out of ten million francs' worth of diamonds set into a pure gold frame. It took the form of a huge looped pendant that reached entirely across the torso to hang in shimmering swags below. Along the bottom hung a series of thirty enormous diamonds, appearing as one observer put it "like huge tears," and heavy ropes of diamonds were arranged across the front and secured in the center with a large diamond clasp. The value was such that it was kept in a bank vault and whenever it was delivered to Otero, it had to travel in a reinforced carriage accompanied by two armed gendarmes.

By the early twentieth century, Cartier was already an institution, helped by the accolade of becoming the official supplier of jewelry to royalty, including King

Edward VII and King Zog of Albania, and also because the firm was not afraid to experiment with new techniques of gem cutting and stone setting. For example, Cartier pioneered the use of platinum, a metal that was harder than silver or gold, and which made articulated settings for fabulous gems much lighter, brighter, and deluxe. The strength of platinum also meant that designs could be more delicate as very little metal was needed to hold a stone in place. Such "invisible" settings were, as Louis Cartier put it, "embroidery rather than armor plating," and this approach led to garland-style festooned necklaces in which diamonds seemed to be floating over the surface of the skin. Cartier's filigree settings and "white on white" style complemented the Edwardian fashion for pale lace and frothy tea gowns, and saw-piercing techniques exaggerated the airy look.

The discovery of gigantic deposits of diamonds in South Africa by the De Beers mining company and

Above: A photograph taken by Alfred Eisenstaedt looking down on the showroom of Cartier's New York store in 1947. **Left**: The "Foliates" diamond and platinum tiara made for Queen Elisabeth of Belgium by Cartier in 1910.

new cuts such as the marquise, baguette, and briolette, together with an international clientele with pots of money, was a winning combination for many prestigious jewelers in Paris, including Louis Aucoc, Bernard, and Charles Mauret. Cartier had the edge though, and language barriers were swept away when a visiting mogul or foreign dignitary was confronted with tray upon tray of glittering gems in the premises on Rue de la Paix.

Wearing a spectacular piece designed by Cartier was one of the ways of gaining social status in the Edwardian demimonde, and U.S. socialites Mrs. Ogden Mills and Doris Duke vied with each other at society functions with their diamond and emerald brooches, tiaras, and rings adorning every finger. Cartier was one of the first jewelry houses to understand the relationship between jewelry and fashion, not least because from 1899 it was situated on the same shopping street as Doucet, Guerlain, and the House of Worth—the leading couturiers of the day—and was canny enough to realize that rich women would want to coordinate their new wardrobes with matching gems. The upswept hair and low necklines, of the Edwardian era called out for extravagant necklaces, and Cartier responded with *colliers de chien* (dog collars), *sautoirs* (rope-style necklaces with a tassel or pendant), and a new design, the Lavalier. Named after the popular actress Eve Lavallière, one of the first women in Paris to bob her hair, the Lavalier was a double pendant, one suspended from the other. The vogue for a graceful, swanlike neck was further exaggerated by the use of Cartier chokers with a black velvet or moiré base that acted as a foil to intricate openwork diamonds and pearls. The firm also specialized in eighteenth-century decorative motifs such as Rococo revival swags, bows, cartouches, and wreath shapes—the same wreath shape that decorates Cartier's iconic red and gold boxes today, and this popular look was dubbed the "garland" style.

By this time, Alfred's son, Louis Cartier, had joined the family firm, and his love of fine gemstones, in search of which he was to travel all over the world to Russia, Egypt, Persia, and Japan, injected a new exotic feel into the work. In 1902, Cartier opened a shop in London headed up by Pierre Cartier, Alfred's second son, followed by one on New York's Fifth Avenue in 1909. Such was the fashion for Cartier diamonds in New York that when the thirty-five boxes were fully occupied at the city's

"You must infect the client with gemstone fever!"
Louis Cartier addressing his jewelry designers

Metropolitan Opera House it was dubbed the "diamond horseshoe." The rise of the tiara as a fashion accessory spurred on by Chaumet (see page 30) also saw Cartier at the forefront of its design when the firm introduced a convertible tiara that could be disassembled into brooches and pendants.

From the start of the twentieth century, Cartier began to make its name with watches; Louis-François's son, Louis Joseph, had anticipated the wristwatch revolution when he set up a watchmaking department in the jewelry house in 1848. In 1888, the first lady's jewelry bracelet watch was created, and innovation followed innovation in the new century: in 1904 the first man's wristwatch with a leather strap for Alberto Santos-Dumont, the aviator who had complained about the impracticality of using a pocket watch while in the air; the Tonneau wristwatch in 1906, which has a deceptively simple-shaped barrel, curved to fit the shape of the wrist with a pair of brackets around a dial with Roman numerals; and in 1919, the first thin, lightweight Tank watch, inspired by military machines of World War I. Cartier watches were becoming so successful that in 1907 the house signed a deal with Edmond Jaeger to exclusively supply the movements.

Cartier was one of the first firms to embrace the Art Deco aesthetic; as far back as 1906, Louis Cartier, in collaboration with designer Charles Jacqueau, had experimented with geometric shapes. After this style of streamlined modernist elegance was showcased at the Exposition Internationale des Arts Décoratifs et Industriales Modernes held in Paris in 1925 it revolutionized jewelry. Here Cartier showed its "panther pavé" technique in which onyx dots were set in a ground of pavé diamonds. New advances in cutting such as the rectangular-shaped baguette gave gemstones a sharper line, complementing the Cubist-inspired Deco settings, and Cartier experimented with bold combinations of color, such as sapphires and emeralds with rock crystal. The discovery of

Tutankhamun's tomb in 1922 created a short-lived craze for Egyptian-style jewelry and Cartier set brooches, pendants, earrings, and hatpins with Egyptian artifacts. In 1924, a masterpiece of modernism was created, the three-band ring and bracelet that combined three colors of eighteen-karat gold to symbolize the different stages of a relationship: white for friendship, rose for love, and yellow for fidelity.

The house continued its watch design, including in 1922 a Tank Louis Cartier with the metal exterior made from eighteen-karat gold, including the casing, ardillon buckle, and circular grained crown set with a sapphire cabochon; the Tank Chinoise of 1926; and the Baguette of 1928, named because its shape resembled that of a baguette-cut gem. In 1942, Pierre Cartier gave all watches super-sophisticated movements made by the deluxe firms Patek Philippe, Vacheron Constantin, and Piguet, and in 1973, when Robert Hocq was named chairman of the company, many of the original watches were reissued, including the Tank, Vendôme, Santos, and Tortue models.

In the 1930s, Cartier developed a range of jewelry in the Mughal style, a highly decorative aesthetic derived from the Mughal Empire that controlled India from the sixteenth to the nineteenth centuries. The goal of Mughal design was to create a sense of paradise on earth by combining sumptuous color with exuberant carving. After Jacques Cartier visited India in 1911, he recognized its unearthly beauty and began to collect stones on his travels among the country's elite. After viewing Jacques' finds, Louis Cartier exhorted his designers, "You must infect the client with gemstone fever!" Accordingly, the carved Mughal stones were interspersed with brilliant-cut diamonds and ribbed and smooth beads, and invisibly set in platinum. Christened "tutti-frutti," this striking style became very much in vogue with Hollywood stars and royalty in the 1930s, including Edwina, Countess Mountbatten, who bought a £900 sapphire, emerald, and carved Indian ruby bandeau from Cartier.

During this period, Cartier moved into the design of whimsical accessories, including, as historian of the company Hans Nadelhoffer describes, "tin-openers with a crowned monogram, gold yoyos (W. K. Vanderbilt bought ten of them), and a diamond belt for the actress Polaire, not to mention gold toothpicks made for King Farouk, and a

Left, from top: 1. The Cartier Tank wristwatch of 1919. Louis Cartier was allegedly inspired by the sleek form of the new Renault FT-17 tanks being used on the Western Front. 2. The Trinity ring of 1924 made of intertwining pink, yellow gold, and white gold. 3. An illustration of the Panthère de Cartier platinum brooch, encrusted with baguette-cut diamonds, brilliant-cut diamonds, with an 8.03-karat sapphire cabochon, sapphire spots, onyx nose, and emerald eyes. **Right**: This Mughal-style "tutti frutti" necklace using amethyst, rubies, emeralds, and diamonds was commissioned from the House of Cartier by socialite Daisy Fellowes in 1936.

silver shoe which it took Cartier's master-craftsman Ferdinand Albouze 180 hours to complete in the firm's workshop." It was also in this decade that the renowned Jeanne Toussaint was appointed director of Cartier's Haute Jewelry in 1933—she was nicknamed "the Panther" by Louis Cartier because of her formidable attitude as she stalked the corridors. The panther motif had first appeared on the face of a wristwatch decorated with onyx and diamonds, but in the 1930s, as the firm began to move away from the geometry of Art Deco, the big cat began to take center stage. Toussaint is perhaps best remembered for the jewelry she designed for the Duchess of Windsor, a.k.a. Wallis Simpson. The Duke of Windsor commissioned many jewels for his wife from Jeanne Touissant at Cartier, including the first fully three-dimensional panther brooch in 1948, and an articulated onyx and diamond panther bracelet designed in 1952 that anticipated Cartier's iconic "great cat" jewels introduced in that decade designed by Toussaint and Peter Lemarchand. Their gold, sapphire, and diamond panthers were a huge success and many of

the original designs are still being produced. Toussaint also introduced bracelets with animal head terminals in carved *pelle d'angelo* coral and diamonds, many of which are still available today.

Cartier is now owned by Richemont, a Swiss-based conglomerate of luxury labels that includes Van Cleef & Arpels, Lancel, Dunhill, Chloé, and Montblanc. It has expanded into 200 retail outlets with flagship boutiques in Paris, New York, and London that sell not only *haute joaillerie*, including the celebrated panther pieces and the iconic Tank watches, but other accessories such as scarves, pens, and cufflinks, and a variety of own-brand fragrances. Great Cartier jewels are still worn on some momentous state celebrations by the world's iconic figures; in 2011, on the occasion of the royal wedding of Prince William of Wales and Catherine Middleton, the bride's veil was held in place by a Cartier tiara, the "Halo" of 1936, originally commissioned by King George VI for his wife and presented by the Queen Mother to her daughter, Elizabeth, on her eighteenth birthday.

1849
HUNTSMAN

Founded in 1849 by Henry Huntsman, this quintessentially English tailor has always been a byword for bespoke, creating clothes that transcend the fickleness of fashion. The original business supplied gaiters, breeches, and equestrian and other sporting clothes to the landed gentry, and in 1865 received a royal warrant for providing said items for the pleasure-seeking Bertie, Prince of Wales, who was crowned King Edward VII in 1901. By 1919, Huntsman was situated at No. 11 Savile Row and in 1921 acquired the distinctive stags' heads that adorn the walls of the shop today (reputedly left behind accidentally by a customer),which, together with the leather Chesterfields and open fire, give it the feel of an exclusive gentlemen's club. Huntsman is known for the uncompromising standards of its bespoke with some very well-heeled customers visiting the shop. In his book *Bespoke* (2009), Richard Anderson, who was head cutter at Huntsman in the 1990s, tells the eponymous tale of "the fourth wealthiest man in England," who walked into a shop in Savile Row and "said he wanted to order some overcoats. The salesman

on duty presented the customer with a book of cashmere swatch samples from which to choose. The customer began flipping through the swatches, occasionally ear-marking one, until he had been through the entire catalog, which contained about 100 samples. When he was done the customer handed it back to the salesman with four samples pulled aside. Chuffed, naturally, for an order of four cashmere overcoats would make any salesman's day, the salesman said, 'Very good, Sir. Those are the four you want?' To which the customer replied, 'No. Those are the four I don't want.'"

Huntsman required, both then and now, three fittings for a suit; at the first, comprehensive measurements are taken—nineteen in all—although some employees have what is called in the trade "rock of eye," the ability to cut a pattern from a combination of basic measurements and innate instinct rather than a standard cutting system. From these, five basic templates are cut, which include three for the jacket and two for the pants; the pieces are "basted," or sewn together with loose white stitches and fitted on the customer, taking heed of the advice written in the *Dictionary of English Trades* (1804) "to create a good shape where nature has not granted one." Huntsman's renowned window-pane check has to be perfectly matched by the cutter who, when striking or cutting out the pieces, allows an extra 4 inches (10 cm) to ensure the patterns line up and pockets and lapels integrate perfectly; cutting out from unpatterned cloth has to be in the same direction to avoid shading; cotton, linen, and silk are cut to allow for shrinkage. The art of cutting is such that, over time, Huntsman's experts have acquired cult status, including Colin Hammick, whose goal was to "improve on the perfect fit," and Brian Hall who was the first to successfully adapt the Huntsman style to women's bespoke

Below: The interior of the Huntsman workshop, photographed in 1957.
Right, clockwise from top left: 1. The interior of the Huntsman store displaying the stag's heads that were reputedly left behind by a customer in the 1920s. 2. The exterior of the Huntsman store. 3. Huntsman's Pashley-Deli bicycle used in the special delivery of suits.

"Within the house line, an individual cutter's hands will make their own tiny indelible stamp…"

Richard Anderson, former head cutter at Huntsman

Far left: The processes of making a bespoke Huntsman suit with the chalk marks indicating areas of adjustment. In 2012, Huntsman was bought by Pierre Lagrange and Roubi L'Roubi who, as a couturier, applies the same bespoke standards to womenswear. **Left**: The pattern pieces of Huntsman's famous customers including actor Gregory Peck and former U.S. President Ronald Reagan.

tailoring. As Anderson writes, "Huntsman's house style was so distinct that if two unacquainted men were walking down the street or sharing the lift in Claridge's, and both happened to be wearing a suit of Huntsman provenance, they would almost always recognize as much. And yet, within the house line, an individual cutter's hands will make their own tiny indelible stamp—an ever-so-slightly rounder or straighter front edge, for example."

From 1932 to 1966, Huntsman was owned by Savile Row-trained cutter Robert Packer, a canny businessman who instilled a fashion sensibility into the brand and, like Kilgour (see page 154), subsequently attracted a glamorous host of U.S. stars including Clark Gable, Gregory Peck, Paul Newman, and Katharine Hepburn. Huntsman's employees, like those of other Savile Row tailors, made regular transatlantic trips to do fittings for and take commissions from their American clients, and the salesmen would tout for new business. In the late 1940s, Huntsman became known for lounge suits with svelte one-button jackets, and pants with one front pleat that had an innovative silhouette described by one U.S. client as "swervy suave severity"; the firm shoulders, tapered waist, and higher armhole had their origins in the tailoring and proportions of the riding coat mixed with a dinner jacket. Packer was also responsible for introducing a system in which every component of the garments was made in-house, rather than relying on Savile Row's body of outworkers, thus

ensuring total quality. Richard Walker, in *The Savile Row Story* (1998), writes, "What Packer put together was a formula for efficiency at any price. Whereas the traditional bespoke suit was put together by an individual coat-maker, trouser-maker and waistcoat-maker, Huntsman opted for a production-line system, with garments progressing along assembly lines of artisans in two workshops. To compensate for any perceived loss of romance, Huntsman stressed traditional techniques, to the point of not electrifying one of its workshops." During Packer's reign, Huntsman received the prestigious commission of designing suits for the 1966 World Cup-winning England soccer team.

Today Huntsman remains a temple to the art of bespoke, a status that was recognized by the fashion industry in 2002 and 2011 when the brand teamed up with the House of Alexander McQueen, an apt collaboration as the iconoclastic fashion designer had trained at Savile Row's Anderson & Sheppard, eventually working on Prince Charles's suits. The result was a series of hand-stitched outfits for the menswear end of McQueen, including a black cashmere overcoat, Prince of Wales check suit, and a velvet dinner jacket. In 2012, Huntsman was bought by the partnership of Pierre Lagrange and couturier Roubi L'Roubi, a specialist in women's bespoke tailoring who took the position of creative director, having formerly worked with Holland and Holland and Henry Poole on ladies' sporting tweeds.

1854
LOUIS VUITTON

Traveling by coach in France in the mid-nineteenth century was an uncomfortable experience. Journeys were long and roads rutted and potholed, which meant that any precious objects had to be packed carefully to survive the rigors of travel. Thus it became customary for all items of value to be transported in made-to-measure wooden boxes that could withstand the journey and the notoriously rough touch of the French baggage handlers. Louis Vuitton, whose name is now synonymous with luxury leather goods, was originally employed as a box maker and luggage packer for Romain Maréchal who catered to Paris's haute bourgeoisie. It was a job in which he reached the giddy heights of packing gowns for the Empress Eugénie, consort of Napoleon III. Vuitton's reputation as the trusted box maker and packer of the empress's possessions convinced him to set up a business under his own name as a *malletier,* or trunk maker, in 1854, and he opened his first store on Rue Neuve-des-Capucines. From the very beginning, Vuitton was a canny operator, astutely marketing himself as a specialist in the "packing of fashions" at a time when Paris was styling itself as the center of haute couture. New sartorial codes adopted by the haute bourgeoisie and fostered by the couturier Charles Frederick Worth led to some fashionable women taking up to five changes of clothes per day when on vacation, and the huge crinoline skirts that were de rigeur at the time were notoriously difficult to pack. The actress Sarah Bernhardt was known to take up to 200 trunks with her when holidaying abroad, many of them made by Vuitton.

In Paris Louis Vuitton invented the first flat trunk, an elegant, streamlined departure from the old-style rustic version. The latter had a domed lid to allow rainwater to drain off and was made of pigskin complete with bristles, the sight of which, as French historian Paul-Gérard Pasols comments, "must haven given travelers a sense, not of the pleasures before them, but of cold, uncertainty, pitfalls to overcome, maybe even of packs of wolves to fight off." Vuitton's trunk was different: flat, elegant, and light, fashioned out of poplar wood covered with waterproof dove-gray canvas with a trim of lacquered iron, and it was ingeniously stackable—a key example of early modernist design. With the creation of this simple yet innovative object, Louis Vuitton managed to establish a crucial link between modernity, luxury, and travel. The company capitalized upon this for more than 100 years, cleverly making the brand highly recognizable on the exterior

with the introduction of the LV Monogram canvas in 1896. This was secured from being counterfeited with a patent that protected the use of the quatrefoils and flowers interspersed with the LV monogram in the popular Japonisme style of the day.

After Louis's death in 1892, his son, Georges, took over and began a series of extensions to the brand, including the Steamer bag of 1901 originally designed to sit inside a Vuitton trunk and hold dirty laundry. It became one of the company's most successful handmade bags; the deluxe version in crocodile or ostrich is still made by one artisan from start to finish today. The Steamer was followed by the Keepall of 1930, a light soft travel bag for weekends away; the classic Noe of 1932 was a drawstring bag of cotton-coated canvas with cowhide trim, originally designed to carry five bottles of champagne (four with one upside down in the middle) but used by women as a handbag when it was fashioned from soft Monogram canvas in 1959. The Speedy, a smaller version of the Keepall, was also launched in 1932 with a shape reminiscent of the traditional doctor's bag and it remains one of the most popular designs today. These luxurious bags were sold in the Louis Vuitton stores that were opening in many major cities, including New York, Bombay,

Washington, London, Alexandria, and Buenos Aires; in 1913, the largest travel goods emporium in the world opened on the Champs-Élysées in Paris. By the cinematic era of the 1920s and 1930s, fans could flip open a movie magazine and peruse photographs of their favorite stars, such as Marlene Dietrich, Cary Grant, and Douglas Fairbanks, traveling from one glamorous location to another with matching sets of Vuitton luggage. Fairbanks, a well-known enthusiast for all things bespoke, including John Lobb shoes, James Lock hats, and Savile Row suits, carried a Vuitton Roma suitcase in cowhide, made for him personally in 1925; it can be seen in the Vuitton Museum in Paris.

After the death of Georges Vuitton in 1936, his son, Gaston-Louis Vuitton, took over the company and a range of monogrammed accessories was developed from coin purses and wallets through to the ubiquitous trunks. In 1959, a suppler and thus more malleable version of the Monogram canvas was introduced; it was used in the Papillon (1966), a barrel-shaped bag with shoulder straps that became the model Twiggy's favorite fashion accessory. In 1987, a new era began for Louis Vuitton when it became the flagship of the publicly traded fashion powerhouse LVMH (Louis Vuitton Moet Hennessy), at first run by Henri Racamier, the son-in-law of Gaston-

Left: Vuitton created a flat, light trunk with a poplar wood frame covered with waterproof dove-gray canvas and a trim of lacquered iron that was easily stackable. **Above right**: A parade of fashionable shoppers outside Louis Vuitton, Trouville-sur-mer, in 1911. **Far right**: Actor and director Pierre Étaix, regarded as the French Buster Keaton, carries a Vuitton suitcase in his movie *Yoyo* (1965).

"Louis Vuitton managed to make a crucial link between modernity, luxury, and travel."

Louis Vuitton, and in 1988 under the aegis of Bernard Arnault. By 1989, Louis Vuitton had 130 stores across the globe and was one of the first luxury brands to penetrate the Chinese market in 1992 when an outlet opened at the Palace Hotel in Beijing. The historic Damier checked canvas, first used in 1888, was revived together with another item from the archives, the Alma bag from 1934. The luxury that the firm of Louis Vuitton continued to represent became more democratic, crossing the boundaries of age, race, and social status, and it expanded onto the catwalk in 1997, when the company invited celebrated New York designer Marc Jacobs to become creative director with the brief to create the brand's first ready-to-wear collection and a contemporary line of shoes and bags.

The first Vuitton collection by Jacobs launched in 1998 and featured the most minimal of bags, a white messenger with a discreet embossed LV logo. Jacobs described his approach, "The first season I tortured myself mentally: 'What should we do? What do people expect?' Well, we shouldn't give them what they expect. What is luxury? We looked at this gray trunk [the original Louis Vuitton design] and thought, 'We've got to start somewhere.' There is no archive of clothes. We had to start from a blank page. So [the model] Kirsten Owen, with that white messenger bag, was the beginning. Everything was internal—the Vuitton label was underneath the buttons. The luxury was hidden, not in your face." Jacobs began to create what can only be described as an alternative universe at Vuitton; on the one hand there were the traditional products that appealed to the most refined of tastes, on the other a brand new fashion-conscious audience, lured in through the avant-garde reputation of the maverick designer.

This approach can be seen at its most effective when Jacobs asked three contemporary artists to experiment with the iconic Vuitton canvas, essentially calling for a reinvention of tradition. Stephen Sprouse came first, a much-lauded figure on the New York fashion scene of the 1980s who had made his name designing stage clothes for Debbie Harry of Blondie. Sprouse was known for his striking graphic prints in contrasting neon colors, including his signature hot punk pink. Arguably Sprouse's best work had been in collaboration with the New York graffiti artist Keith Haring with whom he had produced neon prints of hand-painted scribbles that looked as if they had been lifted from subway walls and made the wearer look as if they had been caught full force in the fire of a spray can. A similar aesthetic was used in Sprouse's

work for Vuitton in which he stylishly defaced the iconic Monogram canvas with neon graffiti for a series of bags launched in Spring/Summer 2001. These were strikingly modern yet recognizably Vuitton: bags that transposed the raw power of a spray-painted subway wall onto the hide of luxurious calfskin.

The second artist working with Jacobs was Takashi Murakami, known for his "superflat" aesthetic, a flattened-out, two-dimensional approach to surfaces based on traditional Japanese prints and what he saw as their modern counterpart, anime and manga. For Murakami, "superflat" also symbolized the blurring of boundaries between high and low culture in post war Japanese society. In 2002, the artist reworked the Monogram canvas into thirty-three colors set against a pure white ground followed by the now instantly recognizable LV cherry print.

The final artist, Richard Prince, had a more conceptual approach, and for Spring/Summer 2008, in collaboration with Jacobs, Prince interpreted his own infamous *Nurse* paintings, begun in 2002 and inspired by

the covers of pulp fiction, and parleyed the imagery into an entire show. Models wore white synthetic transparent coats over neon hand-painted dresses with black lace face masks and white nurse's caps. They carried Pulp Monogram canvas bags that had been faux antiqued with imagery and partially legible fragments of lettering from jokes culled from U.S. magazines or pony skin laser-cut with the Monogram design and embroidered with cartoons from retro *New Yorker* magazines.

Although Vuitton is now a massive organization, bespoke still exists with its special-order bags and trunks, which are all handmade. More rarefied creations also make their mark, creating headlines around the world; for Spring/Summer 2012 Jacobs showed the Coquille d'Oeuf minaudière, a modern version of a luxurious bag. Minaudières are the most precious of bags, originally designed by Van Cleef & Arpels in 1933 as a combination of purse and powder compact. Charles Arpel had spied socialite Florence Jay Gould using a metal Lucky Strike tin to carry her cosmetics and cigarette lighter. As a result Van Cleef & Arpels created the minaudière, a sleek metal box featuring several articulated and hidden compartments that could hold cigarettes, money, and cosmetics, rendered in the most luxurious of materials such as engine-turned gold, sterling silver, or layers of glistening Japanese lacquer. Jacobs's postmodern minaudiere took 300 hours to craft out of 12,500 fragments of eggshell pieced together to form the Monogram pattern. He described it as "the greatest thing we have done in terms of craftsmanship. I felt it was at the zenith of craft and luxury. It wasn't diamonds or crocodile, it was taking an egg—and a hen's egg at that, not one from a rarefied bird—and painstakingly elevating something mundane to an absolute peak."

Today the majority of Vuitton's high output has to be sewn by machine to meet global consumer demand. Arnault says, "Production is organized in such a way that we have unbelievably high productivity. Every single motion, every step of every process, is carefully planned with the most modern and complete engineering technology. A single purse can have up to 1,000 manufacturing tasks and we plan every one." The Vuitton trunk is still made today in a workshop in Asnières-sur-Seine in Paris adjoining Louis Vuitton's family home and using the same production methods. The frame is constructed from African okoumé with a distinctive canvas hinge invented by Vuitton to ensure the rear of the trunk was completely flat when being transported—a metal hinge could damage other trunks or break when being stacked. The frame is covered with waterproofed Monogram or Damier check canvas, which is glued down, and the corners are protected with brass or leather covers. The lozine trim, a mix of compressed cloth and paper, is nailed to the edges of the trunk together with the middle belt of poplar wood. Finally the Vuittonitte cotton canvas or Alcantara faux suede lining is glued over the interior and the Louis Vuitton logoed canvas straps are attached to hold the traveler's clothes. The company's skilled artisans build approximately 500 per year.

Today Jacobs describes Vuitton as, " a great name. A famous unique house that will exist after me. Vuitton is not a fashion company. We make 'fashionable things,' we introduced the idea of fashion, which changes according to the mood of the times, the icons of popular culture. But the heart of the brand remains unchanged and unchangeable, which is just as well."

Overleaf, clockwise from top left: 1. Close up of white monogram Mahina leather bag with brass hardware. 2. A detail of the stamp on a Louis Vuitton bag handle. 3. The component parts of a Vuitton case including the Damier Azur canvas, handle, and closure.

Far left: A craftsman constructs a bag's lock and key at the Vuitton workshop in Asnières-sur-Seine, Paris. **Left**: The distinctive Monogram cloth designed in 1896 by Georges, Louis Vuitton's son. **Below**: The Louis Vuitton Murakami Multicolor Eye Love You bag in white, a collaboration between Marc Jacobs and Takashi Murakami. **Bottom**: Fashion photographer Bert Stern photographed Twiggy for *Vogue* in 1967 holding her favorite bag, the Vuitton Papillon.

1854
OMBRELLIFICIO MAGLIA FRANCESCO

In the little hill town of Gignese in the Piedmont region of northern Italy lies a museum devoted to one of Italy's greatest contributions to fashion, the art of umbrella making. The country's umbrella history dates back to ancient Rome where they were used as protection from the sun and the rain. When in the amphitheater, members of the audience used *umbraculum*, canopies made of hide that could be raised and lowered at will. The practice of carrying an umbrella was revived during the Renaissance; the wealthy Italian city-states were centers of fashion that informed the rest of Europe into the seventeenth century, and in 1608 Thomas Coryat described how "many of the Italians carry fine things which they commonly call in the Italian tongue, umbrellas, that is, things that minister shadow onto them, for shelter against the scorching heat of the sun. These are made of leather, something answerable to the form of a little canopy and hooped on the inside with diverse little hoops that extend the umbrella in a pretty large compass." These umbrellas were made by the "ombrellai," as they were known, based in the Piedmont, and by the eighteenth century the region was the center of Italy's umbrella production. The system operated on child labor, many apprenticed for five years before making umbrellas and traveling to Genoa to sell them on to shops and wholesale businesses that would, in turn, export the items around Europe. The first Englishman to regularly carry an umbrella, Jonas Hanway, actually bought his Piedmontese version from Livorno in Italy (see page 60). The Piedmont ombrellai were a closed community and in order to keep their trade secrets safe they developed a covert language of their own known as Tarùsc that dated back to Roman times; it contained many words for the umbrella including *lùscia* or regular type; *ritúsc* for an umbrella made of silk, and a broken umbrella was called a *rajòn*.

Italy remains an important source of bespoke umbrellas today, and one of the precious few companies that make umbrellas by hand is family-owned company Ombrellificio Maglia Francesco, or Maglia for short. Maglia was established in Italy by umbrella maker Francesco Maglia, who had been producing bespoke work since the age of fourteen when he had been apprenticed to an umbrella maker in the mountain village of Montichiari in Lombardy. In 1854, he became a partner in a small-scale business in Verolanuova, and in 1856 he moved to the ancient university town of Pavia and founded his own-name company. Maglia is based in Milan today and has, since 1993, occupied a premises in the Via Ripamonti, run by the fifth generation of the family, Francesco and Giorgio. Maglia's bespoke umbrellas are made in their workshop in Milan and can be customized according to the specifications of the customer.

The constituent parts that make up a Maglia umbrella are, for the most part, made in Italy, sourced within the

Aurelia   Olga Bellani   zio Francesco   bisnonno Francesco   nonno Angelo

Far left: Founder Franceso Maglia (fourth from left) with his sons Francesco and Angelo, who went on to inherit the family-run firm. **Left**: An original invitation to Maglia Francesco dating from the nineteenth century. **Right**: Maglia use a specialist company to make solid stick handles from a variety of different woods; some can take up to six months to steam into shape.

dal 1854

FABBRICA OMBRELLI

Maglia Francesco

MILANO

country, apart from the Chinese and Japanese bamboo used in some of the handles. The fabric for the canopies is finished, dyed, and printed in Como, a 2,000-year-old Roman town on the shore of Lake Como, one of the centers of the Italian textile industry since the late nineteenth century. All the metal hardware, including the cast iron slider and retractable clasp that opens and closes the umbrella and the brass for the milled crown that holds the spokes together, is made in the town, too, and wood is native, sourced indigenously whether it be cedar, ash, oak, or cherry.

The manufacturing process commences with fabric selection, no longer the traditional triple-woven shantung silk that Maglia originally used in all its umbrellas but a Jacquard mix of Teflon-coated cotton, silk, and wool. At this point, Maglia can provide a little personal touch by matching the umbrella to the customer's jacket lining, and vice versa. The fabric is then sized and cut into trapezoid shapes, and in an adjoining room in the Milanese workshop the wooden parts including the oiled tubular steel frame and the shaft are assembled. Each fabric panel is then sewn and fastened to the frame, making sure that the construction is covered up, and extra fabric is inserted where the spokes meet the fabric. The finished umbrella is inspected for any faults and finally steamed and packaged.

Maglia is renowned for its Solid Stick umbrella, a model in which the handle and shaft are constructed from one piece of wood, including walnut, chestnut, cherry, rosewood, or apple, among the myriad types to choose from. The handles are preshaped by a specialist company that creates the crook by holding it over hot steam. As each type of wood reacts differently to this process, it is a specialist job—some woods take up to six months to acquire the right shape, flexibility, and durability. The handle is finally braided with deluxe materials such as crocodile or finished with tortoiseshell. Maglia creates umbrellas for many upmarket stores around the world, such as Barneys and Bergdorf Goodman, New York, as well as Gucci, Loewe, and Paul Stuart, an exclusive mens' outfitters in the United States. Francesco "Chino" Maglia will also undertake more adventurous private commissions, "We once were asked to make umbrellas with whangee ribs. That was difficult, but not impossible." More recently Maglia was asked by Japanese customers to manufacture frilled lace parasols with bamboo and silver handles.

"The fabric for the canopies is finished, dyed, and printed in Como, a 2,000-year-old Roman town on the shore of Lake Como."

1856
BURBERRY

On January 19, 1912, Edward Wilson wrote in a diary entry of "a constant fall of minute snow crystals—very minute—that glitter in the sun as though of some size, but you can only just see them as pin heads on your Burberry." Wilson was a member of Captain Scott's ill-fated team, and he, like many other heroic explorers at the beginning of the twentieth century, was wearing weatherproof Burberry Gabardine.

Burberry has a long-standing history dating back to 1856, with the first Burberry store opening in Winchester

Street, Basingstoke, Hampshire, a market town some 50 miles (80 km) from London. Founder Thomas Burberry, a twenty-one-year-old draper's apprentice and dressmaker had founded what was to become one of the world's most successful luxury brands. The company gained momentum when Thomas's sons, Thomas Newman and Arthur Michael, joined in the 1880s and began to concentrate on outerwear and sports clothes. Burberry began to expand, and in 1891 opened a second store in Haymarket, London. It is reported that in 1901, the company opened up a competition to the public to design a logo for the brand. The Equestrian Knight was chosen, which illustrates a charging knight on horseback carrying a flowing banner emblazoned with the Latin *Prorsum*, meaning "forward." By adding *Prorsum*, Burberry suggested its progress in manufacturing and invention. From 1909, weatherproof coats designed by the brand were called "The Burberry," and in that same year, Burberry opened its first international store in Paris on the Boulevard Malesherbes in Paris; in 1913, Burberry moved to a larger London premises at 18–21 Haymarket designed by British architect Walter Cave.

Burberry was well known for the invention and innovative use of Gabardine, a porous, triple-proofed cotton cloth, woven from fine compacted Egyptian threads that were welded closely together. Gabardine was different to the customary rubber or oiled silk used for rainwear because it allowed air to reach the body, and so was the perfect material for the manufacture of weatherproof outerwear. In 1868, Burberry set up a factory in New Street, Basingstoke, followed by one in London Street in 1892 to manufacture the cloth that was then exported abroad wholesale. One early advertisement stressed its practicality: "T. Burberry's Gabardine—for

India and the Colonies is the most suitable of materials. It resists hot and cold winds, rain or thorns, and forms a splendid top garment for the coldest climates." Burberry recognized the potential of Gabardine by patenting it in 1888, retaining the manufacturing rights until 1917. Counterfeiting was a problem, even this early on in the company's history; in 1915 an advertisement in *The Montreal Gazette* ran, "Every genuine Burberry coat shows the Burberry label. The clerk will show it for your information."

In a world in which the whole notion of travel was changing with the advent of the automobile, ocean liner, and airplane, Burberry manufactured a variety of outfits for both men and women, including traveling capes in check and the Burberry traveling gown of 1910 in its lovat and cheviot tweed weave, described as "a graceful and easy-fitting model in which supreme comfort is as obvious as elegance of design. Lightweight, warm, and weatherproof." Gabardine was soon used in a range of motoring apparel for early motorists as well as more luxury weatherproof wool garments with leather linings. An entry in an old catalog reads, "Burberry adapts itself to the exigencies of travel in either closed or open cars and at the same time satisfies every ideal of good taste and distinction." In 1912, Burberry patented the forerunner to the iconic trench coat, the Tielocken, a weatherproof coat worn by British naval and military officers during World War I and World War II, and advertised under the title, "The Severest Test." The advert continued, "the severest test that a Weatherproof can undergo is a campaign, involving exposure to every kind of weather for months on end and it is under such conditions that the Tielocken Burberry proves itself "the most effectual safeguard ever invented." It did not have any buttons but

fastened with a strap and a buckle. Between 1914 and 1918, it is estimated that 500,000 coats were worn by officers in combat; the trench coat's association with the officer class also gave it an élan and heroism that appealed to countless men.

Burberry also provided apparel for a whole series of adventurous explorers: in 1910, the company supplied the tents and outfits for Norwegian Roald Amundsen, the first man to reach the South Pole. Amundsen wrote from Hobart extolling the virtues of his Gabardine clothes, "Heartiest thanks. Burberry overalls were made extensive use of during the sledge journey to the Pole and proved real good friends indeed." Captain Robert Falcon Scott, a Royal Navy officer and explorer who led two expeditions into the Antarctic, was sheltered from blizzards in a Burberry Gabardine tent as was Ernest Shackleton on his four expeditions to cross Antarctica. Shackleton's navigator, F. A. Worsley, described wearing "a blouse and trousers fastened securely around neck, wrists, waist, and ankles, so that no air could get in. The Burberrys, being windproof, surrounded us with an invisible garment of warmed air, but, not being airtight, did not make us perspire as furs would have done." On June 9, 1924, British mountaineer George Mallory was last sighted on Mount Everest with his climbing partner, Andrew Irvine, a few yards away from the summit, clothed in Burberry's Gabardine.

With such credentials Burberry was regarded as an expert in the field of weatherproof garments for use in the snow, and soon created skiwear for the general population. The Gabardine ski suits were available in the early twentieth century and became very popular during the 1920s when the vogue for skiing took off for both men and women. Serious skiers were supposed to wear muted colors: "the somber colors of the mountaineer" as one observer put it, as color appeared too vulgar against the crisp white of the snow. Members of the Downhill Club, one of the oldest skiing clubs in the world, founded in Wengen in the Jungfrau in 1925, wore Burberry jackets in gray, black, and bottle green, but Burberry also created ski wear in vivid colors such as bright orange and fuchsia pink. Burberry moved into designing garments for aviators, too; in 1910 aviator Claude Grahame-White, the first person to fly between London and Manchester in less than twenty-four hours, also wore a Gabardine Burberry Aeroplane Outrig; the aviator team of Captain John Alcock and Lieutenant Arthur Whitten Brown wore Burberry aviator suits during the first non stop transatlantic flight in 1919 in a modified Vickers Vimy bomber with an exposed cockpit.

By the 1920s and 1930s, the popularity of playing and watching sports created a demand for functional, durable clothes with a degree of fashionable style. Sportswear became a new clothing classification that had such *je ne sais quoi* that some of Paris's most important fashion designers soon became involved, including Coco Chanel, Jean Patou, and Elsa Schiaparelli. Burberry golfing jackets and coats could be seen on the links and their advertising in both the United Kingdom and France emphasized both the quality of the sports clothes and of the fabrics used.

Left, clockwise from top left: 1. The brand prides itself on great attention to detail in the finishing of its iconic trench. 2. The Burberry Commander II, launched in 1960. 3. The constituent parts of a Burberry trench buckle. 4. Although the firm has become a global brand, it still retains many elements of bespoke. **Below**: Explorer Ernest Shackleton chose Burberry Gabardine over the more traditional fur for his outerwear.

"[Burberry] designed everything from coats for the Antarctic to dresses for a London cocktail party."

Christopher Bailey, Burberry's chief creative officer

Above: The Burberry Prorsum Fall/Winter 2013 Menswear Show in Milan. **Left**: Burberry's creative director from 2001—now chief creative officer—Christopher Bailey. **Right**: The Burberry Prorsum womenswear Fall/Winter 2013 show finale, held in a custom-built Burberry venue in Hyde Park, London, in February 2013.

One such advert stated that "the word 'BURBERRY' is synonymous with PERFECTION."

In 1920, the brand was floated on the stock exchange and became a public company under the name Burberrys Limited. The iconic Burberry check on a camel background has since become an internationally recognized signifier of the brand, featuring on accessories such as umbrellas, scarves, handbags, and luggage, and by the 1990s on myriad products from pants and mini-kilts through to boxer shorts, and ending up in the new millennium on the incredibly successful Burberry bikini. The trenchcoat became a stylish, even glamorous urban raincoat, and was worn by characters in a range of films, including Joanna Kramer played by actress Meryl Streep in *Kramer Vs. Kramer* (1979).The wool-lined weatherproofed cotton raincoat with Burberry check lining and fly front—or Commander II as it was named—was launched in 1960, and its more minimalist lines were echoed in Burberry's structured wool outerwear throughout the decade.

In 1926, Thomas Burberry died and his son, Arthur Michael Burberry, headed up the business until the beginning of the 1950s; in 1955, GUS or Great Universal Stores, acquired the company, the same year that Burberry was granted its first royal warrant by HM Queen Elizabeth II as Weatherproofers. In 1991, the company shortened its name to "Burberry," and in 1997, Rose Marie Bravo, former president of Saks Fifth Avenue, was appointed as chief executive. Her brief was to strengthen Burberry's position as a luxury British brand, building on its heritage. Christopher Bailey was brought in as creative director in 2001 and launched a series of collections that took British tradition as a starting point but gave it a much-needed contemporary edge. In 2002 he stated, "What attracted me to Burberry was the richness of the brand. Not just its archives, but its mentality. The founder Thomas Burberry was a brilliantly innovative designer... In his day motorcars were becoming important, so he pioneered a whole series of clothes for cars that changed the way people dressed. He was also able to design an incredibly broad choice of clothes, everything from coats for the Antarctic to dresses for a London cocktail party."

Bailey unveiled a series of evocative advertising campaigns shot by acclaimed fashion photographer Mario

Testino and featuring models *du jour* Kate Moss and Stella Tennant; the company shortened the name to Burberry in 1999 and opened a flagship store on New Bond Street, London. He also launched the fashion-forward label Prorsum in which, like Karl Lagerfeld at Chanel in the 1980s, Bailey played with the house codes. The trench coat was sexed up with metallic leathers and the check lining turned inside out and used as an exterior print on both men's and women's coats; in 2006, the trench became a silk-faille dress in lilac with a crimson lining and in 2009 it was made body-con in stretch satin. In 2011, Kate Middleton, soon to join the British royal family on her marriage to Prince William, was photographed in a trench with a ruffled hem; it immediately sold out online. Bravo exercised tight control over distribution, refusing to allow Burberry products in stores whose image was not consistent with the increasingly hip brand, although there was little she could do to alleviate its popularity among the "chav" subculture, the British equivalent of "white trash." As she

put it in 2004, "We had this issue with logo-ism that was rampant across the industry. But we know that these things run in cycles, you can have too much of a good thing. We moved on, and we got into a mode of being more discreet with the logo." By 2011, only 10 percent of the company's products displayed an overt check.

In 2006, Angela Ahrendts was appointed chief executive officer of Burberry. She has led the brand through a period of exceptional global growth, with revenues tripling between 2006 and 2013, driven by a focus on culture, core values, and creativity. In 2009, Christopher Bailey was named chief creative officer, a newly created position in recognition of his outstanding contribution to the brand since joining in 2001. In his role he is responsible for all of the Burberry collections and products as well as advertising art direction and overall brand image. Today Burberry has more than 500 stores in more than fifty countries and it is globally recognized as epitomizing the cutting edge of true British style.

1857
BORSALINO

Borsalino is a name that conjures up magical moments from cinema history for the company's hats have been worn on screen by the most shining of stars, from Fred Astaire, Gary Cooper, and Orson Welles through to Al Pacino, Robert De Niro, and Johnny Depp. Celebrated war correspondent Ernie Pyle traveled with a solitary suit, three ties, a generous supply of cheap white cotton socks, and a lightweight wide-brimmed felt hat from Borsalino. Pyle had to buy his Borsalinos in bulk after forgetting to pick them up from hatcheck girls after a hard nights of carousing and most notably left one on the set of a Joan Crawford movie in Los Angeles.

The label's best-known hat is the felted fedora, patented under the name Borsalino and manufactured from 1857. The hat had an unusual silhouette with origins in the violent street demonstrations that took place during the Risorgimento, the nineteenth-cenury Italian unification movement. Alessandro Giuseppe Borsalino, the founder of the firm, had seen the crown of Bowler hats dented by blows to the head and crushed underfoot. He took the

dent and turned it into a design feature, the "vaga" or "crease," an unusual detail that also had a practical use: it made it easier for the man to doff his hat when in the company of a lady. In the later model, the front of the fedora was pinched to create the bozze, two indentations that made the hat even easier to grasp, lift, and replace politely. The fedora was also flexible enough to be folded and stowed away in a pocket while still retaining its shape. A pinch-fronted version with a teardrop-shaped crown was most famously worn by a trench-coated Humphrey Bogart in *Casablanca* (1942) and had a renaissance after being sported by John Belushi in *The Blues Brothers* (1980).

Alessandro Giuseppe Borsalino was born in Pecetto di Valenza on September 15, 1834, in the Piedmont region of Italy, and at the age of fourteen was employed as an errand boy and apprentice at the Campagna Hat Company in the historic city of Alessandria. In 1850 he traveled to France, where he was apprenticed to A. Berteil et Cie. in Paris, a well-known manufacturer and retailer of fur felt hats. After seven years, Borsalino was skilled enough in the trade to return to his native town, and armed with his hatter's licence he set up the first Borsalino workshop with his brother, Lazzaro, in Via Schiavina. The business started small, with Giuseppe making hats while simultaneously training ten workers and completing fifty hats per day, but as staff increased so did output; the eventual 130 employees maintained a daily turnover of 300 handmade hats. Giuseppe realized that if the company were to expand any further, production needed to be increased, and so in 1888 he imported state-of-the-art machinery being used in Denton, near Manchester in England, to manufacture felt hats by mechanically separating the fur from the hide. Denton was at the center of the felt hat industry in

Left: Founder of the firm Alessandro Giuseppe Borsalino was born in Pecetto di Valenza, Italy, in 1834. **Above right**: A Marcello Dudovich-designed advert from 1923, referencing the contemporary debate of creation versus evolution. **Right**: The movie *Borsalino & Co.* (1974) was so named because the director thought the firm's fedora evoked the necessary gangster glamour.

Britain, with the first recorded felt hat being made there in 1702—by 1907 the town made 14.5 million. Legend has it that in 1897 Giuseppe again improved his stock by using British techniques after visiting Battersby & Co.'s hat works in Stockport to investigate how Bowlers were made. He secretly dipped his handkerchief into a vat of the shellac used to stiffen the felt to make the perfect Bowler hat and took the recipe back to Italy. The result was an unmistakably Italian version of the conservative British hat, the Borsalino Trionfo Bowler with a stiffened crown and a distinctive upturned Homburg brim.

The Borsolino Montecristi Panama made from South American toquilla palm fiber was renowned for its handsome ivory hue. The panama was a traditional hat originally brought into Europe from Ecuador by the Spanish conquistadores, who were supposedly so entranced by the delicacy of its material that they thought it had been fashioned from the skin of bats. By the nineteenth century, the Montecristi Panama was an established summer hat notoriously worn by Napoleon during his years of exile on St. Helena, and in 1900 it gained renown in the United States after being worn by President Theodore Roosevelt when visiting the Panama Canal.

Today the Borsolino Panama is still fashioned from the toquilla palm grown on traditional plantations along the coast of Ecuador. The verdant green palm fibers are harvested before reaching the flowering stage, and the yard-long *cogollos*, or sheaths, are cut to reveal flexible filaments of tender palm fiber, which are boiled in clay pots then dried naturally in the wind. The dried straw is washed and smoked over a sulfur brazier, in a process that gives it a distinctive ivory color, and it is then dried again before the premium, or the finest fibers, are selected to be woven into the panama. The Montecristi Extrafine is the lightest weight of panama as it uses the finest of fibers that take the longest to weave, a full six months for one hat. The panama is woven from the rosetta, a web of eight fine threads of fiber that forms the center of the crown, and more fiber is added until the wings or sides of the hat are reached. The finisher examines the hat to make sure that the color is perfect and the weaving is tight, and the resulting shape is lightly blocked or steamed over a wooden head shape. The finishing touch comes when the classic black hat band is hand-sewn on.

At the time of Giuseppe's death in 1900, the company was in great shape; its reputation was such that more than half of its hats were being exported to the United States, Britain, and France. Giuseppe's son, Teresio, took over the running of the company and production continued to increase from 2,800 hats a day in 1901 to 5,500 in 1909. In 1911, the company began to work with painter-turned-poster artist Trieste, born Marcello Dudovich, known as the "poet of the Belle Époque." Dudovich's wife, Elise Bucchi, worked for a number of Italian fashion magazines and using her influence he presented an advertising image to Borsalino that won a competition to launch its Zenit hat, even though he had not officially entered. This began a fruitful relationship through the 1920s, with Dudovich designing a number of successful billboard advertising campaigns for the company. In 1921, *The American Hatter* wrote: "Every Borsalino sold means dollars worth of newspaper advertising, for it is bound to

"Every Borsalino sold means dollars worth of newspaper advertising, for it is bound to make loyal, constant friends."

The American Hatter, 1921

make loyal, constant friends. The satisfied Borsalino customer comes back to you; the price is not the first consideration, but 'ANOTHER BORSALINO' is."

By the 1930s, Borsalino was selling more than two million hats per year, exporting all over the world, and the fedora began its association with the underworld when worn as a status symbol by young French and Italian gangsters in Marseilles and Milan who were nicknamed "Borsalinos." The Borsalino fedora was so popular that inferior copies began to flood the market (as early as 1913, fakes were being manufactured in Melbourne, Australia) and allegedly the Borsalinos devised a test to prove a hat's authenticity to other members of the gang; the first step was to roll the fedora into a cylinder, then into a tight tube, and then pass it through a wedding ring—if it sprang back into its original creaseless shape, it was a real Borsalino.

During World War II with Teresio Usuelli, Teresio Borsalino's nephew, at the helm of the company, the factory suffered the effects of bombing campaigns by the Allied Forces and was partially destroyed in 1944. Like many Italian brands, Borsalino fared well in the 1950s as a result of the "Made in Italy" campaign designed to rebrand the country after the prevalence of Mussolini's fascism; the company launched fifty new hat designs that were exported internationally. In the 1960s, the global decline in hat wearing caused by the more laissez-faire attitude of teenagers and the rise of car owners, who had less need to cover their heads when outdoors, made the

Below: Two examples of the Borsalino Panama. **Below left, from left to right**: 1. A collection of hat molds. 2. Pigments used in the dyeing process. 3. Finished hats are placed to dry on the same racks that were used in the nineteenth century.

BORSALINO   117

company concentrate on quality rather than on the huge quantities they had been manufacturing in the interwar years. Borsalino was also helped by the new nostalgic aesthetic entering fashion through designers such as Barbara Hulanicki at Biba, who, by the end of the decade, were rejecting the hippie look and were rediscovering the golden age of Hollywood.

The company was given a further fillip in 1970 with the success of the cult gangster movies *Borsalino* (1970) and *Borsalino & Co.* (1974), directed by Jacques Deray and starring French New Wave heartthrobs Alain Delon and Jean-Paul Belmondo. The films were named for the hat company after Deray had come across one of the original advertising images for Borsalino by Dudovich; for him, the Borsalino fedora evoked the film noir glamour that he wanted to embrace in his film. Many of Chicago's most infamous mobsters had worn Borsalinos in the 1930s, including Al Capone who sported a Borsolino straw boater and one of its white wide-brimmed fedoras together with his big cigar and cashmere coat. The company was able to supply the correct and authentic styles of hats for both films, and the ensuing publicity campaign included faux gangsters "driving by" cinemas where the film was being shown in period cars and wearing Borsalino fedoras—every 1,000th cinema-goer was given a voucher for a free Borsalino hat.

Today the hat has undergone a renaissance in men's fashion, and Borsalino, now run by the Gallo and Monticone families, remains the gold standard of deluxe headwear. Accordingly the company has undergone a period of expansion, moving into Asia and the United States with more than fifteen stores worldwide. Borsalino felt hats remain unique, with each one taking seven weeks to manufacture and undergoing at least fifty production phases by machine and hand. Borsalino felt is constructed of single short rabbit, hare, or beaver fibers that interlock when exposed to hot water and are then kneaded to create a material of incredible strength. The fur undergoes a series of refining processes known as "white-working," in which it is "blown" to remove any dirt and blown again onto a forming machine that gathers the hairs and draws them inside a bell within which is a slowly revolving copper cone form. Jets of hot water set the felt on the cone, forming a shape that is removed by hand and immersed in hot water, shrunk, and rolled under pressure to make it compact, a process called "steeping." After dyeing, the finished felt is shaped into a hat by being steamed, stretched, and compressed over an aluminum or wooden block, and the brim is cut, set, ironed, and pressed on a wooden flange. The brim is stiffened with shellac and the "black work" begins; the whole hat is rubbed with sandpaper, pumice, or sharkskin depending on the quality to give a smooth finish, blocked again, and then "finished," that is, trimmed with a sewn lining, a Morocco-leather or grosgrain band and ribbon. After a final pressing, the hat is inspected to ensure quality control, packed, and shipped. Sales director Claudio Mennuni says, "Some of the steps we do have to be done the same way we did it fifty, sixty, seventy years ago. We found we couldn't get the same quality using new gear."

"I sometimes think that if my great grandfather walked in he'd feel very much at home."

James Hunter Lobb

H.M. KING GEORGE V

1866
JOHN LOBB

When the celebrated essayist and critic Max Beerbohm was visited by a friend on his deathbed in 1956, his first question was nothing to do with the state of the nation, his beloved theater, or how his many friends in English society were faring, but rather, "Tell me, is Lobb still the best bootmaker in London?"

The story of John Lobb crosses centuries and continents from its founder's humble origins in a small Cornish village to the elegant establishment in St. James's Street, London, today. John Lobb was born in a tithed cottage at 22 Broad Street, Tywardreath, near Fowey in Cornwall in 1829 to a Cornish farm worker. He started work at the age of eleven but after breaking his leg when falling from a hay wagon he was left with a permanent limp. A change of career beckoned, and the young Lobb was apprenticed to a local shoemaker for five years. When his indenture ended, fueled by little more than skills and ambition, Lobb, despite his disability walked the 200 miles (320 km) to London, ending up amid the discreet gentlemen's clubs and bustling coffee houses of St. James's Street. He brushed himself down and presented himself to Thomas, the leading bootmaker of the day, with no letter of introduction or examples of his work as was customary. Thomas sent the scruffy country bumpkin packing; in return Lobb shook his fist and proclaimed that one day he would return with a business that would better them all.

In the mid-nineteenth century, a young man who dreamed of making his fortune had few opportunities for social advancement. There was one irresistible lure, however; the richest goldfields of Australia were being discovered in Victoria and New South Wales and a gold prospector could make at least double the wage of a London workman. Lobb's brother, William, had gone there before him so John Lobb booked the grueling four-month-long passage to Sydney, but once there he realized that the rough and dangerous conditions made it difficult for him to participate with any real success. However, there was one obvious way to make money that suited his particular talents: repairing and resoling the prospectors' tough boots. Accordingly Lobb set himself up in a tent in the major goldfield of Turon in New South Wales and catered to their demands. He also began to make bespoke boots for the lucky prospectors who had struck gold; in the goldfields it had become the practice to celebrate success by commissioning fancy knee-high leather pairs. Lobb also innovated a prospector boot with a secret compartment set in a hollow heel to store gold nuggets. After earning the necessary funds, Lobb set up shop in George Street, Sydney, married the harbor master's daughter in 1857, and, according to settler Nehemiah Bartley, "purveyed the boots of juvenile Sydney swells."

Left, clockwise from top left: 1. and 2. Shoemakers working from a wooden last, a unique three-dimensional pattern of the customer's foot. 3. A leather boot is constructed in the Lobb workshop. 4. The hand-carved shoe last of King George V. **Below**: The exterior of John Lobb Bootmaker at No. 9 St. James's Street, London.

In 1862 the name of John Lobb, Bootmaker, began to be known in London after he showed at the International Exhibition of Industry and Art held in South Kensington in a section devoted to boots and shoes made in the Australian colonies and won a gold medal. He also cheekily created a pair of beautiful riding boots set in a tooled leather box and sent them unannounced to Edward, Prince of Wales, with a request to be his personal bootmaker. The prince was impressed and Lobb was summarily given the royal warrant in 1863. He realized that the time was ripe to return to London, sold the business in Australia, and with apprentice Frederick Richards arrived back in 1866. He set up in premises at 296 Regent Street and began showing work in a series of exhibitions in Europe and the United States, garnering both medals and recognition, including in Paris in 1867, 1878, and 1889, and significantly in Vienna in 1873, at that time one of the most important centers of bespoke shoes in the world and the home of the renowned bootmaker to the kaisers, Rudolf Scheer (see page 50). John Lobb rapidly established itself as the premier boot and shoemaker of the British Empire, providing a bespoke service to the aristocracy, and to the political, business, and social elite. He also contributed an innovative shoe design; a two-tone cricket shoe that was the forerunner of the spectator, a name derived from a spectator standing on the sidelines at an event. The original Lobb shoe combined a white accent with different colored leathers or leather mixed with colored canvas or gabardine.

In 1880, a second premises opened in St. James's Street next to Boodles, a private members' club, founded in 1762 by the Earl of Shelburne, later the Marquess of Lansdowne and prime minister. After the death of the founder, John, his son, William Hunter Lobb, took over in 1895. The firm had its ups and downs during this period, with a successful branch opening in Paris in 1902 while the Regent Street premises closed down. During World War I supplies were scarce, and Brian Dobbs in *The Last Shall be First*, a history of the company written in 1972, writes of how "the hog's bristles used for guiding the waxed thread through the holes punched by the awl in hand-sewing became well nigh impossible to obtain. At a pub in Berners Street one man came up with an ingenious idea. Six noble bootmakers, armed with apples,

Right, clockwise from top left: 1. A vast collection of Lobb hand-hewn lasts. 2. A pair of slippers with embroidered crest. 3. A high Louis-heeled Cromwell-style buckled shoe. 4. Queen Victoria's shoe lasts. 5. A lace-up leather boot with brogued toe-cap. All of these nineteenth-century bespoke examples are from the Lobb archive.

pears, and nuts set out, not for the Western Front but for Regent's Park and London Zoo. With an air of assumed casualness, the party wandered past various cages, until there was no keeper in sight. When the coast was clear they converged on the hog enclosures. Two hogs were lured to the bars by the apples and pears and a selection of sweet hog-like noises. When the poor beasts lurched over, twelve hands suddenly descended and grabbed a handful of hair each. By the time the squeals had subsided, the party was in Regent's Park Road and on its way back to town with a six-month supply of bristles for the West End trade." The interwar period saw the work of Lobb being worn by fashion photographer Cecil Beaton, dancer Vernon Castle, film director Orson Welles, and actress Katharine Hepburn. During World War II the premises at St. James's were destroyed during the Nazi bombing campaign—luckily the firm found new premises only a few doors away at No. 26. In 1945 Lobb introduced the William, a double-buckled monk shoe, and the Lopez loafer in 1950, adding to the repertoire of classic shoes such as the Oxford, a shoe that laces up the front through three or four pairs of eyelets with a tongue to prevent the foot from the pressure of the fastenings. A key feature of the tailored Lobb Oxford is its method of closed lacing whereby the shoelaces are looped through eyelet tabs that are stitched underneath the vamp. In 1926 Lobb's Plain Oxford was described thus, "Made of waxed calf leather, this shoe is correct for any town occasion; although Box Calf is now more used with equal effect if preferred. The smart line is enhanced by the beveled 'waist'—the center portion of the sole which joins the front with the heel— which is a feature of all lightweight shoes."

Well-known patrons of John Lobb have included writer George Bernard Shaw, opera singer Enrico Caruso, Queen Elizabeth II, and the Duke of Edinburgh who, in a letter to the firm, personally attributes his advanced years to his well-shod feet. Dobbs also details a host of nameless others who were a little eccentric when it came to their favorite supplier of shoes: "Requests for Lobb's

laces to be sent 5,000 miles are a common occurrence. The East Indian gentleman with his magnifying glass and the guards officer who tries to tear his shoes apart are not exceptional. Lobb can also tell of an engineer who used to send full blueprints of the shoes he wanted and was prepared to allow no more tolerance than one sixty-fourth of an inch in the making, and of the London man-about-town who places his new Lobb shoes on the carpet and lies on his stomach to inspect them from grasshopper level. One customer, staying in a suite in Claridge's, phoned for a skilled Lobb craftsman to taxi over to his hotel to fit, not a new pair of shoes, but a new pair of laces. The craftsman obliged, of course."

In the 1960s the director of bespoke in London began to experiment with dyeing skins in order to create a rich, lustrous brown to resemble the hues and supple grains of exotic woods such as mahogany. The corresponding director in the Paris workshop was also working along the same lines by using different mahogany dyes on aniline bergeronnette box calf to increase the shine on Lobb's shoes. When London and Paris compiled their findings, the result was Lobb Brown, a deep red-brown color with base tones of black and burgundy that give it a particularly rich intensity.

In 1976 the French luxury brand Hermès (see page 72) acquired John Lobb and began to expand into ready-to-wear. Throughout the 1990s, a series of Hermès-controlled ready-to-wear John Lobb boutiques was opened, firstly in Paris in 1990, then on London's Jermyn Street in 1995, Madison Avenue in New York in 2000, followed by Marunichi in Japan, Hong Kong, Shanghai, Moscow, and Beijing, with a factory in Northampton, England, set up to cater to the ready-to-wear demand. Lobb's ready-to-wear shoes are produced under the very stringent conditions of a 190-step process; output was at one point limited to only 100 pairs per day. Recently John Lobb joined with Aston Martin to launch the Winner Sport, an aerodynamic lightweight calfskin driving shoe lined with sheepskin and a bonded rubber sole, codesigned by Aston Martin's director of design Marek Reichman and John Lobb's creative director Andrés Hernández.

John Lobb Ltd. continues to be independently run by the Lobb family out of the St. James's premises in London. Today prospective customers can sit back into a leather armchair and choose the model, shape, and type of leather of the desired shoe and have their feet measured by the fitter, who takes into consideration every detail of the foot; the outlines are traced into the last-maker's pattern book and as each pair of bespoke shoes can take up to six months to make, a commitment to Lobb is the essence of deferred gratification. The last-maker uses the pattern to release the shape of the foot from a block of maple, beech, or hornbeam to create the last or wooden replica to add to the 16,000 the firm currently has in its storerooms, including those of dancer Fred Astaire and inventor Guglielmo Marconi. The clicker cuts out leather, which has been carefully screened for flaws, and the skins, which have been tanned for up to six months in oak-bark-filled vats so as to acquire suppleness and shade of color, carefully taking into consideration the height and weight of the client. The closer stitches the uppers together, incorporating stiffeners and linings, and nails them to the last before this molded body is passed on to the maker. The maker adds the sole and heel before commencing perhaps the most complicated procedure: the stitching of

Above left: To step into the interior of John Lobb is to step back into a former age of bespoke shoemaking. **Left**: Lobb is passionate about the care of its handmade shoes and sells a range of bristle brushes and shoe crèmes and polishes to achieve the correct finish. **Top**: Lobb is known for a rich, lustrous, mahogany brown. **Above**: A contemporary black leather buckled style.

the insole to the interstitial welt and upper, in which the tension has to be even throughout the shoe. The next step is for the maker to stitch the sole to the welt, add the heel, and finally to polish the shoe. "There is an expression of delight on the faces of people when they buy their first tailor-made shoes from us," says James Hunter Lobb, the great grandson of the firm's founder, who personally signs off every pair before they are presented to the customer. As he puts it, "We've turned our face against machines and machinery and stuck to making [shoes] by hand in the traditional way. The craftsmanship is very much the same, very little has changed, it's all using the same tools. I sometimes think that if my great grandfather walked in he'd feel very much at home."

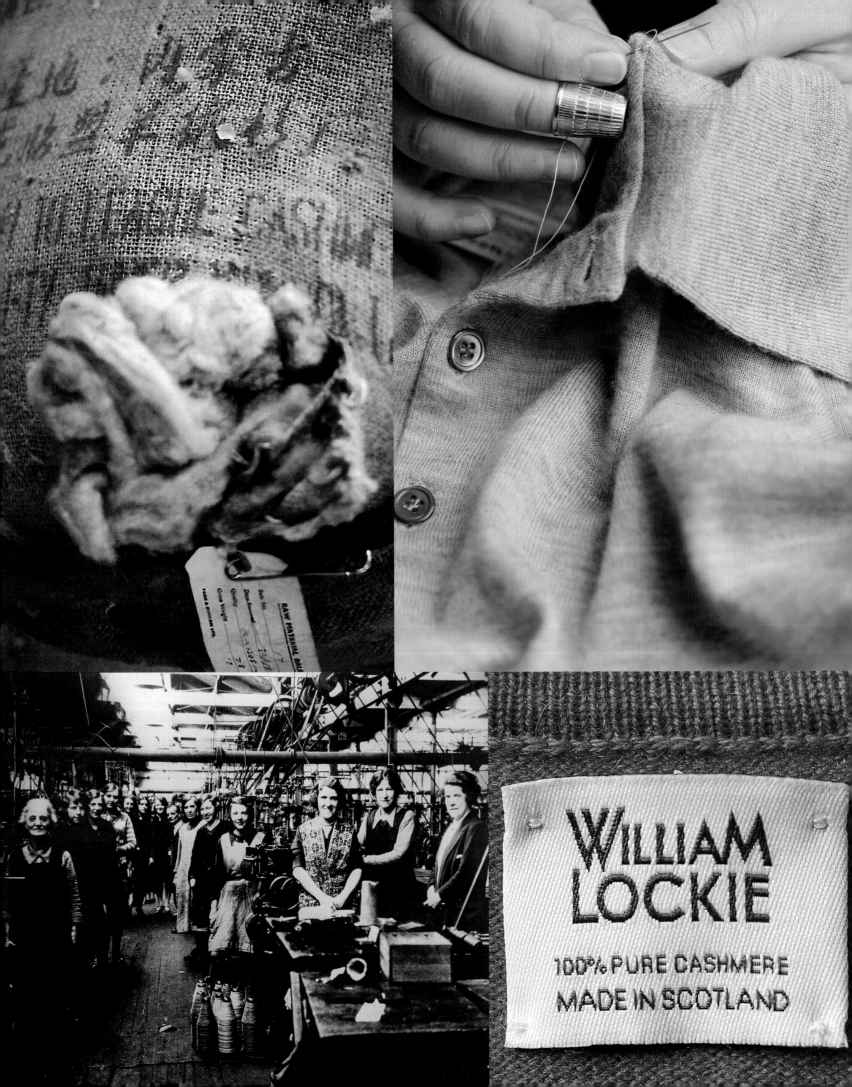

WILLIAM
LOCKIE

100% PURE CASHMERE
MADE IN SCOTLAND

1874
WILLIAM LOCKIE

The world's precious fibers sourced from some of the most remote corners of the world are given the evocative name "noble" and include fine charmeuse silk spun from the cocoons of the Chinese silkworm, linen woven from Belgian flax, and cashmere named after the Kashmiri goat of Inner Mongolia. On the plains where the goats roam, the temperature is notoriously intemperate with extremes of hot and cold that, although harsh, encourage the growth of downy hair on the underbelly of the goat for warmth, protected by a layer of long guard hair that grows over the top. In spring, the soft hair is carefully combed away and sent away to be spun in the Scottish Borders. In this land of rolling hills and rivers teeming with trout lies a firm that has a reputation for knitting the cashmere into some of the finest finished garments in the world much praised for their super-soft feel and resilience—William Lockie.

William Lockie was born in 1835, and after leaving school found employment in the finishing department of a Hawick hosiery manufacturer, Messrs William Laidlaw and Sons, situated first at Cumledge Mill and later at Lynnwood Mill. The Borders town of Hawick was at the center of the woolen industry in Scotland, which had begun to grow in the eighteenth century after Baillie John Hardie installed four knitting frames or mechanical knitters in 1771; as each frame could produce the same amount of work as six expert hand knitters, there had been some consternation when the frame was first introduced in England, which eventually culminated in the Luddite riots (1811–16). In Hawick, however, Baillie's frames were the sparks that lit the flame; by 1812 there were 1,200 frames manufacturing linen, worsted, and lambswool stockings. In 1869, David Bremner, in his study *The Industries of Scotland: Their Rise, Progress, and Present Condition*, described a typical Hawick mill: "On

Left, clockwise from top left: 1. The soft hair of the Kashmiri goat is spun in the Scottish Borders and knitted into garments at William Lockie. 2. One of the secrets to the success of Lockie knitwear is the precision of its hand finishing. 3. William Lockie is known for knitting cashmere into finely finished garments praised for their super-soft feel and resilience. 4. An 1930s photograph of the workforce in the Lockie factory.
Above: In 1874, William Lockie founded the company of Messrs Wm Lockie & Co. as a manufacturer of hosiery.

"The Lockie color palette is inspired by the shifting seasons and rugged countryside."

the floors of the knitting factory, the frames, which are worked by hand, are ranged on either side, each being opposite a window, as a good light is indispensable to the workmen. Though to the uninitiated the knitting-frame appears mysterious and complicated in its working, it is simple in construction, and the process of knitting by it is easily learned. The workman sits on a high stool with his feet resting on a series of treadles, which produce certain of the eleven movements necessary to form each row or 'course' of loops. With his hands he places the yarn over the 'needles,' and works a pair of levers, which complete the operation. The ribbed tops of stockings, bottoms of drawers, and wristbands of shirts are worked on a frame specially devised for the purpose, and the men who make them earn the highest wages in the trade. It is considered a healthy trade, as the air in the workrooms is kept at an equal temperature, and no deleterious substance is used in any of the operations. From the knitters and seamers the work passes to the scourers and finishers, and is by them made ready for the market."

Many such workshops and mills grew up alongside the river in Hawick, changing the face of Scottish textiles from a cottage-based family concern to a vibrant and vital industry, and by the 1870s, when William Lockie began his business, there were more than 250 woolen mills in Scotland. Hawick had turned from an essentially rural district to an industrial one. During the same period, the hosiery industry also began to take off, and at its peak the town was manufacturing one million pairs of stockings per year. There was room for entrepreneurial spirit and Lockie saw his opportunity when Laidlaws abandoned its hosiery work and sold off the equipment. Laidlaw had taken the advice of former weaver James Shield to move into the manufacture of blankets. It was a successful business decision, despite the mill burning down a year later and Laidlaw

having to start anew, for Laidlaw's remained solvent until 1972.

Lockie decided to branch out on his own account in the Fore Row, now Drumlanrig Square, and in 1874 founded the company Messrs Wm Lockie & Co. of Westfield Works on the banks of the River Teviot as a manufacturer of hosiery. His strong business ethic and attention to detail meant that the firm soon found a ready market for its goods. Lockie also took a philanthropic interest in his town but was disinterested in entering local politics despite being a staunch Liberal Unionist. His interest in the conditions of his workers led to his participation in a move to demolish the notorious Auld Mid Raw, a street of pended arch houses and notorious slum-tenements that were eventually removed in 1884 through funds provided by a grand bazaar held in the town hall. After his death in 1900, Lockie's obituary described him as a man "possessed of a great natural shrewdness, and a keen business capability, he rapidly succeeded in building up a large and lucrative business." Lockie had never married so the business was passed to his nephew, Walter Thorburn.

Over the ensuing decades, Lockie survived recessions, take over bids, and the changing landscape of British manufacturing in the 1980s and 1990s. China entered into the cashmere market and cheaper versions of this once-expensive knitwear began to flood the market, causing many of the original knitwear companies to have to lower their standards or fold completely. Lockie remained true to its exacting standards and today manufactures its own-name brand garments and supplying knitwear to Savile Row, including supplies to Norton & Sons established in 1821 by Walter Norton as "Tailors to the Gentlemen of the City of London."

The secret to Lockie knitwear is in its use of the most high-end of raw materials and the precision of the

Above, clockwise from top left: 1. The yarn is knitted tightly so the fiber retains its shape during the making-up. 2. and 3. The knitted garment is carefully measured.

4. Lockie knitwear is unsurpassed in its attention to detail.
Right: A selection of classic Lockie cardigans.

manufacturing process. Lambswool is obtained from specially bred pedigree sheep in South Australia and taken from the soft first fleece of a lamb at seven months old. Camel hair is from the two-humped Bactrian, an ungulate superbly adapted to life in the harsh Gobi desert, one of the most hostile regions on the planet. Like that of the Kashmiri goat, the camel's coat is fit for its environment and consists of the soft underbelly hair, used in Lockie knitwear, and the coarse outer coat. The hair is collected by hand in the early spring and spun into a breathable fiber that is customarily undyed and left its natural golden brown.

Cashmere, the so-called "fiber of kings" is one of the most superior ways of keeping out the cold when woven into a sweater by William Lockie, not least because some say it is eight times warmer than lambswool. Dyed yarns spun from lambswool, Geelong merino—a high-quality Australian wool with an average fiber diameter of 19.5 microns—and cashmere garments are washed in the water that runs alongside the mill, giving a result that is unsurpassed in its softness. The Lockie color palette is inspired by the shifting seasons and rugged countryside. Skeins of purple heather lie side by side with lemon-frost, sky-blue, and loganberry, while traditional materials such as flannel, linen, and tweed provide the reference point for shades of brown, cream, and beige. Lockie uses more yarn than most other manufacturers when knitting up as the garments are knitted tightly so as to retain their shape, thus creating a denser weight and smoother finish; cheaper cashmere knits tend to use the short hairs of the goat's underbelly, are knitted up more loosely, and thus pill and lose their shape more rapidly. The longer strands of downy hair have less weaknesses along the length where they could break, cutting down on the pilling caused by abrasion from wear, whereby the fibers unravel and the loose ends ball up on the fabric surface.

William Lockie remains a privately owned, family firm with workers from the same local families being employed for generations. It is faring well as discerning consumers reject the built-in obsolescence of so much contemporary fashion in favor of authentic luxury goods.

1875
AUBADE

France has a rich tradition of fine lingerie, for its history is illuminated by women skilled in the art of seduction, one of the few routes to female power before the twentieth century. Silk, satin, and crêpe de Chine create an uncompromisingly erotic presence, and for the Gallic women of the eighteenth century, the boudoir was the mise-en-scène for love. This intimate room was a space devoted to luxury, femininity, and mutual pleasure, created for the inhabitants of the finest Loire chateaux. Here a woman could fashion her own artful aesthetic; the original Rococo boudoir was intimate and flirtatious

with gilded mirrors, painted pastoral vignettes, and all manner of trinkets. Madame de Pompadour's boudoir in the Château de Versailles was described as "crammed… with pictures, bibelots, furniture, embroidery, cosmetics, all buried in flowers and smelling like a hothouse." It was here that she waited for the king in her *déshabillé*, described by contemporary writer Horace Walpole as "fantastic nightgowns fastened with a pin." This "sweet disorder in the dress" was the antecedent of French lingerie, for which the Aubade label is known.

In 1875, Dr. Bernard set up a company for the manufacture of corsets, a foundation garment derived from the cotte of the 1300s, a rigid laced tunic of linen stiffened with paste to fit closely to the body, and when the front and back parts of the cotte were laced together, the corset as we know it today began to evolve. In the eighteenth century, the corset began to compress the waist to create an hourglass figure, but it was regarded as a functional rather than a sexualizing device; when Bernard was manufacturing his "robust and austere" corsets, as they were described at the time, it was believed that they were a necessity to lend orthopedic support to the "structurally unsound" and fragile bodies of women.

In 1890s Paris, undergarments began to have a more overtly erotic reputation when the scandalous cancan was performed at the notorious nightclub the Moulin Rouge. The raucous dance allowed spectators full view of stocking tops and frilly drawers; the petticoat in particular played a key role when dancer Saharet kicked up her legs and flashed yards of thrilling frills. Such cascading petticoats of Valenciennes lace began to make their way into fashion and were given the collective name *frou frou*. This evocative word described the sound made when the petticoat rubbed against the coarser material of the skirt

and one gentleman observed, "Take your time to listen
to the music of the fabrics. This music is at the heart
of man's desire." The women of Paris understood the
power of beautiful underwear; historian Cornelia Skinner
wrote how the French woman "was an erotic queen
whose very clothes rustled with innuendo. The lifting
of her skirt was erotic. The act of pulling up the skirt
and petticoat together to just the proper height was an
art. Émile Bergerat, a well-known observer of the passing
scene, used to sit out on a café terrazzo on windy days for
the pleasure of watching ladies defending the honor of
their legs." Parisian writer Octave Uzanne noted how
"the lingerie shops have grasped in a wonderful way that
it is impossible to devise trimmings sufficiently fantastic
or silks sufficiently transparent, to invent enough filmy,
flimsy materials in delicate, dainty colors. French lace,
guipures from Ireland, enchanting laces from Mechlin,
Chantilly, and Alençon, and point de Venise are used to
deck the fashionable beauty."

Many of the most important developments in underwear
happened in France; Herminie Cadolle, a corsetière and
seamstress, patented the first bra, the Bien-Être, in 1889
and one of her first customers was the notorious spy Mata
Hari. The Callot sisters, or Callot Soeurs, used antique
ribbons and lace to trim some of the first pieces of
lingerie; and the original strapless and halter-neck bras
were marketed by Aubade, the company that evolved
from the Bernard et Cie corset company of 1875. The
transformation from the functional to the flirtatious
happened for this French corset company in 1958 when
Claude Pasquier took over and decided on a change of
name; Aubade was chosen as it had a suitably romantic
meaning, a love song that represented lovers breaking
away from each others arms at dawn. It was a circumspect

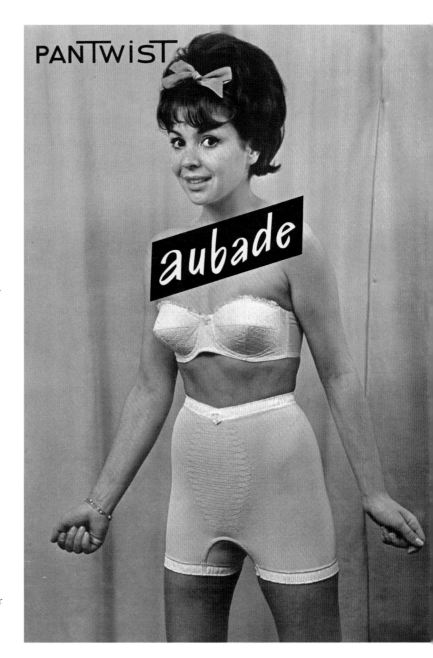

"Take your time to listen
to the music of the fabrics.
This music is at the heart
of man's desire."
Anonymous

Above: Aubade realized that the most seductive lingerie should appeal to the spectator as well as the wearer and pioneered the use of luxurious lingerie for seductive appeal as well as function.

Right: All Aubade bras are individually cut and the constituent parts assembled using a combination of machine, hand-stitching, fitting, and finishing by a team of expert seamstresses.

move as in the 1950s, frivolous underwear had become popular again as fashion entered an overwhelmingly feminine period after the austerity of World War II. Dior had launched the New Look in 1947, which defined the silhouette of the decade with its fitted bodices, cinched waists, and full, frothy, crinoline skirts, a look that reintroduced the *corselette,* or "waspie," into women's wardrobes. Rococo motifs crept back into the bedroom, linking the woman of the postwar decade with the high femininity represented by the courtesans of the past, and the cleavage began to be the defining erogenous zone, with lingerie designers vying with each other to design the most effective cantilevered engineering. Breasts were molded into position with cone-shaped bras; Frederick's

of Hollywood invented the first push-up bra and the shape of underwear began to exaggerate the voluptuous feminine figure.

Aubade was one of the first French lingerie firms to demonstrate that its designs had to appeal to the spectator in addition to the wearer. The era's etiquette books suggested the same thing: that the key to a happy marriage was to remain as if "on camera" even when at home. In Paris, Aubade, with its history of corsetry, concentrated on the craft and fit of the bra and began to manufacture the most exquisite elaborately hand-sewn lace-embellished bra and pantie sets in a wide range of colors that were bought by the discerning *femme fatale*. The finest detailing was incorporated into each bra design: a symphony of bows, pleating, and stitches. One of the most innovatory aspects of Aubade was how it helped to shift the paradigm of underwear from being a functional necessity to a tool in the art of love. This philosophy has extended over the years; Aubade is marketed with direct reference to sexual play. One infamous lingerie advertising campaign of the early 1980s, Aubade pour un homme, was revolutionary in that a besuited man's arm appeared in the frame grasping the model's thigh or stomach rather than the more normal usual, solipsistic pose. Writer Claire Paillochet analyzed it thus at the time, "You might see it as man and woman in their best roles; the great seduction game. She has her hand on his, you don't know whether it is to discourage him or keep it next to her body. Audacious and deliberately provocative, this campaign gives underwear some of the erotic power it might have lost." Aubade's use of the risqué scene continues in the long-running Lessons in Seduction campaign, which began in 1992, to build on the relationship between the wearing of lingerie as the route to the giving and receiving of sensual pleasure. Aubade relates to a woman who is, as the brand says, "at ease with her body, asserts her sensuality, and plays on her natural femininity. She is romantic, provocative, delicate, naughty, gentle, discreet, audacious, and elegant as well as knowing… She is the mistress of her seductive power, wanting to play with and share it with her man, a willing victim in this game." The first Aubade calendar was launched in 1998.

In the 1960s, Aubade became a leader in lingerie invention; it was one of the first to introduce a wider range of colors from the usual white, black, and pastel

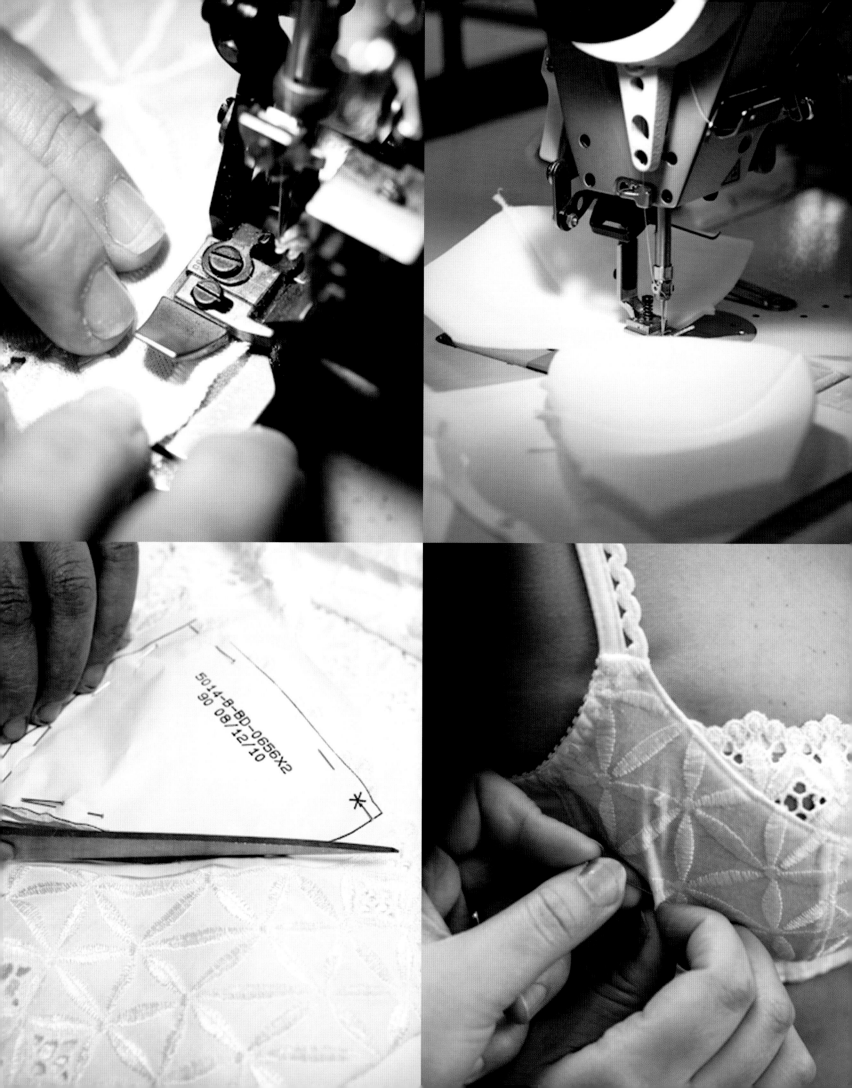

pink, thereby reflecting the dramatic changes that were happening in fashion. The sophisticated woman of the world was metamorphosing into the dolly bird, and androgynous models such as Twiggy introduced a pre-pubescent look that needed only simple underwear to garb it. Miniskirts made suspenders and stockings seem old fashioned and obsolete, and nylon panties and pantihose took over, as silhouettes became less hourglass and more youthful. Aubade was at the vanguard with its Pop art hues and pretty prints using motifs, including flowers and butterflies, that still recur in ranges today whether woven into gauzy black voile or in hand-sewn appliqué.

The 1970s consolidated Aubade's reputation, as fashion designers began to reexamine the past with nostalgia in an era when the optimism expressed by the hippie movement was segueing into widespread political and social discontent. In London, Biba, the iconic label designed by Barbara Hulanicki, began to cite the sirens of 1930s Hollywood with bias-cut liquid-satin gowns and marabou-feathered mules; lacy lingerie also enjoyed a revival after the androgynous tights and panties of the 1960s. French *Vogue* showed the most intimate encounters between tuxedoed men and women in the sheerest of seamed stockings, suspender belts, and killer heels photographed by Helmut Newton and Guy Bourdin. Aubade was one of the first to understand that a great lingerie revival was on its way, and used luscious satins, silk, and crêpe de Chine that mirrored the feel of flesh, decorated with guipure lace, the luxurious trim also known as Venetian lace.

In 1972, Aubade launched one of the first convertible strapless and halter-neck bras, and in 1974 the first Agrafe Coeur bra with front fasteners and appliqué flowers flirtatiously covering the nipples. In 1975, as panties became more miniscule, Aubade developed the first suspender belt bikini, a hybrid that mixed the retro with the contemporary. The company showed it could accommodate switchback changes in fashion, too; when an Edwardian feel entered fashion, most obviously exemplified by the work of English designer Laura Ashley, Aubade responded to this retrospective trend by introducing *broderie anglaise* into its ranges. In 1979, the company catered to the tighter silhouette being displayed in skin tight designer jeans, causing the curse of what became known as the VPL (visible pantie line). Aubade cut the front of the pantie high over the hip and shrank the back to a narrow strip, and the tanga brief or thong was born, an innovative item of underwear inspired by the bikini briefs worn on the beaches of Brazil. By the early 2000s the thong had become the fastest-growing segment of women's underwear, and as women's pants sank lower over the hips, displaying the back of the Tanga, so Aubade began to decorate the rear of the waistband with bows, tassels, cut-outs, and jewels, and created the String Minimum, the smallest G-string in the world, weighing a mere 5 grams. In 1993, the Bahia collection using embroidered cotton was launched, which remains a best seller today.

Aubade remains a French institution exemplifying elegance and refinement, and it has become a shorthand for seduction, name checked in modern novels; writer Susan Fales-Hill, in her novel *One Flight Up* (2011), has her heroine walking "briskly up Central Park West. With each step she was naughtily aware of her new Aubade lace brassiere and matching tanga with its corseted waist. The eight pounds she had lost since the start of her *liaison delicieuse* had given her a new taste for the form-fitting as opposed to the flowing." Aubade continues to use traditional methods of manufacture, with every item of lingerie being individually machine stitched and then trimmed, embroidered, and embellished by hand. Bras such as the understated triangle-shape model have discreet underwiring and whalebones for extra support; the Plunge Bra uses a system of removable supple micro-bead pads to optimize the position of the chest so as to project it to the center and create as much cleavage and support as required. Bras are individually cut, intricately constructed by the hands of expert seamstresses out of fifteen different materials, such as fine-quality Calais lace and Swiss cotton, and are hand-finished with grosgrain ribbon trim.

"Dale continues to use traditional motifs such as the eight-pointed star or Selburosa in its patterned wool sweaters, and they are worn by men, women, and children."

1879
DALE

Norway has a fascinating knitwear heritage dating back to the ninth century; traditionally young women were taught to raise and tend the family's sheep and also how to shear, card, and spin the wool into yarn. Wool was the perfect natural insulation for the harsh winters, and it became the tradition for men to wear woolen sweaters over their shirts and tucked into their pants covered up with a vest and coat. As the lower half of the sweater was invisible, it became the practice to use only one color below the waist, a design feature that remains in traditional Norwegian sweaters; many nineteenth-century sweaters also began to feature two-color designs as the second yarn gave extra warmth in the long, cold winters.

In Norway, knitting is a skill that has been passed down the generations, and for more than 150 years all Norwegian children have been taught to knit in school in the traditional manner: in the round, on small circular needles to create a tube with no side seams and with the pattern repeating around the circle. To create the finished garment, the openings for the arms and front are cut and finished to keep them from unraveling. By the 1850s, many regions of the country had developed their own specialized patterned garments; in Setesdal the patterned knitted cardigan known as the *lusekofte* emerged with its distinctive inset raglan sleeves, "lice pattern" of isolated white or black stitches on a black or white ground, and geometric border around the neck, shoulder, and sleeves. Sweaters made in Fana had allover striped and checked designs with a border of stars across the yoke and the top of the sleeves; Bykle sweaters could be recognized by their zigzag patterns. In the northern district of Selbu it was customary to wear monochrome knitted mittens and gloves to church as Sunday best with patterns derived from nature, including insects and ears of corn, and Selbu

Above left: At Dale, highly trained technicians ensure that every product gets the best possible technical solution and finish. **Below left**: From 1956 onward, Dale began the tradition of creating a jumper for every Winter Olympics, including this design for Innsbruck in 1964. **Top**: An archival image of the Dale factory floor dating from the 1920s. **Above**: Dale of Norway is situated in the mountain village from which it takes its name.

brides were also expected to make gifts of mittens to their male wedding guests.

Skiing was a natural part of life in Norway—in the 1770s one country priest wrote of children "accustoming themselves to the use of skis from the tenderest age. A little fellow, hardly three years old, has both the courage and desire to attach these long shoes to his small feet. He puts them on and immediately goes to nearby slopes. Then he tries to run down on his ski, unconcerned if he falls head over heels a score of times and is buried in snow." As skiing developed as a sport, Norway was at the forefront of developments; the first ski factory was opened by Simen Rustad in 1882 near Lillehammer. In the 1890s, the first women began to participate in the sport of ski-racing, which had previously been seen as a male

Above: Norwegian athletes at the Olympic Games in Cortina in 1956 wearing the first commemorative Dale knit. From left: Borghild Niskin, Inger Jorgensen, Inger Bjørnbakken, and Astrid Sandvik.

Right: A classic Norwegian wool *lusekofte* using traditional motifs.
Far right: A Setesdal pullover with pewter buttons and embroidered ribbon knitted with a heavy-weight Norwegian Heilo yarn.

wearing Norwegian sweaters, and the Setesdal *lusekofte* was immensely popular both in and outside of Norway, almost attaining the status of folk costume. The *lusekofte* became even more commercially appealing when color was added to the design by attaching ribbons or bands of embroidery on black woolen fabric around the neck and the edges of the front opening. The cardigan was also closed with a row of pewter clasps, and this once masculine garment began to be worn by women.

One of the Norwegian names that began to gain global status was Dale knitwear, named after the picturesque village in which it originated. In 1872, Peter Jebsen visited Dale, not far from the city of Bergen, and recognized the potential of the nearby River Dale; with its natural waterfall and system of fjords it was the perfect environment for a textile mill. Accordingly, in 1879, he built Dale Fabrikker, today known as Dale of Norway; in 1912 a new mill was set up to produce a worsted yarn that began to feature in most of Dale's output, and in 1938 the four-ply Heilo yarn was developed, spun from pure virgin Norwegian wool. In the 1950s, Dale began to be more directly connected with winter sport and commenced work with the Norwegian National Ski Team in 1954; in 1956 the company designed the first of a series of Winter Olympics sweaters for the games in Cortina, Italy. The tradition has lasted ever since, and the Dale designs, named after the location of each event, have become highly collectible and include the "Sarajevo," "Calgary," and "Lillehammer," among others. Moreover, Dale sweaters are the official uniform of Norway at every Winter Olympics and they are worn by all athletes, coaches, and support staff.

Today Dale manufactures the Dale Exclusive Collection by hand using traditional Norwegian designs and embroidered embellishments. It continues to use traditional motifs such as the eight-pointed star or *Selburosa* in its patterned wool sweaters, and they are worn by men, women, and children. The company also makes hats, scarves, mittens, leggings, and the yarn and patterns for knitting enthusiasts who wish to create their own Norwegian knitted garments. During the manufacturing process for its high-quality wool products, the raw wool is first thoroughly scoured in which short fibers are removed to create a more durable yarn, cleaned, and then combed and stretched, a notoriously long process that makes the yarn

preserve; the first female ski champion whose name is known was a Norwegian woman, Hanna Aars who wrote of her first race (and possibly the first professionally organized women's race) in 1891, "my parents were not quite sure that such a public appearance could be reconciled with 'real womanliness.' But I managed to wheedle permission and one brilliant winter's day skied off five kilometers to the race. It was terribly exciting to stand at the top of the slope with a number on my breast and wait for the starting signal."

By the 1930s, the popularity of skiing made the mass manufacture of Norwegian knitwear a commercial possibility, helped by the vogue for the sport among Hollywood stars; Ingrid Bergman, Gary Cooper, Clark Gable, and Claudette Colbert were photographed posed on the slopes of the Sun Valley Ski Resort in Idaho

stronger and less liable to fray or pill when knitted up. The yarn is then spun into single lengths and then left to rest for several days before being twisted together to create different thicknesses, usually two, three, and four ply. The dyeing process comes next, using a color palette that ranges from the traditional black, red, and navy through to pastel pinks and turquoise blues. The yarn is left to dry at a regulated temperature so that the color stays fast.

The body, arms, and neck of the sweaters are knitted separately by machine; advanced machines are now being utilized to knit a complete sweater without any seams. The individual pieces are fitted together by hand with the neck and arms being assembled loop by loop, making the seam almost invisible. The final step is the addition of zips, buttons, pewter fasteners, and labels, and the end result is a knitted garment that can last up to twenty years. The company does not stand on tradition though and continues to innovate, including Hilmar Fosse's fluorescent neon color yarn and the Storetind water-repellent sweater, knitted with Heilo yarn treated with

Teflon fabric protector. This innovative garment has transformed the Norwegian sweater into high-tech outerwear by using Knitshell, a three-layer system developed in 2007. Knitshell is comprised of an outer layer of water-repellent 100 percent wool, a windproof Windstopper membrane, and an insulating soft flannel lining used in vests, anoraks, and jackets targeted at the European sports market, including skiing, hiking, and cycling. Every item of Dale of Norway's knitwear carries the Woolmark label, which guarantees that the yarn is made from top-quality 100 percent virgin wool. The company also experiments with different blends: white crossbred wool of a full year's growth and crossbred wool which is shorn in the fall. Consequently Dale yarn is not only stable, but its breaking strength is also about three times that of ordinary wool yarns, giving Dale knitwear exceptional dimensional stability. The garments are fit for purpose and retain their shape so well that they can be passed down through the family for generations to come following the age-old Norwegian tradition.

1879
E. VOGEL

Before the invention of the railway and automobile, all gentlemen who rode wore riding boots. A pair of high-quality boots was a mark of prestige; in the sixteenth century those worn on horseback were highly decorative with scalloped trims and patterned uppers or turnover tops trimmed with lace. After the French Revolution (1787-99), such foppishness was associated with the louche lifestyle of the aristocracy and thus incompatible with the Age of Enlightenment. Simplicity became the order of the day in fashionable menswear; hair was natural and unpowdered, colors were subdued, and there were no obvious trappings of rank. A form of stealth wealth

entered into mens' fashion; it became a matter of cut, nuance, quality of material, and craftsmanship.

By the nineteenth century, such restraint in dress marked out the gentleman. Riding boots were toned down, worn for function rather than fashion, and made from waxed leather with a rigid construction. England had many fine bootmakers; the United States had E. Vogel, a New York firm that today is still recognized as the purveyor of the country's best riding boots, fitted closely to the lower leg so as to communicate successfully with the horse. The original business was set up on Grand Street, Lower Manhattan, in 1879 by German immigrant Egidius Vogel, and it is now run by the fourth generation of the same family. The firm's slogan was "A Commitment to Excellence" and its riding or equestrian performance boots remain of such high quality that they are worn by the United States Olympic Team and medal-winning equestrian athletes, including William Steinkraus who was the first U.S. equestrian to win a gold medal. E. Vogel hand-crafts many styles for equestrians, including high-cut field boots, lower-cut paddocks, and the Western-styled Midwest boot, all customized to perfectly fit the owner; they can be given ribbed soles or better grip in the stirrups, spur rests, swagger tabs, elastic gussets, and three-quarter linings.

Women's riding boots came into general use much later than men's because of the custom of riding side saddle rather than astride. In the eighteenth and early nineteenth centuries, women wore the same heelless kidskin slippers that they wore by day to present a pretty picture when on horseback. By 1848, *Godey's Lady's Book* wrote, "Dark boots should be worn for riding. Ladies who ride much will find the advantage of having a neat kid or Morocco boot." As the century progressed, riding

Below: The founder of E. Vogel, German-born Egidius Vogel.
Right, clockwise from top left: 1. The interior of E. Vogel, a bespoke shoe and bootmaker still owned by the fourth generation of the family. 2. The design of E. Vogel's Three Strap boot is derived from a riding boot of the civil war. 3. E. Vogel's premier equestrian boot, the Fieldmaster, in black French calf with decorative punched toe cap.

"To paw through the rolls of hide in every hue and finish imaginable is, for anyone with a tactile appreciation or sense of smell, nearly overwhelming."

Gary Fisketjohn

Left, from top: 1. One of E. Vogel's specialty boots, the Charlotte. 2. The Hamilton Sport Shoe. 3. The Nantucket loafer with penny strap detail in brown pebble-grain cordovan. **Right, clockwise from left**: 1. A Fieldmaster field boot in black leather with a contrasting pebble-grain cuff designed to conform to the shape of the leg and foot. 2. A leather cutter at work. 3. Finishing after the attachment of the heel.

boots became practical and functional for both men and women when riding was done for sport rather than status. E. Vogel's best-known female customer was Jackie Onassis who had her riding boots custom-made, her wooden last remaining with 1,600 others in the shop's cavernous basement. Jackie was an accomplished horsewoman and wore black reverse calf boots with rather snazzy patent leather tops for hunting—the reverse calf or suede was for protection against thickets and thorns and Vogel customized them according to her specifications with boot straps and spur rests. Apparently Jackie loved these boots so much that when she had a suspected broken foot after falling from her horse, she refused to let the paramedics attending her cut them off. Vogel is so associated with equestrian footwear that today Dean Vogel, the great-grandson of the founder Egidius, says, "I have had customers who ordered boots from us for years on end before they noticed we had shoes in our collection. When they asked how long we had been making shoes, I would say: 'Oh, for about 120 years!'"

As horse transport and riding began to decline as the nineteenth century progressed, more people took to walking the boulevards and broadways of the city, window-shopping at the department store, the new cathedral of consumption. E. Vogel introduced one of the first low-cut wingtip toe-capped shoes, revolutionary in an era when the high-topped button boot held sway and very similar to the Wingtip Derby Brogue with a hand-sewn welt worn by actor James Cagney in the 1930s. The brogue's upper was double-layered with perforations applied to the first layer, allowing water to drain from the shoe without compromising its water resistance, and it can still be bought at the store today.

The process of constructing a Vogel hand made shoe is exactly the same today as it was more than a century ago; the same cutting and stitching machines are still in use. The artisan shoemaker measures the client's foot from

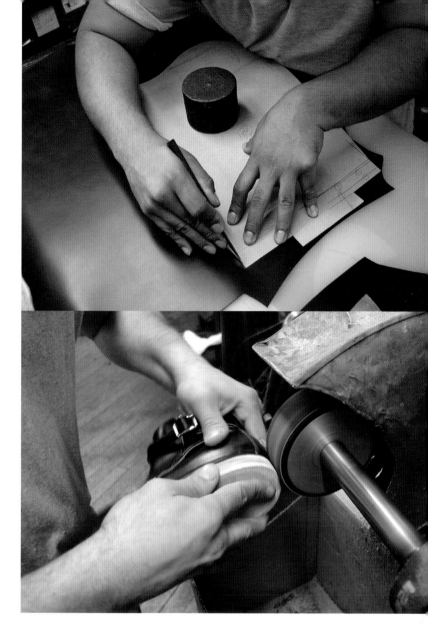

which he carves a last, effectively a wooden copy of the foot that remains on the premises for future commissions. After measuring, the material from which the shoe is constructed is chosen; today Vogel imports fine leather from Europe and calf is the most sought after because of the malleability of the leather, although high-end alligator and ostrich skins are also available. After consultation over the design, a paper pattern is made of the pieces that will fit together to make the shoe; the pieces are cut from leather, stitched together, and shaped over the wooden last to make the finished shoe. Production remains small: 600 pairs of shoes per year and 1,500 pairs of boots.

Vogel shoe styles can also be adapted for sports such as golf; journalist Gary Fisketjon described the process in 2005: "I could've chosen from the more than three-dozen styles on display. Among them are the elegant Soho, the raffish Spectator, the classic Baltusrol, the straightforward

Woodlawn, and the slip-on Hamilton… Store manager Jack Lynch assisted me while I decided on the top and how much of it I wanted to see from above (enough to know it's there, not enough to distract me from a yard-long putt). How many eyes did I want for the laces? Six on each side seemed about right. After driving myself crazy with all the choices, I selected the Palmer for its simple, throwback charm, then picked white calfskin for the body of the shoe and the only hide left of a beautiful green leather from Italy for the heel trim, saddles, and lining. Clients' names are handwritten on the inside of Vogel shoe tongues. Laced up, I felt suitably stylish as I ripped opening drives. My motto: If you don't play well, try to look as if you could have; in these beautiful green saddle shoes I do, and they'll only get better looking with age. If anyone ever questions how they look, well, that's strictly my own fault."

1879
HEINRICH DINKELACKER

Heinrich Dinkelacker calf leather shoes represent the height of the shoemaking craft. They are completely bespoke from the first last to the finish and are one of the finest shoes in the world according to bespoke aficionados. This German company, founded in Sindelfingen and now based in the medieval city of Bietigheim-Bissingen, is one of the last of the traditional shoemakers and makes the Budapester shoe, a double-stitched triple-soled full brogue with open-throat lacing that is shaped by hand on a round toe last to give it a distinctive upturned front and high-walled look. The firm was, until recently, run by Burkhardt Dinkelacker, grandson of founder Heinrich Dinkelacker. After Burkhardt's retirement in 2004, Anton Hunger and Bietigheim-born Norbert Lehmann became partners after being, as Lehmann put it, "captivated by the charm of the traditional methods and the passion put into every shoe." In 2005 investment was provided by Wendelin Wiedeking, a former manager at Porsche who now owns 30 percent of the company.

The renowned Dinkelacker Budapester is handmade in the city from which it takes its name—Budapest—the so-called "Paris of the East" and is then sent to the firm's showroom in Germany. The factory is set away from the grand avenues and elegant riverside boutiques of Budapest in a quiet leafy suburb and it employs thirty-five artisans, some of whom have been working there for more than fifty years. This is the heart and soul of Heinrich Dinkelacker, where all its bespoke shoes are made. One journalist described how, "Visiting the factory is like stepping back in time. The sounds of hammering and the pungent odors of glue and leather fill the air. The veranda on the third floor is taken up by shoes that have been placed in rows to dry. Piles of leather are weighed against

> "Visiting the factory is like stepping back in time. The sounds of hammering and… odors of leather fill the air."

iron weights on enormous scales. The craftsmen here do most of their work with tools that their grandfathers might have used: hammer and anvil, nails, shoemaker's awl and twine, brushes, and, last but not least, the trusty old Singer sewing machine."

Each shoe undergoes a rigorous process of 300 individual steps; firstly the foot is measured in the shop by the managing director and bespoke shoemaker Christoph Renner, who personally takes an hour with the feet of his customers. Dinkelacker prides itself on fit and comfort and has a vast orthopedic knowledge that is used during this period of consultation. The next step is to make a three-dimensional foam bed from which a raw last is formed and a sample shoe fashioned from foam rubber. Any corrections can be made with putty, and from all this information a plastic last is made from which any customer can keep commissioning bespoke shoes.

Left, clockwise from top left:
1. Dinkelacker uses vegetable-tanned leather infused with its natural oils, and new shoes are polished for twenty minutes by a specialist polisher to ensure a smooth and shiny surface. 2. Each pair of shoes is painstakingly hand-crafted using traditional methods to guarantee quality. 3. Every sole and heel is crafted out of pit-tanned leather from the Rendenbach tannery founded in Trier, Germany, in 1871.

There are sixty styles in addition to the Budapester to choose from, including side-buckled Monks and classic Oxfords. Leather can be polished Italian buffalo calfskin in which the grain is more pronounced, French aniline, or naturally dyed calf or cordovan from the Horween Leather Company founded by Isidore Horween in 1905 and one of the last tanneries left in Chicago, Illinois. After the order is placed, the leather is steamed so as to make it malleable enough to work on, the upper is clicked, and the pieces stitched together. The upper is then pulled over a last, clamped into position, and secured with lasting nails to assume its shape where it remains for several days before the shoemaker stitches or inseams the welt to the upper and insole. A cork insole or foot-bed is added for insulation, grip, and good posture—literally putting more spring into the customer's step—and the insole and leather welt are hand-stitched to the outsole. This is a tough task, since the waxed thread has to be stitched through the welt, insole, and upper. The thread is knotted after every stitch for durability. The outsole is hand-sewn or outseamed onto the welt, and depending on the shoe style, more than eighty brass pins are hand hammered onto the sole to reduce the wear when walking. The heel of the shoe is built up with layers of leather, and the shoe is finished. The finishing process involves smoothing down the edges of the heel and sole, and then the black sole edge color is applied freehand with a brush. A specialist polisher polishes the shoe for twenty minutes to achieve a high gloss before it is inspected and signed by the hand of the artisan. Renner explains why the process is so rigorous: "If you pay for custom-made shoes, you have the right to expect something special. The same process, the same attention to detail. Nothing more than solid artisanry combined with high quality. Then people come back again and again. We have customers who wear their shoes for twenty years and only need to resole them every once in a while. And besides, it's good for one's feet. It's they who carry us through life, after all."

Right, clockwise from top left:

1. The Rio features an upper of top-grained, fully dyed calf velour leather, the flesh side of which has been turned out and dressed to a velvety finish. 2., 3., 4., and 5. The creation of a classic and robust Budapester full brogue with its double sole and inverted seam above the sole. It can be recognized by the high forward-facing toe, Derby shaft, mounted heel counter, and wing cap.

1881
BULGARI

Richard Burton quipped that he introduced Elizabeth Taylor "to beer and she introduced me to Bulgari." The Italian jewelry house was a favorite of Taylor's—according to Burton, "Bulgari" was the only word she knew in Italian. He bought her a Bulgari emerald ring to mark the start of their affair on the set of the movie *Cleopatra* (1963), filmed in Cinecittà in 1962, and from then on, punctuated their romance with a treasure trove of ravishing Bulgari gems. In her book *My Love Affair with Jewelry* (2002), Taylor wrote: "Undeniably, one of the biggest advantages to working on *Cleopatra* in Rome, was Bulgari's. I used to visit Gianni Bulgari in the afternoons and we'd sit and swap stories." Burton bought her a pair of emerald earrings, an emerald and diamond necklace to match the ring that she wore in an audience with Queen Elizabeth II, a 65-karat cabochon sapphire and diamond sautoir, and an unusual turquoise and gold mirror. Taylor's personal collection also included a gold Serpenti bracelet watch with a head and tail studded with diamonds, iconic "coin" necklaces from the 1980s, and a set of white and yellow diamond earrings, ring, and brooch.

The great jewelry house of Bulgari, beloved of film stars and socialites, came from simple origins. Its founder, Sotirios Voulgaris was born into a family of itinerant silversmiths from the remote mountain village of Kalarites, which lies wedged into a rim over the Kalaritikos gorge in the Epirus region of Greece. Today the picturesque village of Kalarites is an agrarian community known for the rearing of sheep, but it was once steeped in the traditions of gold and silversmithing; the fruits of such labor can still be seen in the churches and monasteries of the region.

From the first settlement in the thirteenth century, Kalarites was occupied by Turkey and was part of the powerful Ottoman Empire. In 1821, Greece declared war

Below left: Elizabeth Taylor wears a diamond and emerald necklace and matching earrings from Bulgari, bought by Richard Burton, after they met on the set of the film *Cleopatra* in 1962. **Right**: Taylor and Burton's relationship was commemorated with magnificent jewels from Bulgari. This emerald and diamond necklace was Burton's wedding gift on the occasion of their first wedding in 1964. **Below right**: A diamond, emerald, and ruby "lion-mask" hinged bangle *c.* 1960s in the form of pavé-set diamond lion-masks, with cabochon emerald eyes, wearing baguette and circular-cut diamond collars.

and fought for independence; the Peloponnese and the Gulf of Corinth became the first regions under Turkish rule to break free in 1829. As the empire ailed, remote areas of Greece, such as Epirus, became increasingly dangerous; the mountains served as the outposts of bandits who made incursions into the villages, robbing the inhabitants of their possessions. The silversmiths who moved around the region selling their precious wares were obvious targets, and on one occasion, Sotirios's grandfather, Konstantinos Voulgaris, returned home only to be robbed of his every possession including his clothes. The family abandoned their villa (it can still be seen next to the Fitrou fountain in Kalarites) and left for Paramythia, where the first Bulgari shop is still trading.

Konstantinos's son, Giorgos, married Helen Strugari, and in 1857, the couple had their only son, Sotirios. At the age of twenty, he moved with his parents to the Greek island of Corfu where they established a shop, and then moved on his own to Naples in 1881. Disaster struck when Sotirios was robbed, so he headed for Rome and began selling small silver *objets de vertu* on a stall in Via Sistina, a street of magnificent palazzos in the heart of the city, and with business partner goldsmith Demetrio Kremos showed artifacts in the window of a shop, Kindili's at Trinità dei Monti. The first shop under Sotirios's own name in its Italianized form opened at 64 Via Sistina; Sotirios Voulgaris was now Sotirio Bulgari, and as Rome transformed into an international city of style, the shop became part of the evening's "promenade," during which tourists and Romans wandered the city streets "to see and to be seen." In 1881, Jorgen Wilhelm Bergse wrote, "Along Via Felice and Via Sistina, up on Capo le Case and on the steps of the Piazza di Spagna, the place is teeming with pedestrians of both sexes and all

ages, from every nation. Artists go there to see the sunset, breathe the fresh evening air, and listen to music. The Romans go to criticize the women's clothes and gossip. The wealthy Americans and Englishmen show off what they can buy with their pounds and dollars."

In Bulgari's, the promenaders could buy all manner of silver jewelry, including buckles, belts, and bracelets, plus tableware and antiques. Business was brisk, and by 1899, shops had opened in many of the chic towns of Italy to cater to the wealthy, including in St. Moritz, San Remo, and Sorrento. As a new century beckoned, Sotirio began to consolidate his budding empire; he sold off the shops outside Rome and concentrated his business into one high-end boutique at 10 Via Condotti in 1905, which was run with his two sons, Costantino and Giorgio; Via Condotti was a calculated choice as it was a street that specialized in jewelers and silversmiths. Sotirio named his new venture The Old Curiosity Shop, after the novel by Charles Dickens of 1840, clearly indicating that this was no ordinary jewelry boutique but an eclectic collection of expensive embossed and engraved silver, antiques, and, of course, curiosities. The shop also began to establish a reputation for fine gold and silver jewelry set with gemstones—by the 1920s, this had become its prime focus after Costantino and Giorgio became a united force buying some of the finest gems in the world under the expert eyes of their father. The 40-karat octagonal Egyptian Pasha diamond was acquired from King Farouk

and bought from the Bulgaris by the Woolworth heiress Barbara Hutton, at that time one of the richest women in the world, who had it recut (losing two karats in the process) and set into a ring.

The influence of Art Deco began to be felt in Bulgari's designs during this era; the company created French-inspired modernist pieces with geometric gem settings and the "white-on-white" style of diamonds set in platinum pioneered by Cartier. Watches also entered the repertoire, with geometric cases fashioned from platinum or white gold and the face and bracelet pavé-set with diamonds. Bulgari also used calibre-cut colored gemstones in stylized floral motifs, beginning its association with brightly colored hues that became its trademark in the postwar years of production. The company also catered to the flapper, the newly "hard-boiled" woman who drank cocktails and smoked openly in public (formerly the preserve of the prostitute), by crafting bejeweled cigarette cases from silver and gold encrusted with rubies and diamonds.

After the death of Sotirio in 1932, Costantino and Giorgio decided to revamp Bulgari's image by renovating the interior and the exterior of the Via Condotti store using Italian marble and transforming the company logo to "BVLGARI" using block capitalization in the manner of the Latin alphabet. Bulgari was making its first tentative step into inventing a truly Italian style of jewelry that was to flourish in the 1960s. Rather than being a follower of

the French houses, Bulgari began to create styles based on the heritage of Greece and Italy; the coiled serpent or Serpenti, the ancient Roman symbol of immortality, appeared in flexible polished yellow-gold three-coil bracelet watches from 1949. The Serpenti snake design bracelet had coils in gold mesh that wrapped around the wrist, or were made using the tubogas technique, wherein long strips of gold with raised edges were wrapped around a core of copper or wood. The copper or wood core is then removed by being simply drawn out or dissolved in acid, leaving a flexible gold coil. In 1962, Elizabeth Taylor's Serpenti watch was made from 14-karat yellow gold with the head in white gold, set with round and marquis-shaped diamonds and emerald eyes; the head of the serpent opened to reveal the hidden dial.

Bulgari's reputation grew in the 1950s as Italy's image of *la dolce vita* spawned many homegrown stars who rivaled those of Hollywood. Sophia Loren and Anna Magnani wore Bulgari jewelry, which, like Salvatore Ferragamo shoes and Giò Ponti's furniture, had a certain cachet. By the 1960s, the Bulgari brothers had created a recognizable Italian style, incorporating a cabochon-cut colored gem as the centerpiece of the design rather than the traditional faceted diamond, with aesthetics being the reason for its choice rather than any intrinsic worth. Whereas the House of Dior based its elaborate pieces on motifs taken from nature, Bulgari looked to the glories of ancient Greek and Roman art and architecture, and strong geometry began to mark out its designs. This was never more successful than when Giorgio Bulgari's son, Nicola, who with his brothers, Paolo and Gianni, headed up the family firm in 1967, created the Gemme Nummarie range. Nicola was a collector of ancient coins and cleverly revived their use in jewelry in the manner of ancient Roman work, Italian goldsmiths of the eighteenth century, and the Italian jeweler Castellani in the nineteenth century. Bulgari placed patinated coins—both ancient and modern—into gold frames that hung from heavy, highly

Below: Italian actress Gina Lollobrigida examines a jewel in the Bulgari boutique on Via Condotti, Rome, *c.* 1950s.
Right, clockwise from top left: 1. Bulgari ring in 18-karat yellow gold set with pavé diamonds. 2. and 5. A craftsman at work on a diamond in the Bulgari workshops in Rome. 3. and 4. Inspecting the setting of a completed bracelet.

polished gold chains, yellow-gold rings, earrings, and bracelets, and they were sold in many European locations such as Paris and Geneva, as well as in the first U.S. outlet, which opened in the Pierre Hotel in New York in 1970. This boutique was luxuriously fitted out in Italian beech wood and cream carpeting to highlight the stunning color of the stones, including turquoise, amethyst, and citrine. This was also the decade in which Bulgari launched the iconic Black Face wristwatch.

In the 1980s fashion maven Diana Vreeland noted, "Everything is power and money and how to use them both. We mustn't be afraid of snobbism and luxury." The powerful female executive wanted the status of a designer name in her jewelry but also pieces that could segue easily from office daywear to evening opulence. Bulgari provided exactly this in 1982 with the Parentisi Collection, the first of a series of related collections launched throughout the decade and into the 1990s. These were modernist, modular jewels in combinations of platinum, gold, coral, and steel, with graphic shapes and interlocking hinges that, because of their repeating patterns, could be fitted together in a variety of ways and clearly displayed all the house codes for those in the know.

In 1984, the brand diversified into fragrance with Bulgari, which was reformulated in 1994 after the success of Eau Parfumée au Thé Vert, created by the renowned "nose" Jean-Claude Ellena, and inspired by the fine teas he had savored at Mariages Frères in Paris. A whole series of popular fragrances emerged, including Bulgari Pour Femme in 1994, and a year later Bulgari Pour Homme. Today the firm is run by Sotirio's grandsons, Paolo and Nicola Bulgari, and their nephew, Francisco Trapani, who is chief executive. Bulgari is one of the largest jewelry houses in the world, having diversified into scarves, bags, eyewear, and luxury hotels, where, it is said, Bulgari jewelry can be ordered via room service. In 2011, Bulgari joined the fashion conglomerate LVMH as the biggest family shareholder after the Arnault family. Bulgari remains true to its roots: as Trapani says, "In our creations you can always find a sense of volume, a passion for linear and symmetrical forms which are the precious legacies of our roots. Bulgari is a brand that in well over a century of existence has contributed to the history of jewelry through a strong and constant innovation in style and design."

"Bulgari… has contributed to the history of jewelry through a strong and constant innovation in style and design."

Francisco Trapani,
chief executive of Bulgari

Below: Cary Grant and co-star
Eve Marie-Saint in Alfred
Hitchcock's *North By Northwest*
(1959). Grant wore a Kilgour suit
throughout the film.

Right: A wool basket-weave,
three-piece suit made by Kilgour,
French & Stanbury in 1959.
Basket-weave is a plain weave
with paired warps and wefts.

1882
KILGOUR

Cary Grant is waiting at the side of a dusty road; a crop duster flies idly overhead. The film is *North By Northwest*, directed by maestro Alfred Hitchcock in 1959. Grant is wearing a medium-gray, lightweight-wool, single-breasted suit with a three-button fastening and notched lapels, and it has to be the most refined suit on film. As he runs from the airplane and dives into the dust to dodge the bullets, he reveals forward-pleated trousers cut high to give room in the thigh and a jacket with no vents. Arthur Lyons tailored this iconic suit for Kilgour, French and Stanbury of Savile Row, London, after being personally selected by Grant for his role as Roger Thornhill. The actor was allowed to keep the suit once the shoot was over—he made sure it was written into his contract.

Kilgour, French and Stanbury was an obvious choice as, according to writer Temple Fielding in 1959, "their understanding of American tastes is such a special asset." The tailors specialized in a glamorous version of bespoke

Savile Row style that was imported into Hollywood by stars wanting to display their English elegance on the silver screen. In the 1930s, Ronald Colman, Leslie Howard, and Bing Crosby visited Savile Row and bought bespoke suits from Kilgour, a company that had been in existence since 1882 but had really come to the fore during this decade. Fred Astaire was a returning customer and had first been introduced to the company in 1923 after he and his sister, Adele, had become the toast of London in a production of *For Goodness Sake* at the Shaftesbury Theatre. Edward, Prince of Wales saw the show and invited the stars to supper; Fred was so taken by the dapper aristocrat's style that Edward introduced him to one of his favorite haunts, Kilgour. Here Astaire had his tailcoats cut, including the one worn in *Top Hat* (1935), which had the sleeve head enlarged to accommodate his dance moves.

The company's reputation had moved from traditionalist to modernist after the original business of T. & F. French, established in 1882 with a well-established gentlemanly clientele, merged with A. H. Kilgour to become Kilgour & French in 1923, and in 1925 it joined forces with Fred and Louis Stanbury, a pair of émigré tailors from Hungary. Fred was a stickler for detail and meticulous in his bespoke work; Louis was a consummate showman at front-of-house, always there with a memorable quote such as, "It is for me to make my customer into an Adonis. It is not easy, but I must." They attracted some of the world's most powerful men, including Joseph Kennedy, father of president JFK, and the Aga Khan who famously married Rita Hayworth in 1948. In 1937, the house showed the brothers' worth by undergoing a name change to Kilgour, French and Stanbury and cultivating a more youthful clientele with what were deemed "ultra-modern clothes for the most dashing type of young man."

"It is for me to make my customer into an Adonis. It is not easy, but I must."

Louis Stanbury

In 1968, U.S. men were given more instant access to the delights of Kilgour tailoring when the company sold ready-to-wear suits under licence at Barney's department store in New York. The suits were sold in the store's English Shop, which also merchandised a range of garments by Burberry, Aquascutum, and DAKS.

In London, Kilgour was appealing to the new peacock male; in 1967 men's magazine *Penthouse* wrote, "Whoever heard of swinging in Savile Row? But Louis Stanbury has proved that a super bespoke tailor can run up a few numbers for the switched-on set." Kilgour was prepared to break the rules, and many an eyebrow was raised in Savile Row when the company pioneered research into man-made fibers in collaboration with ICI in 1969. In 1974, Kilgour employed one of its former apprentices Tommy Nutter, who together with another Kilgour apprentice, Edward Sexton, had gone on to revolutionize menswear in the 1960s with a modern take on tailoring. At Kilgour, Nutter designed a Prince of Wales check suit for Ringo Starr, with wide lapels and Oxford bags, before leaving to open his own business, Tommy Nutter, at 19 Savile Row.

In 1998, Kilgour took a different direction with the employment of Carlo Brandelli as creative director with the remit to transform the company into a global luxury brand. He gave good press, championing the single-button suit for its elongation of the torso saying, "If you don't have an athletic figure, we'll give you one." This lean

Left: The exterior of Kilgour at No. 8 Savile Row, London. **Right**: Bespoke tailoring at Kilgour. The term "bespoke" originated in Savile Row when cloth for a suit was said to "be spoken for" by individual customers. **Far right**: After the cutter measures the client, a paper pattern is made from which the cloth is cut.

silhouette with structured shoulders and a fitted, shaped chest remains the distinctive cut of the Kilgour suit today with a color range of deep navy, tonal gray, and black.

In the 2000s, Kilgour French and Stanbury entered a new era; in 2003 the name was changed to one simple word—Kilgour—and in 2008, after the business was bought by JMH Lifestyle, it began to move back to its refined bespoke roots. Today, every element of a custom-made Kilgour suit is made by hand, from the cutting of the high-quality cloth to the finishing. It remains one of the few Savile Row establishments to implement the "one tailoring one unit" mode of production in which the same tailor takes eighty hours to complete one suit at the premises at 8 Savile Row. Bespoke shirts come in myriad styles; customers can choose from cotton, silk, or voile in an unlimited color palette, twelve styles of collar, French

or button cuffs, and detailing including mother-of-pearl buttons and the opportunity to include a personalized monogram. The U.S. connection is still there; Kilgour visits the United States three to four times a year and takes commissions from its overseas clients, consulting on the detail of lapel and shoulder drape, and remaining the epitome of English sartorial craftsmanship refreshed with the currency of contemporary design. As Kilgour puts it, "Our tailoring is designed to make one disappear into one's surroundings, a bit like urban camouflage. Our garments are all about the detailing, the quality of the cut, and luxurious fabrics. We work on the inside of the garment more than on the outside. We strive to make garments that are about a restrained luxury: the shape is beautifully structured, and the detailing on the inside harks back to bespoke principles."

1883
LUCCHESE

The cowboy boot may be an instantly recognizable symbol of Texas but its evolution has been gradual. The first cowboys were Mexican *vaqueros* renowned for their skills at driving huge herds of longhorn cattle across the state in the nineteenth century. High-heeled, steel-reinforced boots were key to their success: a slim toe fitted snugly into the stirrup and a low undercut heel kept it there; an arch with a steel shank applied pressure on the bar of the stirrup when mounting, dismounting, and guiding the horse. Thus the constituent parts of the cowboy boot developed, and were finally fashioned from heavy leather with a wide top and slick leather sole enabling the cowboy to slip his feet out of the stirrups and make a rapid escape if the horse ever buckled beneath him. By the end of the nineteenth century, the demand for cowboy boots became so great that any bootmaker worth his salt and with a bit of business acumen set up alongside one of the great trails across the Rio Grande. Here a cowboy could drop off a pair of boots for mending or commission a new pair to be picked up when he returned. One such bootmaker still exists, the Lucchese Boot Company of San Antonio, Texas, established in 1883 by

Samuel Lucchese and his brothers Joe and Mike, Italian immigrants who had entered the country from Sicily in 1880. San Antonio was the chosen destination because of its proximity to the army post of Fort Sam Houston, and it was a prime route for cattle being driven into the state of Kansas. Cowboys would have their feet measurements taken and then sign them as a form of contract for the commissioning of a Lucchese boot—they remain the only records that survive from the early history of the company. Lucchese earned its reputation among the U.S. cavalry, too, by making bespoke boots for officers either traveling through or based in El Paso, Texas.

Although founder Samuel was a mere fifteen years old he was already devoted to his craft and refused to use any but the finest grade of leathers, a stance his grandson, Sam Lucchese Jr., was determined to retain when he took over the company in 1969. In 1976 he stated, "We're not talking hamburger leather. McDonald's dictates what a lot of boots are made of: the more hamburgers they sell the more hamburger leather on the market. We make ours of imported French or Italian calf. It's like the difference between baby's skin and that of a forty-year-old man."

From early on, the Luccheses also realized that it was unrealistic for one man to make a boot from start to finish; some craftsmen were good at making uppers and others good at making soles and heels. A system was set up whereby a team made a boot rather than an individual. In the years leading up to the outbreak of World War I, the Lucchese Boot Company employed fifty workers who made up to thirty pairs of boots per day and, by 1919, hatbands and belts. As the railways expanded and encroached upon the preserve of the cowboy, the demand for the boot began to slow. Lucchese's streamlined system of manufacture meant they were one of the few original names to survive.

Left: A portrait of Italian immigrant Sam Lucchese who founded the Lucchese Boot Company in 1883.
Right, clockwise from top left: 1. A row of finished crocodile skin boots. 2. Working on the first stages of a boot in the Lucchese factory. 3. A pattern is machine stitched. 4. A worker reinforces the sole of a boot. 5. Completing the stitched pattern on a boot.

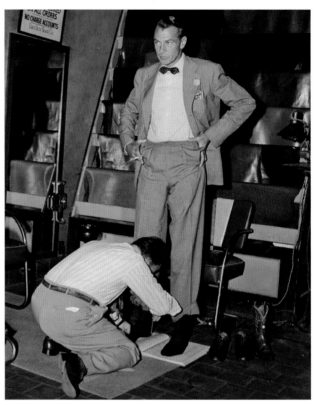

"Hands out-perform machines."

Sam Lucchese Jr.

Above: A Mexican *vaquero* painted by Frederic Remington, a celebrated American painter of the Old American West *c.* 1890s.
Above right: American actor Gary Cooper, star of many iconic Westerns including *High Noon* (1952) being fitted for a pair of Lucchese boots.

Right, clockwise from top: 1. With the exception of its hand-driven lemon wood pegs, every inch of a Lucchese boot is made of the finest leather. 2. and 3. The Exotic Western boots come in a range of deluxe skins, including full quill ostrich, burnished ostrich leg, and alligator with De Soto stitching.

In 1923, the ill-health of Lucchese's founder, Samuel, meant that son Cosimo Lucchese took over the operation. He was even more of a stickler for quality than his father, and because of this, production dropped down to only seven or eight pairs of boots per day. The high quality demanded a higher price but it worked; Sam Lucchese recalls that Cosimo "felt a pair of boots he made belonged to him until he decided that they fit you properly and that they looked good on your feet. His only advertisement was his product. His boots looked so good that his friends could not stand it until they got a pair."

The exceptionally high quality of the Lucchese boot saved the brand during the Depression of the 1930s, and Hollywood created a global demand for the style when the cowboy became one of the first movie heroes. Characters such as Bronco Billy, Tom Mix, Roy Rogers, and Gene Autry rode the range in Western shirts, ten-gallon hats, and increasingly decorative boots, creating a modern style of masculine appeal and a new interest in the cowboy boot. By the 1940s Lucchese boots were being worn by Presidents Roosevelt and Lyndon Johnson and movie stars Gene Autry and John Wayne, and the company created what many believe to be the pinnacle of cowboy boot design, a series of forty-eight boots in homage to each U.S. state with inlays of the state house, flower, flag, and bird.

The Lucchese family's dedication to its craft and to its customers has continued to keep the business alive. In the early 1960s, the founder's grandson and namesake Sam Lucchese Jr. realized that the company had to expand in order to survive beyond its loyal but aging customer base. The challenge was to create a standardized sizing system for what was a custom-fit boot, and to this end he began to study the relationship of the boot to the foot in more detail. A study in foot dynamics from the University of Rochester was key. Sam recalls, "The idea of it was that people are like horses in that they have a gait. Their feet may be the same size but because Charlie walks with a certain gait, he is going to wear his shoes differently. Sitting him down and measuring his feet in a static position does not provide comfort or support or what is generally put under the big umbrella of 'fit.'" After six years of study, the result was the renowned Twisted Cone Last, contoured to mirror the human foot, taking into account the tendons and bone structure and used in all Lucchese boots. The company also introduced the inseamer machine to sew a tighter and thus more leak-proof inseam.

In 2008 Lucchese marked its 125-year anniversary, and in May 2009 the Texas House of Representatives and Texas Senate passed legislation officially recognizing Lucchese and securing its place in Texan history. Today the company recognizes that a fine boot takes time; twenty-one days from the first careful selection and cutting of superb leather, to the hand-driven lemon wood pegs and final meticulous finishing of each boot. A favorite saying of Lucchese's is "Hands out-perform machines"; quite simply there is no substitute for the experienced hands of an artisanal bootmaker and the key elements of all Lucchese boots are still handmade. Every pair is hand-inspected, not once, but twice; leather seams may be skived by machine but the process is repeated a second time by hand. As Lucchese states today, "In virtually every one of our procedures, we rely on human hands to complete the task to near-perfection."

1889
LANVIN

The loving bond that the unassuming Jeanne Lanvin shared with her daughter was the key to her lasting success and it was duly venerated in the original Lanvin logo. Drawn by the modernist illustrator Paul Iribe, it depicted a united mother and child dressed in matching outfits, and it was just such clothing that launched Lanvin's career. In 1867, Jeanne Lanvin was born in Brittany to journalist Constantin Lanvin and his wife, whose name remains unknown. She was the eldest of eleven children and at the age of thirteen was apprenticed to the French modiste Suzanne Talbot for whom she worked as an errand girl; three years later Lanvin trained in millinery at Madame Félix in Paris, and in 1885, with the backing of a client, opened her own millinery workshop in an attic on Rue du Marché Saint-Honoré.

By 1889, Lanvin had set up a small business on Rue du Faubourg Saint-Honoré, and in the same manner as former milliner Coco Chanel, she turned it into a fully fledged fashion house, creating the most exquisitely embellished couture—the House of Lanvin remains the oldest one still working in Paris today.

In 1895, Lanvin married Count Emilio di Pietro and in 1897 gave birth to daughter Marguerite, a.k.a. Marie-Blanche, who was to have a huge influence on the direction her career would take, for the unabashedly romantic mother and daughter outfits that Lanvin designed for her own wardrobe caught the eye of the count's wealthy friends who commissioned copies for their own infants and coordinating clothes for themselves. By 1908, Lanvin had opened a childrenswear department

Far left: French couturière Jeanne Lanvin, photographed by Boris Lipnitzki with her daughter's cat, France, in 1932. **Left**: The original Lanvin mother-and-child logo designed by modernist illustrator Paul Iribe. **Right**: A typically romantic tiered dress design in the neoclassical style by Jeanne Lanvin, *c.* 1910.

within her millinery boutique, followed by womenswear in 1909. In the same year, Lanvin improved her dressmaking and millinery credentials by joining the Chambre Syndicale de la Couture Parisienne and officially becoming one of an elite band of couturiers in Paris. The designer's methods were unusual in that she did not sketch her ideas or work them out by draping material on a mannequin; rather she related her ideas to a team of expert artisans who then visualized them on her behalf. A she described the process to *Vogue* magazine in 1934, "I act on impulse and believe in instinct. My dresses aren't premeditated. I am carried away by feeling, and technical knowledge helps me make my clothes become a reality."

Lanvin's early designs were influenced by the escapist orientalism that Paris-based designer Paul Poiret had introduced into European fashion; fashion historian Georgina Howell describes how "the theatrical came into the forefront of fashion. The modern woman in the gaiter suit turned into a beautiful barbarian in the evening, in a costume that might have been deigned by Bakst. All Paris came out with evening dresses in tiers of shot tulle or silver lace and tea-rose brocade, with Turkish trousers of looped chiffon, lamé jackets, wings and trains of sparkling chiffon, turbans, and fountains of ostrich feathers."

Lanvin was an important proponent of this trend, and women loved her clothes for they were, quite simply, beautiful. She used the most expensive of fabrics, including silk, taffeta, velvet, lace, and tulle, and had her atelier fashion them into jejeune silhouettes that flattered the figure and created an aesthetic of youthfulness that had incredible appeal. In 1913, Lanvin created her legendary *robe de style*, an alternative to the simple streamlined shapes that other more modernist designers, such as Chanel, were showing in Paris. Lanvin's innovative silhouette was eighteenth century in origin,

with a fitted bodice, dropped waist, and full, billowing skirt in the manner of a Rococo pannier; she repeated the style throughout her career, and although this seemed rather picturesque and out of touch, it actually anticipated Dior's Corolle line, or New Look as it was dubbed by the press, in 1947. At a time when applied decoration was being rejected in favor of Bauhaus-inspired geometry, Lanvin blazed her own trail, creating fantasy gowns with bouffant crinolines in 1919, and picture dresses overlaid with lace and embroidery inspired by a personal archive of costume and fashion illustrations that dated back to 1845 and the objets she had found on her travels around the world. By 1914, her orientalist eveningwear showed her debt to the culture of the Far East; the use of quilted satin and the kimono sleeve, for example, were recurring elements in her work well into the 1930s. In 1936, she created an evening jacket in citron-yellow satin covered in parallel rows of topstitching, with kimono sleeves cut all in one piece with the fronts and the shoulder seams left open to display the upper arms.

In 1916, together with Jeanne Paquin, she pioneered the chemise, a dress that was cut very loosely and belted under the line of the breasts with a flat front and back; *Vogue* noted it as "practical, being perfectly adapted to the demands of modern-life, comfortable, graceful and economical. Moreover it's smart." Many actresses adored Lanvin's work, most notably Yvonne Printemps who became a living advertisement for the label, appearing in the press under the banner "Dressed both for town and the theater by Jeanne Lanvin"; when Printemps appeared in the movie *Les Trois Valses* (1938), her entire wardrobe had been hand-crafted by the Lanvin atelier. Fashion historian Dominique Veillon writes, "Rumor had it that when the actress left for a tour of the United States, she demanded to take eighty gowns from Lanvin with her. It was also whispered that Sacha Guitry, that eternal and incorrigible lover, swore by nobody but Lanvin, entrusting her with exclusive responsibility for dressing his four successive wives, the most recent being Genevieve de Sereville."

Lanvin's use of embellishment was the best in Paris, recognized by its application of intricate ribboning and lavish embroidery and trim, clearly displaying her roots in millinery. After falling in love with nineteenth-century

Above: Jeanne Lanvin kneels to drape fabric on a model during a fitting in Paris, *c.* 1930s. **Right, clockwise from top left**: 1. The dropped waist detail of a silk *robe de style, c.* 1927. 2. Detail of the Lesbos wedding dress of 1925, incorporating silk, satin, pearls, glass beads, and metallic thread. 3. Silk crêpe and lace sleeve detail from 1924. 4. A sequinned wool crêpe evening gown from 1937.

"I act on impulse and believe in instinct... I am carried away by feeling, and technical knowledge helps me make my clothes become a reality."

Jeanne Lanvin

Above: The Lanvin Menswear Showroom in Savile Row, London, photographed in 2008.

Right: Alber Elbaz used 1930s sketches from the Lanvin archive for this collection shown in Paris in 2007.

French painting, including the Impressionists, the couturière built up her own impressive collection by artists who experimented with the relationship between color and the dappling effects of light across the surface of a scene, including the work of Édouard Vuillard, Pierre-Auguste Renoir, Henri Fantin-Latour, and the mystical Symbolist Odilon Redon. Accordingly, Lanvin experimented with the play of light and shadow on fabric using appliqué, mirrors, sequins, beading, ruffles, and free-flowing ribbons at the neck and hem of each dress, many with layers of organza that appeared like the petals of a Polignac pink rose. Her orders were so prodigious that three ateliers were opened purely for embroidery, and multi-needle sewing machines were introduced to keep up with the demand for the quilted components of cloaks and other forms of outerwear. After being inspired by the fifteenth-century frescoes of Renaissance artist Fra Angelico, Lanvin set up her own dye factory in Nanterre, on the outskirts of Paris, to experiment with color and to ensure the house's palette could not be replicated by any other designers. In this way, she invented Lanvin blue, a clear forget-me-not color that reappeared consistently in her work, including in her schemes for interior decoration. At the Nanterre factory, the technique of ombré was refined, whereby the color was dyed so as to graduate from light to dark or in stripes of varying shades.

Lanvin was the first designer to see fashion as a lifestyle that had the potential to encompass every aspect of life. Accordingly, Lanvin Decoration was founded in collaboration with designer Armand-Albert Rateau at 15 Rue du Faubourg Saint-Honoré in 1920; Lanvin Sport was established at the same address in 1923 and launched golfing sweaters for women, with collars and cuffs and "a primrose wool jersey dress embroidered in checks of gold and silver thread" to wear on the links; and in 1926, Lanvin Tailleur/Chemisier was followed by Lanvin Fourrure and Lanvin Lingerie. When Lanvin Homme menswear entered the repertoire, the couturier was in the unrivaled position of being the designer who could not only clothe every member of the family but decorate their house too. In 1927, the House of Lanvin launched their first fragrance, Arpège, again devoted to Jeanne's daughter, the couturière having been inspired by the sound of Marie-Blanche practicing her scales on the piano. In the interwar years, Lanvin opened boutiques in the most chic of resorts on the Côte d'Azur—Nice, Cannes, and Biarritz—and dressed royalty and celebrity clients including Mary Pickford and Marlene Dietrich.

In 1946, after the death of Jeanne Lanvin, Marie-Blanche duly took over, employing Antonio Cánovas del Castillo del Rey of Spain as the house's designer until her death in 1958, when cousin Yves Lanvin inherited the business. Castillo was followed by Jules-François Crahay, whose first collection of 1964 was regarded as a success, continuing the house codes of opulent fabrics, historically inspired silhouettes, including a revival of the Edwardian leg o' mutton sleeve, and rich surface detailing. After Crahay came Maryll Lanvin from 1983 to 1989, who was succeeded by the prestigious name of Claude Montana, one of the innovators of the 1970s, who launched his first collection for Lanvin in 1990. Montana stayed for a mere three years, and during this time Lanvin passed through multiple ownership, at one point concentrating on ready-to-wear rather than couture; the business eventually landed with investor group Harmonie S.A., which appointed Alber Elbaz as Lanvin's artistic director in 2001. Moroccan-born Alber Elbaz rejuvenated the company, reintroducing Lanvin's heritage use of luxurious embellishment with the employment of paillettes, beading, and grosgrain ribbon. Fabrics included heavy duchesse satin used in Elbaz's signature cocktail dresses and taffeta fashioned into deluxe trench coats. The designer introduced his own deconstructionist touches with washed silk faille, tarnished metal beads, and frayed collars. After the launch of Elbaz's first collection, *Vogue*'s André Leon Talley wrote that "the debut of Alber Elbaz at that house was an elegant reality check—we could practically hear a crack of thunder over the Petit Palais."

1890
EDWARD GREEN

The town of Northampton in England has been a center of shoemaking since the Middle Ages; the location was perfect for tanning leather as the tanneries could use the bark of the indigenous oak trees and water from the local River Nene. Northampton was also relatively near to London, where hides could be bought from the city's butchers and transported back for tanning or, by the nineteenth century, sourced from the town's covered cattle market. In 1452, the assizes or traveling English courts regulated the trade of the cordwainer, the title given to the manufacturer of fine leather shoes as opposed to the cobblers who repaired them.

Once the tanneries were established, cordwainers began to set up workshops in the town because leather was so readily available. Records show that by 1642 production was in full flow as 4,000 shoes and 600 boots were made for the army, followed by another enormous order for Oliver Cromwell's army in 1648. By 1831, it was estimated that one-third of all the men living in Northampton were shoemakers who tended to work from home in their cellars or small garden sheds. The more commercial shoe manufacturers were only so in name; in actuality their warehouses were set up to receive the finished shoes from the local artisans, which were then inspected, packed up, and dispatched. By the nineteenth century, many shoemakers banded together and opened their own small factories with machinery used for some of the processes, and the town began to gain a reputation for such high-quality footwear that it was described as having an intricate "sixty-four stiches to the inch."

Edward Green's workshop was established in Northampton in 1890 with the intention of "making the finest shoes, without compromise." In the 1930s his sons took over the business, and Cyril Green made the philosophy of the company clear when he wrote in their in-house journal Evergreen: "We are young enough to be conversant with present-day ideas and needs, but old enough to apply the principles of shoemaking correctly, and I am sure that it's this combination of new and old which has helped us to retain our customers and add so many new ones as each year passes." Customers included Edward, Duke of Windsor, known for his love of the finest handmade shoes and who favored the Edward Green Harrow loafer, a slip-on, low-cut, laceless shoe with a full strap and hand-sewn vamp, and writer Ernest "Papa" Hemingway who wore his handmade and very comfortable shoes to Harry's Bar in Venice. The comfort of the company's shoes was derived from their legendary lasts, many of which were developed and refined in the 1930s. Edward Green's lasts fitted the foot very

Below: Founder Edward Green of a company known for making "the finest shoes for the discerning few." **Right, clockwise from top left**: 1. A row of finished shoes available from Edward Green's shops in London and Paris. 2. Each pair of shoes takes several weeks to complete. 3. The shoes are Goodyear welted. 4. The tools of the trade used to work on high-grade skin.

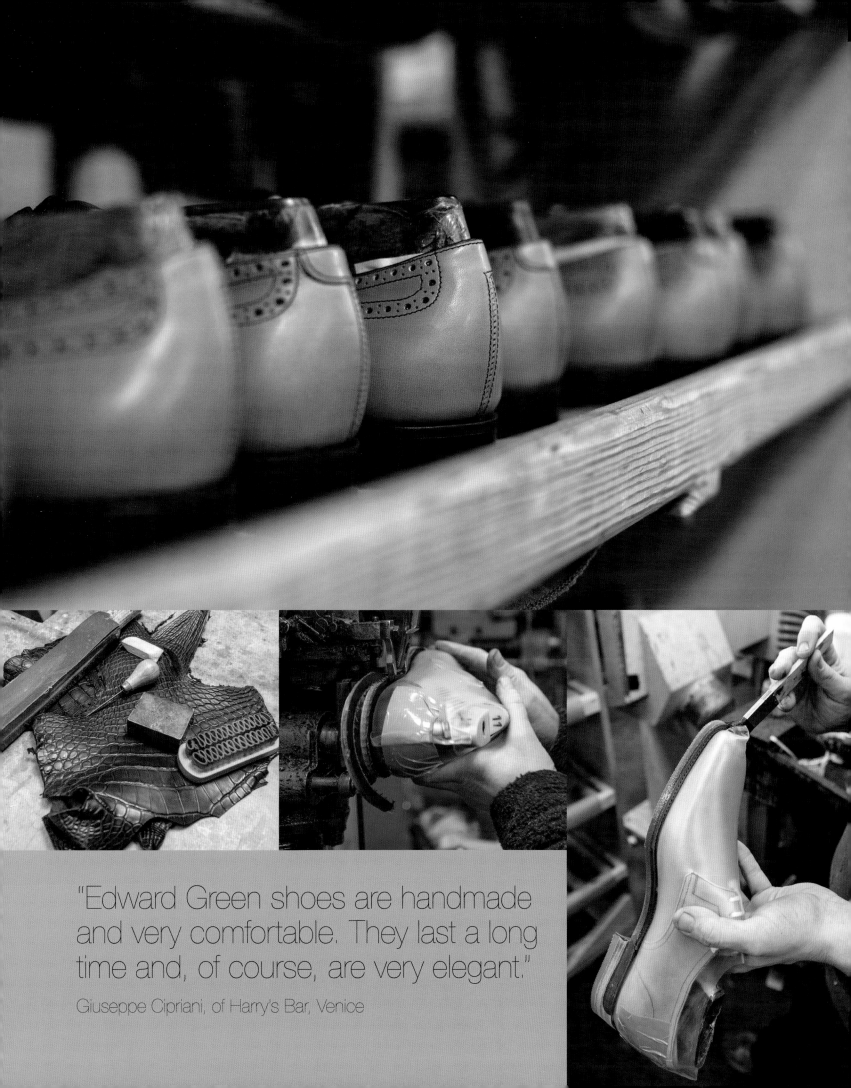

"Edward Green shoes are handmade and very comfortable. They last a long time and, of course, are very elegant."

Giuseppe Cipriani, of Harry's Bar, Venice

comfortably by mirroring its shape, such as in the round-toed classic English 202, still used extensively today to create the perfect city day shoe.

During World War II, the company, like many in Northampton, was turned over to the war effort and manufactured military boots. Immediately afterward, as mens' tastes in footwear shifted overwhelmingly to shoes, Edward Green did the same by focusing on developing a wider range of shoe styles. In 1977, the business entered a new era when the Green family sold out to former belt salesman and leather accessories entrepreneur Marley Hodgson, owner of the U.S. company Trafalgar Limited and later Ghurka, a label renowned for its high-quality leather utility-inspired bags. It was a short-lived arrangement, however, and Hodgson sold on to Czechoslovakian émigré and bespoke shoemaker John Hlustik in 1982. After studying shoe design in Italy and working in Spain, Hlustik brought a Mediterranean sensibility to the traditions of Northampton shoemaking, introducing chisel-toed lasts such as the 888 with a longer Italianate toe shape, updating the traditional Windsor blucher with elaborate broguing, and overturning the English prejudice against brown shoes. Etiquette dictated that a gentleman wore black shoes by day and never wore brown ones in town or after 6 p.m.; this was considered a true breach of sartorial style, an egregious social gaffe only committed by the nation's hoi polloi. In 1926 for example, one author of an English etiquette book described how "I actually saw a man in the Carlton Hotel entrance hall one night last summer wearing brown shoes, a dinner jacket, and a straw hat," adding, "he was presumably an American but even so!" However, by the 1960s, well-heeled Americans also heeded this rule; in an article in *Time* magazine analyzing the style of the new president, John F. Kennedy, titled "Well Suited for the White House," the author described "the most clothes-conscious occupant of the White House since Martin van Buren who showed up for church wearing a velvet collar, a lace-tipped cravat, and yellow kid gloves," adding, "Kennedy has a profound sense of what is proper, and what is not, and his associates have been startled to discover that he does not hesitate to make his views known. One evening a close friend of his showed up at an informal dinner wearing a dark blue suit and dark brown shoes that just missed being black. The president noted the shoes and shook his head sadly, 'Uh-oh,' he said, 'Not for evening.'"

However, in Italy and Spain it was customary for well-dressed men to combine a pair of brown shoes with a navy suit; Hlustik, unbound by tradition, wanted to display the depth of color of his mahogany-hued fine calfskin shoes, especially after he had innovated a method of antiquing the leather. The rich brown shoes were a success and helped gentlemen to break what many believed by the 1980s to be a rather stuffy arcane rule. At the same time, Hlustik also realized that the Edward Green shoe company needed to return to the founding father's emphasis on quality and began to seek prestigious locations in which to sell what he described as "a very elegant shoe, neither heavy and clunky nor slick," including London's Burlington Arcade, a covered and discreet parade of boutiques built in 1809 to unite Piccadilly and Bond Street. After his death in 2000, Hlustik's partner, Hilary Freeman, took over the reins of the company, and in 2004 the factory moved to larger premises on Cliftonville Road in Northampton where the ready-to-wear and made-to-order shoes are manufactured. In 2009, the firm opened a second shop on Paris's Boulevard Saint-Germain.

At Edward Green, shoes are handmade, in the main, and hand-finished by a team of craftsmen, and when machinery is used it is guided by hand. The company uses only the highest quality of calfskin for durability, and as the quality control is so high, only 250 pairs of shoes are completed every week. Each calf hide makes a maximum of three pairs of shoes, and as every hide is different, the arrangement of the pieces has to be carefully decided upon according to grain and stretch. The upper is clicked, or cut out, vamp first followed by the quarters and then the rest of the component pieces, before the leathers are hand-sewn into the upper using pig's bristle as a needle. Edward Green shoes are Goodyear welted, a method by which the sole and the upper are stitched onto a welt, or strip of leather, that forms the supporting structure of the shoe, allowing the sole to be detached easily for repair and remade many times over. A spokesman for the company says, "Lots and lots of men are so fond of their shoes they really want you to go to the most extraordinary lengths to preserve that shoe rather than to have a new pair. We do try awfully hard to and we do get them back after twenty years or so."

Finally the shoes are polished and repolished, rested, and repolished until the trademark translucent patina develops. It was an obvious fit when Edward Green looked into its shoe archive to collaborate with the Hardy Amies label in 2011, for fashion designer Amies who has dressed Queen Elizabeth II was a man who was known for his strong opinions on the polishing of shoes. As he proclaimed in his tome *ABC of Men's Fashion* (1964): "It should be noted that the surfaces of the material in men's costume are predominantly matte. The silk of his tie, and the leather of his shoe or boot, are welcome light-reflecting contrasts. This is just one reason why well-polished shoes are essential." He added, "It is totally impossible to be well-dressed in cheap shoes."

Above left: A pair of burnished brown leather chisel-toed brogues, the pierced holes originally designed to allow water to drain from the shoe. **Top**: A spectator shoe is a leather summer shoe with white cotton canvas or khaki twill. **Above**: A full-brogue spectator shoe in dark oak calf leather and white suede with a darker edge to the sole.

1895
BERLUTI

The Italian house of Berluti, based in Paris, is well-known among connoisseurs for its exquisite handmade men's shoes. Customers all over the world positively venerate the unique streamlined toe-capped Berluti Oxford with an upper made from a single piece of leather with three eyelets and no visible stitching, glossed to such a finish that it reflects like a Venetian mirror. The Duke of Windsor, one of history's most suave fashion plates, wore this irresistible shoe throughout the 1920s.

Alessandro Berluti was born in Senigallia, an Italian port on the Adriatic Sea, and was apprenticed to a local wood and leather worker. He gained an innate understanding of the properties of wood that was to prove especially advantageous for his career in shoes when making lasts, wooden models of the client's foot on which the leather for the shoe is fitted. In the 1880s he left the village and

went on the road to seek fame and fortune with his shoemaking tools on his back. Along the way he met a group of traveling players with whom he lived and worked for several years, making shoes for their performances. By 1895, Berluti was in Paris working as a bespoke shoemaker in his own atelier, measuring, cutting, and polishing shoes and, after exhibiting at the World's Fair in 1900, he began to gain an international reputation. His atelier became shoemaking's best-kept secret as wealthy men made their way there to be fitted for bespoke shoes. After his death, Alessandro was succeeded by his son, Torello, who opened the first Berluti boutique on Rue du Mont-Thabor in 1928, cleverly situated in the vicinity of some of the city's most high-status hotels.

Berluti began to be known for distinct types of male footwear with Goodyear welted soles, including the Pope shoe made out of a single piece of seamless leather, the laced moccasin, and the Napoleon III, an elastic-sided shoe that the Duke of Windsor described as "something simultaneously modern and mischievous." Celebrity clients flocked to Berluti over the next three decades, including President John F. Kennedy, Aristotle Onassis, singer Frank Sinatra, and the Hollywood actor Yul Brynner, who was known for his penchant for exotic skins, including shark, ray, and elephant ear. Today the Berluti Oxford is the stage shoe of choice for Bryan Ferry, erstwhile lead singer of Roxy Music, and off-stage he sports Berluti loafers with cashmere socks bought from the boutique in Conduit Street, London. Ferry says: "I prefer proper leather shoes. Berluti do a very slim, pointy shoe, which I like."

In the 1960s, the leadership of the firm moved down a generation to Torello's son, Talbino, who introduced prêt-à-chausseur at lower prices to expand the customer base, with a visual measuring process of standardized foot

Below: Many well-known names have walked through Berluti's door, from the Duke of Windsor through to artists Jean Cocteau and Andy Warhol and singer Frank Sinatra.

Right: Berluti's wooden lasts, a unique three-dimensional pattern of the client's foot from which the shoe is made.

types. The assistants at Berluti were said to be able to tell what was the most suitable form of footwear as soon as the customer's shoe was taken off; it was either "pretentious," "intellectual," "fragile," "masochist," or even more bizarrely, "unpleasant." This rather original taxonomy had been created by the legendary Olga Berluti who still has a hand in making the bespoke shoes today. As a child, Olga would sit entranced in the workshop of her grandfather and father, lapping up every detail of the making process. She was instructed to polish scraps of leather and, after hours of this simple manual work, she developed her polishing techniques that, according to Olga, include burnishing each pair of bespoke shoes by moonlight as the rays of the sun are too harsh. As she explains, "First, you wash the shoes. Then you must expose them to the rising moon, in the first quarter of the lunar cycle. The moonlight penetrates to the heart of the leather, et voilà!"

Olga Berluti officially joined the firm in 1959 and introduced the trademark "shine" on the finishing of the shoe's Venetian leather by using a selection of oils, pigments, and creams kept in vintage Guerlain perfume bottles to bestow the same rich patina as found on antique furniture. She was also responsible for introducing an innovative color palette, including smoky-blacks, yellowy-greens, red, royal blue, and pinot-noir purple, and at the age of seventeen created a flat-tipped moccasin for Pop artist Andy Warhol, who had been brought into the boutique in Paris by his friend, fashion designer Yves Saint Laurent; the Andy model can still be bought at Berluti.

In 1993, fashion conglomerate LVMH acquired the firm from Olga Berluti after Bernard Arnault, a long-term fan of the shoes, saw opportunities to expand the brand while retaining its core values. In 2012, Arnault's son, Antoine, became CEO of Berluti with Olga as chairwoman, promising never to compromise on the quality of the brand saying: "Berluti was untouched. LVMH bought it and it was one of the few brands that felt like an almost divine name, quite untouchable—and that's where you want a brand to be, in luxury it has to feel almost

inaccessible. A pair of Berluti shoes has this flair, these nuances in color and patina, so I thought: 'What if we took this *je ne sais quoi* and turn it into a menswear brand?' We know this is a segment of the market that lacks a real good player, a house that allies to authenticity and tradition, but with style and sophistication. It's usually either–or."

Accordingly, the Arnaults have appointed as creative director Alessandro Sartori to use the firm's backstory as the foundation for the creation of a range of menswear and accessories to complement the shoes, as bespoke is notoriously difficult to scale up. The same trademark narrow silhouette that makes a Berluti shoe instantly recognizable has been used in sharp Irish tweed suits, navy and slate-gray cashmere coats, and casual calfskin jackets; the same high-quality patinated leather has also been used for briefcases, laptop covers, and weekend bags. The logo is the epitome of discretion: a stitched slash.

Throughout the 1990s, in her eighteenth-century Marais atelier, surrounded by the lasts of Pablo Picasso, Jean Cocteau, and the Duke of Windsor and watched over by a dummy dressed as a samurai, Olga Berluti experimented with tattooing and piercing shoes after being inspired by the tribal scarification of one of her African clients. The resulting Warrior Collection of 1995 presented entirely bespoke shoes with a distinctive unilateral seam stitched from the arch to the toe; the Piercing Collection treated leather as a couturier treats fabric, gathering it in an asymmetrical fold across the upper leather to be pierced with a stitch at the side. Each pair was worked on by four Italian artisan shoemakers for six months, fashioning shoes that Olga describes "like a skin with wounds, scars, gashes, and piercings: a gangster's shoe." The Tattoo Collection applies the ancient tradition of tattooing to the skin of the shoe to create personalized images or text chosen by the bespoke client. Bryan Ferry had his green patinated shoes tattooed with a skull: "I thought they were rather rock 'n' roll, so would be great on stage. They've been on stage a lot since then."

Olga Berluti has encouraged the cult of Berluti by setting up a club for her VIP enthusiasts, Swann, named after Marcel Proust's upper middle-class dandy in the first volume of *Remembrance of Things Past* (1916). Swann members meet monthly to discuss this most beautiful of footwear, the evening ending with a ritual polishing of

Left and Below left: A shoemaker at work on the rue Marbeuf in Paris. In 2012, Antoine Arnault took over as CEO and began reinventing the label, launching its first ever advertising campaign, starring actor Jeremy Irons. **Below**: A selection of Berluti brogues and monk-strapped shoes. Berluti also launched the Sartori menswear collection in 2012 that includes Italian tailoring and knitwear.

their prized Berluti shoes with cream wrapped in Venetian linen, followed by Dom Perignon champagne in homage to the great English dandy George "Beau" Brummell. Olga Berluti says, "The alcohol makes them shine more. And, *en plus*, it's an elegant gesture. Last year, we went to Venice, and there they were, all these grand aristocrats, washing their shoes in champagne and floating about in gondolas, waggling their toes at the moon."

Berluti prides itself on innovative design using traditional methods of manufacture. Each pair of bespoke shoes takes nine months to create from the initial *diagnotique du pied,* or foot diagnosis, a process that Olga Berluti insists on, as for her "there is nothing more vulgar than a man uncomfortable in his shoes." The next step is the choice of hide, whether a deluxe alligator or ostrich skin or fine calf, and the color of the patina from natural through to a more jewel-bright hue. The form or last is then carved from wood and the shoe built up from leather. The leather is tanned using the Venetia process,

allegedly washed in the lagoon of Venice and buried in the snow at Cortina to make it supple. The final touch to every hand-finished shoe is the insertion of a slice of leather under the sole to provide a little extra support, but also, according to an age-old tradition of shoemaking, to hold the sole of the shoe.

Today Berluti still offers its renowned repatination process. After a pair of shoes has been purchased, Berluti recommends that they are worn several times without polishing and then brought back so that the wear can be expertly checked and, if necessary, to alter the color on request. The polish can be stripped back and redyed in layers, and polished to achieve the desired depth and effect. The shoes still hold their magic; in 2013, journalist E. J. Dickson described a pair of men's purple lace-ups in the window of Berluti's new branch in London's Conduit Street as, "Long-toed, high-topped, burnished to the shade of ripe figs, these are story-book shoes, shoes to go skipping to hell in."

TWENTIETH CENTURY

Fashion's luxury powerhouses emerged during this time period, as the business of couture expanded. For the first time many had women at their helm, including the ubiquitous Coco Chanel who launched her atelier in 1909. As globalization has demanded more goods for less money, bespoke has struggled in a market that demands fast fashion rather than quality. There are success stories, however, of brands that have weathered the storm by creating the best of quality goods and many of these continue to innovate.

Left: The iconic Hermès Birkin bag, launched in 1984.

CHIPPEWA

Chippewa manufactures the quintessential U.S. work boot from fine full-grain leather with rustproof hooks and eyes, tempered steel shanks, and long-wearing outer soles. This most masculine of footwear has been worn by loggers, riggers, soldiers, and bikers: men who have fully participated in the evolution of the country from a wild frontier to a global superpower.

The Chippewa Shoe Manufacturing Company, named after the local Native American Chippewa tribe who lived and traded fur pelts on the southern shores of Lake Superior, was originally set up by J. B. Piotrowski and John Andrejski in Wisconsin in 1901 to cater to Midwestern and Canadian loggers. Logging boots had to withstand one of the toughest forms of manual labor as cutting pines for the pulp and paper industry was a risky business; the hours of the lumberjack were long, axes and handsaws were sharp, and the hauling of the timber over rough skid roads or balancing on the log to roll it into the water was heavy on the feet. Camps were so remote that one pair of boots could potentially be worn for months on end, so they had to last. From the outset, Chippewa's rugged Logger Boot, with its tough double and triple leather midsoles and hand-plugged outsole spikes, was considered the best in the business. The company started off by trekking to remote timber camps to measure the workers' feet, provide custom-made boots, and repair those that were worn. From its inception, the company was a success, originally employing a mere seven workers, and soon grew to a workforce of 300 who produced more than 1,000 pairs of boots per day; in 1910 the five-story factory in Chippewa Falls increased daily production to 2,500 pairs.

In 1914 the company issued the trademark "Original," which was added to the company name to read "Original

Left: In *The Wild One* (1953), Marlon Brando's countercultural uniform of rolled Levi's 501s, Perfecto leather jacket, and heavy oil-tanned cowhide Goodyear-welted Chippewa boots inspired a generation of teenage rebels.

Top: The Chippewa Shoe Manufacturing Company was named after the local Native American Chippewa tribe.
Above: The founders of Chippewa, J. B. Piotrowski (left) and John M. Andrejeski (right).

Chippewa," thereby preventing counterfeiting. During this time, the demand for the Chippewa field boot increased exponentially as a result of the United States entering World War I; the company manufactured the boot for both the Allied and the U.S. military forces. During the Depression years, when logging was hit by the ensuing economic chaos, the oil fields became a major area of employment, supplanting cotton as a key industry in states such as Texas. The first unlicensed oil rigs operated under harsh conditions, but because unemployment was so high, many men were prepared to work whatever the circumstances. In the early days, steel-toed boots were virtually non existent; men came to work in cloth caps or felt hats and rubber boots with serrated bottoms for grip that offered no protection from falling debris. The Chippewa Logger boot with its protective steel-reinforced toe, was fit for the purposes of safety, but workers found

Below: The original Chippewa Engineer boot with a Woodmans heel and rubber top lift. **Bottom**: Chippewa developed the Logger boot for the lumberjacks of the great upper Midwest in 1901. **Right**: An advert for Chippewa ski boots from 1949 built with steel-reinforced arches and wrap-around straps. **Far right**: In the 1940s the company developed the fleece-lined Arctic boot with a square lug at the toe and grooves in the soles for the ski-bindings of the U.S. 10th Mountain Division.

"No matter how tough the going, the feet always feel happy and comfortable."

Chippewa advertising from 1946

the metal toe cap made their feet feel cold in winter. The ordinary leather boots were warmer but had no protection, so a wide-topped overshoe caught on with a steel toe for safety and a felt lining for warmth. Chippewa took this shape and developed a brand new buckled black leather boot—the Engineer. This innovative design was a combination of an English riding boot last with a stovepipe leg shaft that could be easily pulled on and off, with buckled leather cinches at the ankle and knee. The name derived from the coal men and engineers who rode the rails stoking the firebox of the train with coal; they took to wearing Chippewa boots because they protected their legs from the heat and hot embers.

The Engineer became the boot of the roughneck and roustabout, rugged men who lived by their wits in the oil fields doing difficult and dangerous jobs in the wilds of Montana and North Dakota. The boot developed an outlaw reputation that made it the footwear of choice for a new generation of cowboys who rode the range on a motorbike rather than a horse; it had the requisite thick black leather to prevent foot injuries and the stovepipe shape meant the foot could be easily pulled out in anticipation of an accident. Consequently the Engineer, advertised in 1953 as crafted from "oil-tanned cowhide," became a biker's boot worn by gangs all over the world as a mark of allegiance to their tribe.

In the 1940s, Chippewa developed the fleece-lined Arctic boot with a square lug at the toe and grooves in the soles for the ski-bindings of the U.S. 10th Mountain Division, a mountain warfare unit trained to fight under the most adverse weather conditions who were parachuting behind military lines during World War II; the cold-weather boot is still used by the U.S. service on tours of duty in the Antarctic. For its diamond jubilee in 1976, Chippewa introduced the Minus 40 boot, super-insulated with a thick dual lining of lamb shearling and wool felt and full leather Goodyear-welt construction; it was followed by the Minus 50. Chippewa also developed the SAC 600 high-altitude Flight Boot for the U.S. Air Force in extreme weather conditions; it was the first insulated boot with a quilted lining of Feutron or spun nylon felt and Insolite foam.

The rise of the suburban middle classes in the 1950s and paid vacations for blue-collar workers meant that many Americans had money and leisure time to pursue

their hobbies. Fishing and hunting took off to such an extent that it was estimated that one quarter of the nation's men participated in this recreational activity. Chippewa invested in innovative outdoor boot technology and launched models such as the Chippewa Snake Boot, with rubber outsoles developed for outdoorsmen who wanted protection from the strikes of venomous snakes while out in the wilds. The Kush-N-Kollar was also introduced, a padded collar designed to reduce the stress on the Achilles tendon while hiking and to reduce the "break-in" time for new boots. It was trademarked by the U.S. Patent Office in 1972 and used on the bellow-tongued Chippewa Backpacker along with the durable Vibram sole.

In 1984, Justin, a heritage name that had been manufacturing cowboy boots since 1879 on the Chisholm Trail, bought the Chippewa Boot Company and, by uniting two such great U.S. names, brought strength to both. Chippewa continues to build on its reputation for toughness with its range of classic silhouettes made from heavy-duty oiled leather with Vibram outsoles, Goodyear leather welts that with wear conform to the shape of the foot, solid steel shanks for strength and rigidity, hardware made from brass milled studs and good quality nickel, and heavy duty laces that stay tight because they have a waxed coating. Boots are made using a mix of machine and hand processes. Once the component pieces for each boot are cut, they are sorted and the quarters stitched before the hardware, foxing, and hard counters are attached to the upper. All the uppers in Chippewa boots are hand-lasted; the back quarter of the boot is attached to the insole to keep the upper from moving or twisting during the lasting process and then it is sent to the power toe laster. This machine puts leather over the toe of the last to give the boot its shape and form. The sides are then pulled up with pliers and stapled and the excess leather trimmed off. The leather welt is inseamed or stitched to the uppers and the whole pressed before the heel is positioned and the steel shank applied for support. A layer of foam padding is applied for additional comfort, all cemented and pressed so that every layer is bonded solidly to make up the bottom of the boot; the mid sole is stitched to the welt and the outsole is cemented to the mid-sole, pressed, trimmed, and sanded, before the boot finally finished.

Chippewa is one of the greatest U.S. heritage brands, with a long and fascinating history of rugged design innovation mixed with social responsibility. As the company puts it, "The foundation for Chippewa's success as a true American brand is rooted in our authenticity, entrepreneurial spirit, sound business strategy, and our unique contemporary perspective of the 'American Endeavor.'"

1906
SCULLY

One of the greatest legacies of U.S. fashion is Western wear—a dress code derived from the cowboy. Iconic items such as the Stetson hat, pearl-snap cotton shirt, and cowboy boot have influenced designers for more than 100 years, despite being originally developed for the practical necessities of life on horseback by the first cowboys or Spanish *vaqueros*. The cowboy hat, for example, was a derivation of the tall-crowned sombrero, and by 1870 had developed into the Stetson with a deeper crown and trimmer brim. Richard Henry Dana was one of the first to chronicle early cowboy fashion in his seminal book *Two Years Before the Mast* (1840), documenting life as a sailor on a trading expedition on the ship *Pilgrim*, calling in on many of the coastal towns of California. In Santa Barbara, Dana described a form of dress "which we found prevailed through the country; broad-brimmed hat, usually of a black or dark brown

color, with a gilt or figured band round the crown, and lined under the rim with silk; a short jacket of silk, or figured calico (the European skirted body-coat is never worn); the shirt open in the neck; rich waistcoat, if any; pantaloons open at the sides below the knee, laced with gilt, usually of velveteen or broadcloth; or else short breeches and white stockings. They wear the deerskin shoe, which is of a dark brown color, and (being made by Indians) usually a good deal ornamented. They have no suspenders, but always wear a sash around the waist, which is generally red, and varying in quality with the means of the wearer. Add to this the never-failing poncho, or the *serapa*, and you have the dress of the Californian." Many of these elements found their way into the dress of the cowboy; the brimmed hat with the gilt band, the shirt, vest (waistcoat), chaps, and moccasin shoes.

In 1906, Scully was established in Napa, California, and began to manufacture gloves and jackets hand-crafted from the highest grade of leather which it sold from a horse and buggy. In 1918, Scully expanded production to include driving gauntlets for the first motorists, baseball mitts, and some of the original leather flying helmets and flight jackets for early pilots who needed apparel to keep them warm in the open cockpits of their airplanes. One of the first intrepid airmen was Richard E. Byrd, who learned to fly during World War I and became a flying instructor for the U.S. Navy. After several flights over the North Pole—there is much controversy as to whether he was the first person to reach the North Pole by air—Byrd was inspired to make one of the first twentieth-century U.S. expeditions to the region in 1928, following in the footsteps of Charles Wilkes in 1840. This pioneering polar explorer

Below left: Inside the Scully workshop in Napa, California, where leather gloves and jackets were made from 1906. **Right**: Polar explorer Admiral Richard Evelyn Byrd photographed in 1926 wearing a leather flying cap by Scully that now resides in the Smithsonian Institution. **Below right**: A commemorative award celebrating Scully's contribution to American exploration and endeavor.

left New York harbor in a Norwegian sailing ship, *The City of New York* formerly known as *Samson*, and set up a base camp on the Ross Ice Shelf. There expeditions set out by snowshoe, dog-sled, and airplane, with Byrd's pilots dressed for the occasion in leather gear by Scully including Byrd's leather cap that now resides in the Smithsonian Institution.

In 1938, aviator Douglas "Wrong Way" Corrigan became a U.S. folk hero after an unusual transatlantic flight in a modified but rather battered Curtiss Robin monoplane and a leather flight jacket by Scully. Corrigan had been trying for three years to persuade the Federal Bureau of Air Commerce to allow him to fly from the United States to Ireland but had been refused because the condition of his plane made ocean crossing hazardous, and also because of the disappearance of Amelia Earhart over the Pacific in 1937. He was allowed to fly from New York to Long Beach and after setting off was last seen disappearing into thick fog heading east. Just over twenty-eight hours later he flew into Dublin, and after landing, explained that he had "lost his way" because he had set off in fog, his World War I compass had stuck and because of the way the fuel tanks were mounted on the front of the airplane he could only see out of the sides. Corrigan returned home to New York on a steamer to a million-strong crowd cheering his name and a ticker-tape parade down Broadway.

The company continued its association with aviation during World War II when the Scully bomber jacket in zip-up brown lambskin leather with a cotton tan lining was issued to U.S. flight crews. Today Scully aviation artifacts are considered of such historical significance that several are displayed at the Museum of Flight in Seattle. The same model of bomber jacket, with its distinctive

... a Leather Legacy

Left: An advert showing an array of Scully products, including the Windtite flying helmet made of cordovan with a lambswool lining, a favorite among pioneering aviators. **Below right**: From left to right, Val Kilmer, Sam Elliott, Kurt Russell, and Bill Paxton were dressed in authentic Western wear by Wah-Maker, a subsidiary of Scully, for the gritty Western movie *Tombstone* (1993).

top zip pockets and elastic knit cuffs and waist, is still produced by the company today. Scully had also added men's and women's Western leather jackets to its repertoire in the 1920s that also remain in production.

In the 1980s, as the businessman became the epitome of modern masculinity taking over from the *Boy's Own* heroes of the inter war period, Scully expanded its range to include well-crafted luggage, briefcases, portfolios, wallets, and bags crafted from the highest-quality leather. The three-button hacking coat of the 1950s took its cues from the "ducking brush" leather or canvas coat worn by the original cowboy out on the range, as did the leather vest, originally a garment bought from the local dry

goods store with pockets for the watch and stock book. The revival of interest in the Hollywood Western also fueled demand for the look and the theatrical garb of the first global cowboy star, Tom Mix, in his white suit, red-patent boots, and diamond-studded belt buckle, began to be shaken off in favor of a more authentic image. The "frontier" look also hit fashion catwalks with the designs of Ralph Lauren.

Anticipating a trend, Scully purchased Wah-Maker, a company that produced authentic "Old West" clothing. Wah-Maker was clued up on original patterns and textiles of the Old West after spending a year researching historical Western clothing up to 1910, using period photographs and examples in archives and museum collections. This was unusual as most Western wear was based upon styles from the 1930s through to the 1950s. Scully went back further to a period when the authentic Western cowboy lifestyle evolved.

The resurgence of the Western in the 1990s, spearheaded by Clint Eastwood's *Unforgiven* (1992), was a boon to Wah-Maker it was commissioned to clothe the actors in authentic period garb—as Dan Scully put it, "It doesn't hurt for people to see Clint Eastwood in our pants." Wah-Maker went on to dress the cast of *Tombstone* (1993) and *Wyatt Earp* (1994). Scully recognized that "the big thing in Western movies now is authenticity. At first we had the "B" movies with Gene Autry wearing flowered shirts and wild outfits. Now we're coming back to the old traditions and people want to see the real cowboy. After the consumerism of the 1980s, people have come back to real American values. They're looking to go back to the way it was."

"It doesn't hurt for people to see Clint Eastwood in our pants."
Dan Scully

Wah-Maker's real cowboy clothes: vests, hats, and banded collar and bib-fronted shirts are still successful today and have been followed by Western clothing such as the Engineer and Lawman shirt based on frontier styles and made from traditional materials as worn by gold miners, wranglers, and ranchers. Scully's contemporary and Western leather collections still use premium-quality A-grade skin and continue to be hand-crafted by artisans. The company says, "Since no two leather skins are alike, each Scully leather good has a unique character."

1907
TROENTORP

The clog is the ultimate heritage shoe and for centuries has been worn as work wear all over Northern Europe. When few could afford enough leather to cover the entire foot, it was an inexpensive alternative to walking barefoot and was both waterproof and durable. Wood, whether it be beech, birch, sycamore, or alder, was readily available. The only downside was the clog's rigidity, which could prove uncomfortable when walking over long distances, therefore the shoes tended to be worn with thick socks and with straw stuffed down each side. Clogs were originally made by hand and each pair had to be cut and cured from the wood of the same tree at the same time to prevent uneven shrinkage. A saw was used to rough out the shape and then chisels hollowed out the internal space. Today the machine has taken over and most clog soles are industrially produced, unless they are hand-crafted in Sweden by Troentorp. In 1907, local farmhand-turned-cobbler August Johansson founded this unique company, named after its place of origin in the village of Troentorp. Johansson was interested in developing a more efficient way of carving the traditional Swedish clog after having been apprenticed in the evenings to a clog cobbler in Kringelstad, a nearby town. He introduced an effective plane to smooth the raw alder wood, a homemade band saw, and a wind-powered lathe. In 1920, the weather-dependent lathe was replaced by a 2 horse power oil engine, which remained the lathe's source of power until electricity was introduced in 1940.

The original Troentorp clogs were made entirely of alder wood, chosen by Johansson for it lightness, absorbency, and strength. In later years leather uppers were combined with a unique orthopedically correct alder wood base developed in 1957, curved to fit to the instep of the foot thereby fully supporting the back. The

"There are not many other brands produced in small, family-owned factories, and we have been walking on wood for more than 100 years."
Paul Macliver, owner of Troentorp

Left: The traditional Troentorp clog has weathered the storms of recession and gains particular popularity when a natural look pervades fashion, such as in the 1970s when the brand achieved style status. **Above**: The first clogs were made in Troentorp near Bastad more than 100 years ago in a small factory set up by August Johansson who learned his trade from a local cobbler.

uppers are wet lasted or soaked in water before being stretched onto the last (a wooden foot form), rather than the usual nailing, to give a long-lasting natural shape and a closer fit to the foot. Once the uppers are dry, the lasts are removed and the uppers are hand-hammered to the shoe. Troentorp explained the process: "The leather must be treated as a living material and when lasting the shoes one must be careful since the level of stretch in the upper will depend both on the skin that is being used, and where in the skin the upper has been punched out. This is a very important stage in the production since it will ensure the clogs get a good fit and retain their shape."

In 1942, the ownership of the company changed hands when August's sons, Stig and Bjore, took over the production of Troentorp's hand-crafted, nailed, and wet-lasted clogs, along with their first full-time employee, Sven Persson. Unfortunately in 1958 the factory was destroyed by fire, but during the rebuilding process the brothers decided to turn a potential disaster into an opportunity for improvement. A designated drying room was included in the rebuild to improve the stability of the wood before it was worked on and the whole process was streamlined. By the early 1960s, production was slowly climbing; clogs were beginning to move from a humble working shoe to a fashion item for both men and women as the optimism of the space-age 1960s began to dissipate. High heels were being decried, most notably by Australian feminist Germaine Greer whose dazzling tract *The Female Eunuch* was published in 1971. This polemic against patriarchy and its relationship with capitalism decried the fashion system as one of many cultural institutions that suppressed women by promoting ideals of beauty that were impossible to live up to. The clog stepped forward into a starring role: for men it was a rite of passage for any self-respecting hippie; for a woman, clog wearing was a badge of feminism. The clog became the shoe of the women's movement, which itself, ironically, influenced mainstream fashion. Traditional

Swedish brands became astonishingly popular, including Troentorp, which began to reimagine the clog with a series of innovative styles, colors, and design elements. The Wright clog of 1966 had a tailored weave across the front leather sheet of the upper; the Audobon laced clog was launched in 1967, and the Mariah clog sandal followed in 1973. By 1977, the 150 artisans at the Troentorp factory were manufacturing more than half a million pairs of clogs per year, including the new Mary Jane clog launched that same year.

In the early 1980s, the demand for clogs faltered and, despite the success of the Rembrandt and O'Keefe clogs of 1982 and the black-soled Monet clog of 1983, production at Troentorp had to be pulled back and the staff decreased. In the 1990s, the closed-back casual Van Gogh and sturdy Picasso clogs were developed; the Picasso cleverly targeted the work wear market, so the company could remain unaffected by the vagaries of the fashion market, and has a steel heel and toe cap with the traditional wet-lasted cowhide upper and anatomic foot bed.

Today the clog has been reinstated in global fashion as a classic form of footwear, since clogs have an authenticity that seems appropriate during a recession. Troentorp continues to last the course because its clogs are designed with integrity; the anatomic alder wood sole gives optimum comfort to the foot and Troentorp always uses nails in the clogs' construction, unlike cheaper stapled clogs. Production methods have changed little over the last 100 years, from the initial sawing and drying of the logs—a process that can take up to five weeks—to the milling of the lengths of alder to create the innovative instep. The sole is glued onto the wood, milled again, and the nailing groove, or distinctive decorative strip, put on the heel. Finally the alder wood is polished and varnished. The soles have been refined with a 1-inch-thick (2.5 cm) heat-bonded polyurethane sole with a non slip tread to cut down on noise when worn on a hard surface. Paul Macliver, the owner of Troentorp today, believes the secret to Troentorp's longevity is "comfort, quality, and tradition. Our clogs have been hand-crafted in the same small Swedish factory since 1907. There are not many other brands produced in small, family-owned factories, and we have been walking on wood for more than 100 years."

Left, clockwise from top left: 1. Cutting out the leather uppers of the clog. 2. Rows of wooden soles awaiting the attachment of the upper. 3. The moisture-absorbing alder wood used in the sole is dried before being worked on.

Above, from top: 1. The Troentorp Edith laced clog boot with a heel shape designed to give support to the back. 2. The Mary Jane Clog Sandal with a wet-lasted cowhide upper. 3. The Nelly closed-toe t-strap sandal with a raspberry suede upper.

1909
CHANEL

In the 1920s, the aesthetic of modernism invaded design; streamlined, geometric, and Cubist-inspired forms entered the visual vocabulary of designers and was later dubbed Art Deco. The fashionable body shape for women followed the same clean lines, all svelte serpentine slimness; Cubism made flesh. Women cast aside the over-stuffed splendor of Edwardian fashion in favor of a more minimalist look that showed off newly tanned and toned bodies fresh from the tennis court or ski slope. With eyebrows arched, their lips painted carmine, a brilliantine kiss curl against their cheeks, no discernible waist, and breasts bound flat, women presented a sportif, youthful silhouette, the epitome of modernity in an increasingly urban world.

Coco Chanel's designs were the fashion that defined this aesthetic revolution, as British *Vogue* put it, "The straight line is her medium." Her neat chic poverty de luxe look had the same elegant lines as a Le Corbusier chaise longue, a Manhattan skyscraper, or Louise Brook's bob. The color black had only formerly been used for mourning dress; Chanel made it elegant and wearable in any place, at any time. As she put it, "I imposed black; it's still going strong today, for black wipes out everything else around." When *Vogue* published an illustration of her chic crêpe de Chine little black dress in 1926, accessorized with a single strand of pearls and a streamlined cloche hat, it added the epithet that compared Chanel to the celebrated motor car, "Here is a Ford signed Chanel."

For Chanel, fashion had to be effortless and practical as well as chic, and her first designs were loose and informal requiring no corset—as she put it, "Nothing is more beautiful than freedom of the body." The budding couturière used the knits and flannels usually found in an Englishman's sportswear and casual clothing, for example

her lover Arthur "Boy" Capel's polo shirts; in 1925 she introduced a version of her classic two-piece knit suit with a collarless jacket and braid trim based on the traditional loden janker jacket she had seen worn while traveling in Switzerland, a suit that has been a mainstay of the house ever since.

Gabrielle "Coco" Chanel had emerged onto the fashion scene from humble origins having been born in 1883 in Saumur, France, in the poorhouse run by the Sisters of Providence. After the death of her mother, Chanel, at the age of eleven, was sent to an orphanage in the medieval village of Aubazine run by the Sisters of the Congregation of the Sacred Heart of Mary, and at the age of eighteen she attended the Nôtre Dame school in Moulins where she was given instruction in sewing. Her first paid employment was in a drapers on Rue d'Horloge; by 1909, her drive and ambition was such that

she had opened a millinery shop in the Paris apartment of her lover at that time, racehorse enthusiast and textile heir Étienne Balsan, at 160 Boulevard Malesherbes. It was here that Chanel began to promote her own pared-down style, one that went against the grain of the frills and furbelows of the prevailing Edwardian look for, as she believed, "nothing makes a woman look older than obvious expensiveness, ornateness, complication." In 1910 Chanel Modes formally opened at 21 Rue Cambon with the backing of Capel and, over the years, expanded into numbers 23, 25, 27, 29, and 31. Here she created hats, and as the millinery side of the business became more and more successful, Chanel began designing simple sailor blouses and uncluttered dresses in navy and gray using jersey fabric manufactured on circular knitting machines by the French textile brand Rodier. In 1913 she established a fashion boutique in Deauville followed by

one in Biarritz in 1915, and in 1918 officially registered as a couturière, with a maison de couture established at 31 Rue Cambon, Paris. This was the year, according to the designer, that she "woke up famous."

Perfume played a huge part in Chanel's success: in 1921 the couturière launched Chanel No. 5, a groundbreaking fragrance developed with perfumer Ernest Beaux of Grasse saying, after French poet Paul Valéry, "A woman who doesn't wear perfume has no future." Flowery scents were the norm in overblown orientalist bottles—Chanel wanted to do something different; as she put it, "I don't want hints of roses, of lilies of the valley. I want a perfume that is composed. It's a paradox. On a woman, a natural flower smells artificial. Perhaps a natural perfume must be created artificially." The resulting perfume, with its spicy bouquet composed of more than eighty ingredients—including jasmine, ylang-ylang, Centifolia rose, and clove combined with aldehydes, organic compounds similar to alcohol—was

revolutionary and stood out from the market with its minimalist name and modernist bottle. Today it is believed that a bottle of Chanel No. 5 sells every thirty seconds.

Fashion and fragrance were not the only cutting-edge products created at the House of Chanel; it also pioneered an innovative approach to jewelry. Chanel's poverty de luxe aesthetic was translated into costume jewelry after the shrewd designer eschewed the use of real gems in favor of ones fashioned from glass, in her words "because they were devoid of arrogance in an atmosphere of too easy luxe." The breakthrough collection was launched in 1924, designed in collaboration with the Maison Gripoix, a pioneer in the manufacture of poured-glass jewelry. *Harper's Bazaar* greeted the resultant gems in styles that ranged from Indian and Baroque to Renaissance as "the most revolutionary designs of our time." The use of the faux pearl became one of the most recurrent themes in Chanel's haute costume jewelry, interspersed with metal

and red and green poured glass and crystal beads influenced by the Byzantine treasury of St. Marks in Venice. In 1929, Chanel pinned a huge brooch to her beret, influencing a whole generation of women to follow suit.

In 1932, the London-based Diamond Corporation Limited commissioned Chanel to apply her talents to real gems instead of faux, since they thought she could update the image of the diamond. Chanel created a ravishing collection based on the cosmos. Earrings took the shape of stars and necklaces of comets left trails of sparkling diamonds around the throat. The most spectacular design was the Comète necklace of 1932: a star with a cascading trail of diamonds that was worn curled around the shoulder and neck with the tail resting above the breast. Janet Flanner in *The New Yorker* wrote, "With that aggravating instinct to strike when everyone else thinks the iron is cold that has, up till now, made her success, she has, at the height of the depression, returned to precious stones 'as having the greatest value in small volume'; just as, during the boom, she launched glass gee-gaws in an epoch of 'too easy luxe.'"

In 1933, Chanel commissioned one of the twentieth century's greatest jewelry designers, Duke Fulco di Verdura, to create pieces for the house. She commissioned him to design jewelry for the boutique and to reset the dazzling jewels given to her by a series of generous admirers. Fulco observed the gems from one of her wealthiest lovers, the Duke of Westminster, and reputedly said, "The thought of designing something for all these different stones is too enervating," and recommended treating them simply, almost as if they were mere baubles. He designed a single chain containing all the differently colored precious stones in an exercise in understatement, blurring the boundaries between costume jewelry and

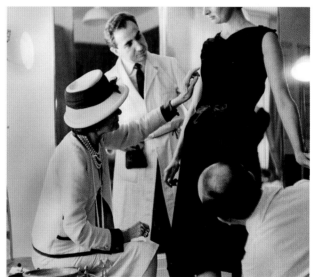

CHANEL

Below: Elizabeth Taylor wearing Chanel with husband No. 4, Eddie Fisher, in the early 1960s. **Right, clockwise from top left**: 1. A 1996 version of Coco Chanel's classic bouclé wool suit designed in stark monochrome by Karl Lagerfeld. 2. Detail of the white braid trimming. 3. Close-up of the sleeve of a red bouclé wool suit with gilt buttons dating from 1960. 4. The intricate handwork of Chanel is displayed in the pink edging of the buttons on a tweed suit of 1960.

"I imposed black; it's still going strong today, for black wipes out everything else around."

Coco Chanel

"the real thing." Other jewels were made into a cuff featuring a large Maltese cross, which went on to be a trademark motif at Chanel.

One of Chanel's most successful designs was the iconic 2.55 bag, named after the month and year of its release. The designer first came up with the idea for a practical shoulder bag in 1929 when "sick and tired of holding my handbags and losing them, I stuck a strap on them and wore them slung across my shoulder." Her first shoulder bags were made of black or navy jersey, and when revisited by the designer in 1955 they became objects of luxury and desire with the introduction of quilted leather, or matelassé, gilt fastenings, and the ubiquitous long, gilt chain handle interlaced with black hide. As Chanel put it, "I know women. Give them chains. Women adore chains." The inside of the bag was still eminently practical with three discreet flap pockets: one for lipstick, one zippered for security, and one totally secret, perhaps for the adoring aide-mémoire of a lover.

After the 2.55 bag came shoes to match; the Chanel slingback was designed in 1957 by Massaro of Paris as a comfortable alternative to the incredibly successful but uncomfortable Italian stiletto. She employed the Parisien *bottier* Raymond Massaro from Rue de la Paix, an atelier founded in 1894, now owned by Chanel, to supply boots, pumps, and mules for a list of wealthy clients, including, over the years, the Duchess of Windsor, Marlene Dietrich, Elizabeth Taylor, and fashionista Daphne Guinness. The Chanel slingback sandal, or *soulier* as she called it, had a small heel and a soft broad strap, and was bicolored in beige with a distinctive black toe. Massaro explained, "The black, slightly square toe shortened the foot. The beige melted into the whole and lengthened the leg. It was a very pure design, accentuated by the fineness of the straps. We rejected the idea of a buckle, which looked a little bit old-fashioned, preferring instead to add a little elastic on the low-cut inner side. This elastic adapted to the shape of the foot, adjusting its every tension and following its movement." The choice of beige was key to Chanel's design; as she put it, "I take refuge in beige because it's natural." (In fact, the house launched a Beige perfume in 2009). Chanel liked the fact that beige suggested the color of the skin of her wealthy white clientele in addition to optically lengthening the leg.

The shoe had a black toe cap for functional reasons —it meant the shoe did not get dirty or scuffed while traveling, and it was inspired by the black leather toe cap that Chanel had noted worn by staff on the Duke of Westminster's yacht.

Massaro's slingback formed part of a whole ensemble that was set to successfully relaunch the House of Chanel after the designer's rather dubious activities during World War II. Chanel had remained in Paris after the city's occupation by German forces in 1940 and was ensconced in the luxurious Ritz Hotel with Hans Gunther von Dincklage, rumored to be a German military intelligence officer. At the end of hostilities, Chanel's diminished popularity led to an enforced period in Switzerland, after which she returned to Paris and launched a comeback collection with mixed success. The determined designer decided to update her easy-to-wear trademark looks, believing they had a USP that provided a counterpoint to the restrictive silhouette of Dior's New Look. Her classic tweed suit, developed in the 1920s, was reborn with a collarless cardigan jacket trimmed with braid and lined

with silk, the hem weighted with a chain so it hung perfectly on the body, two front pockets, and gilt buttons. The suit became a symbol of postwar status for thousands of women when worn together with Massaro's slingback shoe, both now among the twentieth century's most copied designs with countless manufacturers launching their own versions.

After Chanel died in 1971, her atelier was headed up by a series of designers, including Philippe Guibourge in 1975. In 1983, Karl Lagerfeld took over and totally revamped the brand; the culture of visible wealth that flourished in the 1980s was creating a veritable logomania, and the designer transformed the House of Chanel from what had become viewed as a rather matronly label into one of *joie de vivre* and youthful cool. Double "C" logos were fashioned into earrings, bracelets, and pendants, and Chanel's most enduring house codes, including the classic tweed suit, the camellia, and the slingback, were revitalized; Lagerfeld enlarged the 2.55 bag into attaché dimensions and created the female executive's equivalent of the briefcase. The Chanel logo became an exaggerated feature,

Left: The pristine surroundings of the Chanel handbag atelier.

Below: A quilted Chanel bag papped on the streets of Manhattan, New York, in 2012.

CHANEL 197

with the gilt chain plumped out to almost ropelike proportions. Lagerfeld explained his direction in 2010: "I play with Chanel's elements like a musician plays with notes. You don't have to make the same music if you are a decent musician."

In 2002, Chanel founded Paraffection, a subsidiary company set up to preserve and promote the heritage, craft, and manufacturing skills of artisan workshops associated with fashion, thereby ensuring the traditions of haute couture were saved for posterity. Under its umbrella came the costume jeweler and button maker Desrues, established in 1929 and acquired by Chanel in 1985; Desrues created the first collection of buttons for Chanel in 1965 and today fashions the most exquisite types from copper, pewter, silver, mother-of-pearl, jet, wood, galalith, and glass. Lemarié the feather-maker—a company dating back to 1880 when most fashionable women's hats were ornamented with dyed feathers—was bought in 1996. The atelier of Maison Michel the milliner—in existence since 1936 and known for its straw hats with huge brims in the 1970s whose invisible stitching was achieved by vintage

Weissmans straw sewing machines—was acquired by Paraffection in 1997. The historic embroidery house of Lesage—founded in 1868 by Albert Michonet, who worked for Empress Eugénie and her couturier Charles Frederick Worth—and the shoemaker Massaro of 1947 became part of Paraffection in 2002. The gold and silversmiths Goossens, which collaborated with Coco Chanel on her jewelry line from 1955 until her death in 1971 was followed by Guillet, the 1869 maker of fabric flowers; embroiderers Montex; Causse the glove maker, founded by Paul Causse in 1892 and run exclusively by the family until 2003; and Barrie Knitwear established in Hawick, Scotland, in the 1870s. Bruno Pavlovsky, the president of Chanel said: "The acquisition of the Barrie business by Chanel is all the more natural as the factory has worked with us for more than twenty-five years, producing cashmere knitwear including Chanel's iconic two-tone cashmere cardigans. Through this acquisition, we reaffirm our commitment to traditional expertise and craftsmanship, and our wish to safeguard their future and support their development."

Below: The founder of L.L. Bean with his grandchildren, from left to right: Leon Jr, Leon Sr, Tom, and Jimmy Gorman. **Right**: The footwear that launched the L.L. Bean brand, the adaptable Maine Hunting Boot, a hybrid of the galosh and leather hiking boot for hunting in wet weather. **Below right**: Leon Leonwood Bean testing wooden duck decoys.

1912

L.L. BEAN

Since the nineteenth century, the United States' huntsmen have regarded Maine as a wild paradise abundant with game. The development of the railways made it possible to board a train at Boston in the evening and arrive in the state of Maine by the next afternoon to hunt moose, bear, wolves, and wildcats, or fish the Kennebec River for striped bass. Every year the Bangor and Aroostook Railroad published a pamphlet for tourists titled *In the Maine Woods* that, in the 1908 edition, described how "seekers for moose, deer, or bears can count on splendid results in northern Maine for many years to come, even though industrialism should push further and further into the forest, and civilization tame a wider border of what is now a wilderness, unfettered and untouched." By the early twentieth century, hunting and fishing camps and game lodges had sprung up all over the state to cater for the out-of-state visitors, and, by 1912, they could buy all manner of gear from the rambling emporium of L.L. Bean.

Leon Leonwood Bean, born on Howe Hill in Greenwood, Maine, on October 13, 1872, was a clothier with his own outlet, the L.L. Bean Pant Store, selling shoes and work wear at 74 Main Street, Auburn, before moving to a wooden building in Freeport, Maine. He was a passionate deer hunter and trout fisherman but grew tired of returning home from the thrill of the chase with blistered feet. His leather boots were waterproof but as the leather hardened when drying they began to chafe his feet. Bean's goal was to design the perfect all-weather hunting boot and one day, as he put it, "I took a pair of shoe rubbers from the stock on the shelves and had a shoemaker cut out a pair of seven-and-a-half-inch tops. The local cobbler stitched them together." L.L. Bean's boot, essentially a hybrid of a galosh and a leather walking boot, would have remained a simple domestic product, personally engineering for his own comfort, if it was not for local dairyman Edward Conant, who liked the look of them and commissioned a pair. Conant returned them a few months later with the note, "I wore these boots two weeks moose hunting last October and then put them right into hard service on the milk farm right up to the first of March. Your shoe is not only OK for hunting, but it is the lightest and best-wearing farm shoe I have ever had." The shoes had been returned for no other reason than to have the rubber soles replaced and were thus deemed a resounding success. This was the genesis of the Maine hunting boot sold through L.L. Bean from 1912 and advertised in 1914 as "Designed by a hunter who has tramped Maine woods for the past nineteen years." For the purposes of marketing, the weight of the boots was emphasized: they were as "light as a pair of moccasins with the protection of a heavy hunting boot," weighing "only 33 ounces to the pair." The advertisement continued, "Outside of your gun, nothing is so important to your outfit as your footwear. You cannot expect success hunting big game if your feet are not properly dressed." The boot had tremendous adaptability; in

"Your shoe is not only OK for hunting, but it is the lightest and best-wearing shoe I have ever had."

Edward Conant, who commissioned the first pair of L.L. Bean boots

winter the rubber soles stopped the boot drawing in water and the tread kept the hunter from slipping when on bare ground. The only downside was that the boot had no thermal properties but the company suggested wearing a pair of thick socks for insulation. Advertising material was sent to out-of-state hunters who had to apply for a license to hunt before traveling to Maine—the beginnings of the mail-ordering empire the company eventually consolidated across every state of America and beyond.

The Maine Hunting Boot was followed in the 1920s by the Hunting Pant, Auto Sweater, and other outdoor wear including the Winter Sport Cap in high-grade glove leather trimmed with lambskin, looking not unlike an aviator's cap with its ear protectors, and the Deer Hunting Cap advertised as giving "almost absolute protection against accidental shooting" in red felt with a black elk leather band and visor. In 1927, the wind-resistant Chamois Cloth shirt was launched by L.L. Bean made of fine-grade

seven-ounce cotton flannel with a raised nap on both sides that gave it the soft feel of chamois leather. The shirt remains a best-seller today and comes in a range of colors other than the original Olive Drab, the only hue available until a red version was launched in the 1950s and advertised in 1960 as "a good fishing shirt as red repels black flies. Also safe for dragging in deer without a coat." In the same year, the Maine Duck Hunting Coat appeared in the L.L. Bean catalog for the first time made of olive green waterproof cotton duck or canvas with a contrasting corduroy faced collar. The ergonomic design featured an extra pleat at the shoulder and a gusset under both arms so the hunter could swing around while aiming his gun without any physical restriction. In 1947, it was renamed the Field Coat with an additional rubberized game pocket in the manner of an English shooting jacket. Jim Gorma, author of comprehensive history of L.L. Bean *Guaranteed to Last* (2012) writes, "At Bean, heritage garments like the field coat present an interesting balancing act for product managers who want to retain the item's traditional appeal while updating it as better processes or materials become available, or as trends and lifestyles change."

Today the leatherwork and stitching on the boots take place in a factory in Brunswick. The clicking is done by machine, and the pieces are then planed and beveled to create smooth seams, before being machine stitched by 1940s sewing machines. Brass grommets are punched into the leather upper into which a lining is sewn and the rubber bottom added, previously having been manufactured in a small factory on Westminster Street in Lewiston. It is a testament to L.L. Bean that in these days of global outsourcing the Maine hunting boot is still made in Maine.

Throughout the 1940s the gregarious L.L. Bean was gracing the pages of many U.S. publications, including *Life* magazine, which profiled his business in an article in 1941 titled "Maine's Bean Outfits"—the journalist described the firm's mail-order catalog sent out from Newport twice a year as "more heady than love, ladies, or liquor" and described how every item within its 300 pages had been personally tested by Bean; customers were even invited to try out the waders and fishing rods in a pond adjacent to the store.

In the ensuing decades, the participation of more and more Americans in the "great outdoors" and the start of the back-packing craze in the 1970s meant the company diversified into camping equipment and other types of sporting gear, including the down-filled nylon trail model vest of 1971; L.L. Bean even launched a range of dinnerware. In 1961, when President Kennedy moved from his Senate Office to the White House, he is said to have taken only one piece of furniture with him—the L.L. Bean, or presidential rocker, with its angled steam-bent back posts, and Malaysian rattan seat and back to provide the support he needed for his aching back. The company also inadvertently became part of the preppy trend in fashion when mentioned in Lisa Birnbach's *The Official Preppy Handbook* published in 1981; the author described the Newport store as "Prep Mecca" continuing, "A middle-of-the-night pilgrimage here is one of the Prep's rites of passage." The "middle-of-the-night" reference was entirely correct, for in 1951 L.L Bean removed the locks from the doors of his Freeport store

and ordered that his store remain open twenty-four hours per day for every day of the year. Since then the store has reputedly closed only twice, as a mark of respect when President John F. Kennedy was assassinated in 1963 and the day of L.L. Bean's own funeral in 1967. Today it is the most popular visitor attraction in Maine, with an estimated three million visitors per year. The store's open-door philosophy remains, not least because the company has a huge online presence, still shipping its traditional U.S. work wear to all four corners of the globe. As the great U.S. folk hero L.L. Bean put it, "Sell good merchandise at a reasonable profit, treat your customers like human beings, and they will always come back for more."

Left, clockwise from left: 1. An L.L. Bean fishing outfit from the 1940s including a woollen shirt, twill hat, fishing blouse with a rod-holding tab at the left shoulder, duck-cloth pants, and rubber boots. 2. A pair of mail-order lambskin slippers from 1941. 3. L.L. Bean's original worsted yarn hunting gloves with leather palms, fingers, and thumbs available by mail order in the 1940s. **Below**: A Maine hunting boot with a rubber sole, leather and canvas upper, and rawhide laces.

1913
PRADA

Fratelli Prada was a small and exclusive shop founded by the Prada brothers, Mario and Martino, in 1913, in the Galleria Vittorio Emanuele II, a vaulted four-story double arcade of boutiques in central Milan. The business was set up to resemble an elegant library complete with leather-bound books, and within these sophisticated walls Fratelli Prada sold its own shoes, handbags, and luggage, made from exotic leathers such as walrus skin, and a range of imported luxury goods. La Scala's set designer Nicola Bemis painted a mural of an ocean liner as a backdrop to display the deluxe steamer trunks that Prada had imported

from the United States from Hartmann, a company founded in Milwaukee, Wisconsin, by Bavarian trunk maker, Joseph S. Hartmann in 1905. Mario Prada had discovered labels such as Hartmann when he traveled the world in pursuit of beautiful objects to appeal to the tastes of his wealthy and exclusive clientele. Writer Tibor Michaels describes a visit to the shop in the early days: "'Sclur' [sic] Mario, which is the Milanese equivalent of the word 'signore,' was always there in the front, receiving his valued customers with something special to show them. Tortoiseshell combs, brushes of all kinds, ladies' toiletries, samples of exotic skin or high-quality leather trunks for gentlemen. It soon became the habit for the well-off to drop into the store before embarking on a trip. The scent cloud of self-confident society women, the shine of La Scala's gala nights, and the world of elegant upper- and middle-class salons surrounded its paraphernalia."

Milan had been a center of fashion since the Middle Ages; by the Renaissance it gained a reputation for the artisanal crafting in small-scale workshops of luxury goods that were sold directly to customers through Milanese boutiques, or from 1865, in Alle Città d'Italia, the first Italian department store, opened by the Bocconi brothers and now known as La Rinascente. Fratelli Prada was never at the cutting edge of Milanese fashion and not much changed after the death of Mario Prada in 1958. It had always been a staunchly patriarchal business; paterfamilias Mario Prada was a traditional Milanese man who believed a woman's place was in the home—thus it was ironic that his daughter, Luisa, took the reins, followed twenty years later by her daughter, Miuccia, in 1978.

Miuccia Prada's background was entirely different; perhaps in defiance of her privileged conservative background she had become an ardent feminist and

studied political science to PhD level at the University of Milan, and mime at the avant-garde Piccolo Teatro di Milano under director Giorgio Strehler—she even worked briefly for the Communist Party. Many young men and women in Milan were politically active in the early 1970s during the *anni di piombo*, or "years of lead," with both right- and left-wing extremists manning the barricades in an attempt to transform the Italian state according to their own visions. Miuccia Prada was among them, protesting and handing out pamphlets allegedly while dressed in Yves Saint Laurent. Perhaps this accounts for the nonconformist spirit that seems to find embodiment in Prada's designs, which, unlike other Italian labels such as Versace, do more than just state the obviously erotic. The designer's work has always challenged bourgeois notions of taste and, decries the prevailing tenet that there is an implicit incompatibility between fashion and feminism.

The catalyst for Prada's international success was the meeting of Miuccia Prada and her business partner and husband, Patrizio Bertelli. Bertelli was a leather goods entrepreneur, owner of the firm I Pellettieri d'Italia and one of Fratelli Prada's suppliers; it was his business acumen and Miuccia's quirky creativity that made their relationship an inspired union. The first global hit was an androgynous, ascetic backpack fashioned out of black Pocono nylon, a material manufactured by a parachute company with additional leather trim. This object of absolute discretion was a slow-burner but became the bag that defined the 1990s and the complete antithesis of the flamboyant, logo-laden bags of the decade before. Prada had realized that the 1980s trappings of luxurious excess were anathema in the 1990s; there was a call for a global change in consciousness of which Miuccia, with her political leanings, would have been aware, a move toward

"I had to have a lot of courage to do fashion because in theory it was the least feminist work possible."

Miuccia Prada

spirituality, sensitivity, and eco-awareness rather than shopping, and a change in the vocabulary of design had become necessary. The Prada backpack led the way; it was an *oggetti di lusso*, or luxury item, but one deliberately difficult to decipher, that was a coolly ironic accessory. This broke the rules of conspicuous consumption with its subtle understatement—for where were the usual designer logos; the flashy fabrics; the leather, fur, and feathers? The iconic Prada backpack was modernist, lightweight, fashioned out of cheap industrial material, stamped with a diminutive logo, and presented in austere graphic black. This was anti-fashion *in extremis*, but luckily for the lifestyle consumer, reassuringly expensive enough to separate the fashion cognoscenti from the witless hordes, "a bag for the connoisseur rather than the consumer," as Miuccia Prada explained. Fashion journalist Lisa Armstrong attempted to enlighten her bemused audience about this pared-down aesthetic in an article for *Vogue* in 1995: "Eighties snobbery may have been simplistic, but it was democratic, easily grasped by everyone. This new version, by contrast, has taken to its heart a completely different system of status

Below: The iconic Prada backpack manufactured in Pocono nylon.
Right: Prada's A-line uniform-inspired dresses with coordinating gloves and clutch bags.

Far right: Backstage at Prada's Fall/Winter 2011–2012 show in Milan. A model in a shift dress covered in oversized paillettes holds a top-handled snakeskin clutch bag.

symbols that, far from being recognized from the other end of Bond Street, couldn't be identified from next door."

If this was a bag of lifestyle choice, what sort of lifestyle did it signify for the 1990s consumer? The answer was minimalist—the designer's response to environmental disaster, world recession, and global poverty. Minimalism was a canny way of selling fashion, and such an ethos was socially acceptable in a climate of New Age "green-ness" and recycling mania. Minimalism's new take on modernism was the perfect way to make women appear both chic and environmentally aware, and the Prada backpack was a textbook example of such a cutting-edge style. The bag became fashion's equivalent of downsizing: a hands-free option for the city nomad; an example of stealth wealth in the midst of a culture suffering from pre-millennium tension; the bag equivalent of the waif, the new breed of model cantering down the runway and appearing in Calvin Klein's grungy advertisements in the shape of Kate Moss. This was a bag for a more sober world, where "ostentation is not simply unaffordable but passé," as journalist William Langley put it. Minimalism was not really anti-fashion, however; it was just a new vocabulary with which the consumer had to get to grips. Its plainness was deceptive and the mask of puritan abstinence it presented slipped when one looked at the price tag. But for most of the population, Prada poverty-chic was indistinguishable from the real thing, making the style perfect for the increasingly violent city streets.

The designer's forceful desire for change meant that Prada did not stop there: in 1983, a second shop opened on Via della Spiga in Milan followed by others in Florence, Paris, Madrid, and New York City; a successful shoe line was launched in 1984; and the first collection of womenswear debuted in 1989 at the Prada headquarters at the Palazzo Manusardi, Milan. Here the Prada aesthetic began to take shape; a mix of elegant, almost demure Milanese tailoring in unusual, yet subtle, color combinations with techno prints mixing nostalgic references from the 1950s to the 1970s. Her Fall/Winter 2011 collection was a case in point, described by fashion journalist Hilary Alexander as "slightly sci-fi, evoking the 'space-age' uniforms of early television series, but at the same time harking back to the grace and swing of the Jazz Age and Charleston eras." The same cut-and-paste attitude was applied to Prada's

shoe design; in 2004 Prada launched a hybrid of patent-leather brogue upper and brothel creeper that was a curious mix of two classic men's shoes, one conservative and the other counter cultural. Its towering triple-decker layers were picked out in tan, white, blue, and gray to create a futuristic postmodern shape that even incorporated a layer referencing the rope sole of the espadrille. This was a cultural currency both eclectic and uncompromisingly modern; in an interview with *Vogue* in 2009, the designer explained that her work was "about what I like, but also analyzing what is and isn't trendy and why people like something, trying to find a way to look at it from outside,

researching new ideas on beauty and femininity and the way it is perceived in contemporary culture." Influences have variously included 1950s Americana as displayed in the Rocket Mule of 2012, Abstract Expressionist painter Mark Rothko, Roman gladiators, the nylon uniforms of fast-food operatives, Peggy Guggenheim, Joan Crawford, 1960s Formica, Japanese robots that took the form of the saffiano leather handbag charms in 2005, and a more general aesthetic of mixing the utilitarian with the deluxe as seen in the 2000 Prada bowling bag in black ostrich-skin. As the designer explained, "I have always thought that Prada clothes looked kind of normal but not

quite normal. Maybe they have little twists that are quite disturbing, or something about them that's not quite acceptable. Prada is not clothing for the bourgeoisie."

In 1993, the Miu Miu brand was launched with the intention of targeting a younger customer base—the name derived from Miuccia Prada's childhood nickname— followed by Prada Sport, or Ligna Rossa in 1997 with its red strap logo, featuring semitransparent or silver nylon, Teflon-coated piuma tracksuits with drawstring bottoms and storm pockets developed for extreme conditions. Prada also launched its first menswear collections in this decade. For many years, the company has been involved in the arts with the Prada Foundation, which has sponsored artists such as Dan Flavin, Louise Bourgeois, and Vanessa Beecroft, and video artist Francesco Vezzoli. Its architectural projects have included a ten-year collaboration with the celebrated Dutch architect Rem Koolhaas on the Prada store design. Koolhaas designed both the New York and the acclaimed Los Angeles boutique on Rodeo Drive with a front designed to be entirely open to the outside air. Brands expert Mark Tungate describes how "a subtle wall of air keeps breezes and raindrops at bay when needs be—and at night an aluminum screen rises from the ground to seal off the space. Shop windows are giant reinforced potholes set into the floor, so customers trot over the mannequins below. The interior is pure science fiction. Plasma screens blink fragmentary images and clips of the day's news, and glass changing rooms turn opaque at the touch of a floor switch. Lighting controls enable customers to see their desired garment at various times of the day. Elsewhere, laminated screens change in tone and hue depending on how many bodies are present." As Koolhaas put it, "we give people the freedom not to shop by devising alternative sources of interest." In 2009, the Prada and Koolhaas collaboration culminated in the Prada Transformer, a portable pavilion that takes the form of a tetrahedron with one hexagonal face, one cross-shaped face, one rectangular face, and one circular face. The pavilion can be flipped over by cranes so that the walls become floors and vice versa, creating an entirely new viewing experience each time. Today Prada and Bertelli describe their fashion colossus as a brand that moves "from fashion to communication, from the pursuit of excellence to technological advancement, from architecture to art."

Left: Launched in 1993 as a secondary brand to Prada, the edgier ready-to-wear Miu Miu now has stand-alone status. Fall/Winter 2013/2014. **Below**: A hybrid brogue/ brothel creeper/espadrille launched in Spring/Summer 2010. **Bottom**: A Miu Miu runway show of Fall/Winter 2013, displaying the label's quirky accessories.

1914
E. MARINELLA

At the turn of the twentieth century, the gentlemen of Naples were Anglophiles when it came to matters of dress, looking to Savile Row and St. James's Street in London for their sartorial cues, fine leather shoes, and silk accessories. In 1914, on the eve of World War I, tailor Eugenio Marinella, at the age of thirty-four, decided to bring London more directly to the Neapolitans by opening a shop on the Piazza Vittoria on the elegant waterfront, the Riviera di Chiaia overlooking the Bay of Naples, a popular promenade for the haute-bourgeoisie of the city. E. Marinella, framed by an entrance of polished wood and Calabrian marble, sold ties, cologne, and leather accessories displayed in eighteenth-century mahogany cabinets, and after the opening, the elegant establishment was described by the press as "a corner of London in Naples." Customers learned menswear's new rules, including the "four-in-hand" knot, the typically British mode of tying the tie.

Originally E. Marinella specialized in handmade shirts stitched and fitted out of a workshop attached to the business premises by artisans from Paris who had been invited to Naples to teach local Italian workers the secrets of the trade. Eugenio journeyed to England to seek out the best suppliers and imported fine printed silk from the Pennine town of Macclesfield, the center of the silk-weaving industry in Britain after Charles Roe built the town's first water-powered mill in 1744. Adamley, a 300 year-old mill located 2 miles (3.2 km) outside Macclesfield, became the supplier for the printed silk of E. Marinella ties and today it has a comprehensive archive of designs dating back to the early nineteenth century that are regularly consulted by the current owner, the grandson of Eugenio, Maurizio Marinella.

Macclesfield silk is used to make the seven-fold tie, a veritable origami of silk that many consider the pinnacle of the art of neckwear construction. A square yard unlined sheet of silk carefully cut on the bias is accordion-folded in on itself seven, and occasionally nine times for added heft or bulk at the knot and to prevent twisting. The tips and edges are hand-rolled and hand-stitched, leaving an entirely silk tie without the wool interlining or acetate on the tie blade of ready-made versions.

The shop survived both World Wars and global recessions but production problems, as a result of the shortage of raw materials, meant that by the 1950s shirts had been slowly phased out in favor of ties. The label received welcome publicity for its neckwear in 1948 after Enrico De Nicola, the first president of the Italian Republic, began to sport Marinella ties. A century later, E. Marinella is still in the same spot with a reputation for making the most beautiful hand-cut ties, scarves, and handkerchiefs, plus cologne, watches, and leather accessories. In 2011 this Italian version of English style was imported back to London when the Marinellas opened a premises at 54 Maddox Street.

From the age of ten, Maurizio spent time in the shop absorbing its atmosphere and learning the family business from the inside out. Today he describes its take on gentlemanly style as "very classic and very conservative," an image shored up by the fact that E. Marinella ties are habitually worn by some of the most powerful men in the world. In the 1980s Francesco Cossiga, president of the Republic and personal friend of the Marinella family, adopted the habit of presenting any visiting dignitaries and heads of state with a box containing five Marinella ties, which duly appeared around the necks of President Clinton, Helmut Kohl, Jacques Chirac, King Juan Carlos of Spain, and Prince Albert of Monaco. When the G7 was held in Naples in 1994, the organizers gifted every head of state six Marinella ties, garnering worldwide publicity for this hitherto relatively unknown name and setting in stone its reputation for the most refined Italian elegance. Celebrated film director Luchino Visconti, well known for the cinematographic elegance displayed in the film *Death in Venice* (1971), ordered his ties from E. Marinella complete with matching Indian silk handkerchiefs, and Greek shipping magnate Aristotle Onassis used to buy twelve black ties in one fell swoop; apparently he favored this funereal color so that in business negotiations his rivals could not guess his mood. As Maurizio Marinella puts it, "My grandfather taught me that ties are really the one unique fashion statement allowed to men. The tie a man chooses is his personal signature." Accordingly, Marinella has compiled a Tie Decalogue, or the ten commandments of tie etiquette, that runs as follows:

1. As in all things, for the tie it is a matter of size: the correct one should be between 8.5 and 9.5 cm at its widest point.
2. The knot: don't tighten it too much and always untie

"The tie a man chooses is his personal signature."

Maurizio Marinella

Top: E. Marinella's ties have a stylish, understated aesthetic. **Above**: A selection of Marinella colognes, including 287, which takes its name from the number of the original shop on Riviera di Chiaia in Naples.

Right, clockwise from top left: 1. and 3. The pattern is used at the cutting-out stage. 2. All patterns are aligned when the tie is pinned and stitched. 4. Silk scarves patterned with the Neapolitan *cornicello* or "little horn."

it in the evening so the tie can hang during the night.

3. Use the correct material: silk jacquard for regimental ties, a lighter silk foulard for prints, a pattern for elegant formal ties, lined wool or Scottish motifs for winter and sports clothing.

4. A tie should be suitable for every occasion: a light, patterned tie for the morning, a darker tie for the evening.

5. Follow your instinct when it comes to choosing a tie. "It has to be an irrational action."

6. Absolutely avoid wide and showy patterns, ties with only a central pattern, and pale and anonymous ones. Remember that the tie reveals the personality.

7. Plain ties should have definite colors; patterns such as lozenges, paisley, and rhomboid should be small, and transversal lines should have two or three colors at the most.

8. The color of the tie must stand out against the color of the suit and the shirt, without clashing. The color should be darker than the shirt and more intense than the jacket. It is often the only colored note of serious clothing, but be careful not to exaggerate! Avoid pea green, canary yellow, fire red, and sugared almond pink in favor of darker but not anonymous colors.

9. Avoid the overlap of a tie with a thick pattern on a squared shirt or the combining "all-stripes" of a regimental tie with stripes on a shirt and jacket.

10. Never coordinate the tie and the small pocket handkerchief: it is a useless anachronistic affectation. Always avoid a too obviously affected overall look and opt for relaxed elegance. It's easy to be fussy about ties; they are such flimsy things. One can become obsessive about getting the length right, or fiddle with the knot throughout the day. The latter, of course, undermines any impression of easy style. A perfect dimple, equally, can suggest a little too much thought and preparation.

In recent times, Maurizio Marinella has introduced own-brand Chiaja cologne and watches; tourists had been advised to leave their expensive timepieces at home after a spate of robberies in the city of Naples so Marinella supplied his customers with cheap, plastic watches for free. They became collectible souvenirs, and, observing their success, Maurizio saw that there was demand for a well-designed Marinella watch and launched a Swiss-

made steel-cased wristwatch with a classic face. Cufflinks and charms are part of the repertoire, too, reflecting Neapolitan culture and history as seen in the use of the Marinella flower and red coral. In Greek mythology, after Perseus decapitated Medusa, he laid her head on the banks of the river and her blood turned the weed into red coral. Today coral is worn to ward off danger and disease.

E. Marinella prides itself on the most personal of service; the founder Eugenio's motto ran, "A good entrepreneur should aim to pamper his customers." Accordingly, the shop opens at 6:30 a.m. so customers can drop by on their way to work in the morning, and once there they can choose from the hundreds of silk samples on show. Measurements are taken to ensure a perfect fit, a pattern is made and cut out, the tie is then basted, adjusted, and hand-sewn, and if not seven fold, lined, or self-tipped with the same fabric. The majority of customers order bespoke, but there are ready-made ties on offer that can be altered to each customer's specifications from specialists such as Drakes, a company specializing in handmade ties founded in 1977 by Michael Drake, Jeremy Hull, and Isabel Dickson. During the rush of Christmas shopping, when queues literally snake down the street outside this tiny shop, Maurizio Marinella provides *sfogliatelle*, a traditional Neapolitan pastry filled with ricotta and candied fruit, and coffee to the people in line. Although branches of the company have opened in Tokyo (2007), Lugano (2010), and London (2011), Maurizio refuses to expand the brand into airport concessions or sell online despite repeated offers of a buy out, saying: "I've never been interested in advertising, and the idea of franchising makes my skin crawl. We have had potential buyers from Australia, Japan, and China, and recently we had a serious enquiry from a Russian company which actually offered an astronomical sum. We receive about one serious offer a month. But it is simply not possible for me to sell the shop. This is where I have my life, and I also believe that it would be like selling a piece of Naples's history."

1914
SALVATORE FERRAGAMO

The Ricostruzione period of 1945 to 1965 was one of unparalleled economic and cultural change in Italy, a time of social and material revolution after years of Fascist rule. After World War II, Italy underwent a political and social reorientation supported by economic aid from the United States, which, in an attempt to boost postwar trade, helped to regenerate large areas of the Continent. This was a favorable time for Italian progress and Italian fashion, in which shoes had always paid a pivotal part, began to strengthen as an industry. Italian shoemakers had enjoyed an enviable reputation for their craftsmanship

Below: A 1938 platform sandal designed for singer Judy Garland in layers of cork covered in colored suede.

Right: Salvatore Ferragamo with dancer Katherine Dunham at a shoe fitting posed for publicity in Florence, 1950.

since the establishment of medieval guilds in the country's major cities, and one of the most remarkable artisans of the twentieth century was Salvatore Ferragamo, a.k.a. "the Shoemaker of Dreams."

Ferragamo is said to have created his first pair of shoes at just nine years of age—a tiny pair of white communion slippers for his sister, put together from canvas and cardboard. After his apprenticeship in Italy to a local cobbler and an upmarket Neapolitan footwear retailer, Bonito-born Ferragamo (1898-1960) migrated to the United States in 1914, like many young Italians in search of the American dream. Ferragamo realized that U.S. methods of mechanized shoe production were the most advanced in the world and wanted to educate himself in its industrial processes. He found a job at the Boston factory of Queen Quality, a popular footwear brand, but soon realized that any factory-produced shoe, however efficiently made, would never reach the high standards of his hand-crafted version. As he put it, "They were good shoes by the parameters of machine-made footwear, but not to me, to me they seemed heavy, gross, awkward, not to be compared with those I had seen in Naples, and far, far below the level of excellence I had set myself."

In 1914 Ferragamo moved with his brothers to Santa Barbara, California, and set up an exclusive business specializing in handmade shoes and repairs for customers associated with the emerging movie industry. One brother was working in the props department of the American Film Corporation and persuaded it to commission several pair of cowboy boots for a Western that was to be in production. It was Salvatore's big breakthrough, and from then on, the heroes of the corporation's popular Western sagas were shod in Ferragamo boots, apparently so comfortable that the director, Cecil B. DeMille, was

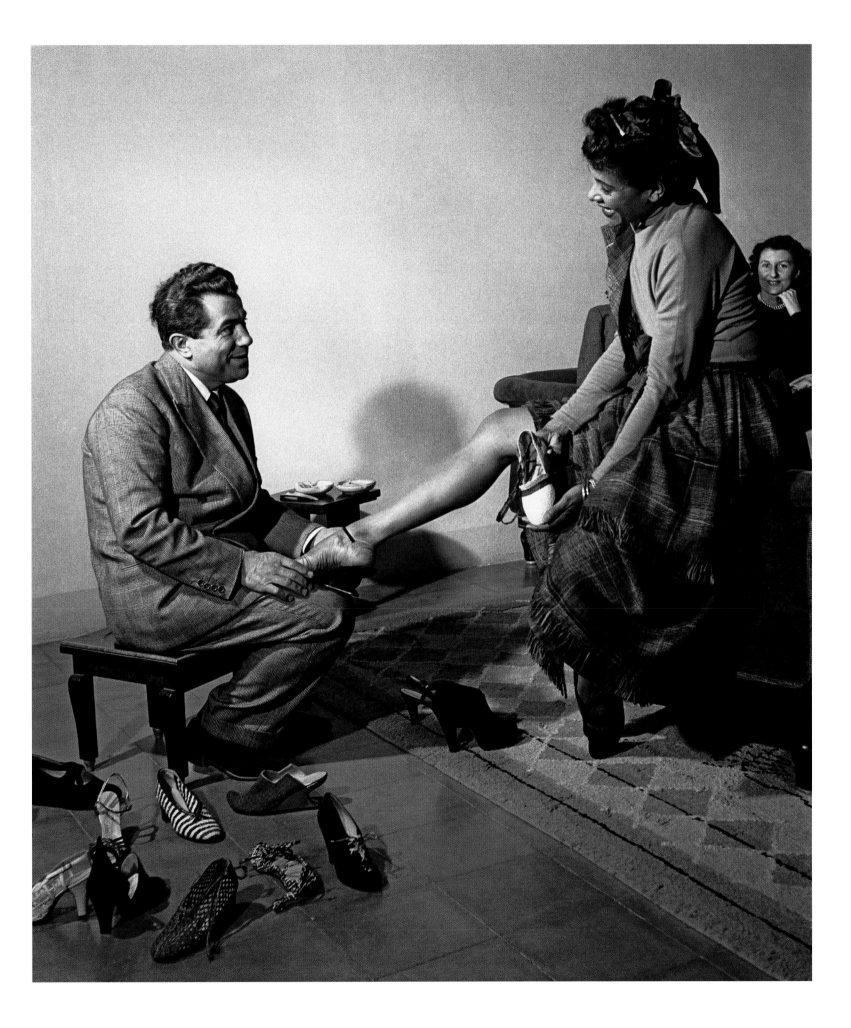

Above: Audrey Hepburn was a huge fan of Ferragamo heels and ballet flats, seen here with the shoemaker in 1954. **Right**: A selection of Ferragamo shoe lasts, three-dimensional wooden patterns of some of the world's most famous feet including those of actresses Greta Garbo and Gloria Swanson. **Far right**: The Ferragamo shoe workroom in Palazzo Feroni, Florence, c. 1937.

heard to comment, "The West would have been conquered earlier if they had had boots like these." Ferragamo's fame spread fast among the movie crowd based in Santa Barbara, and his business became a veritable shoe shop to the stars, catering to such clients as Mary Pickford, Pola Negri, Clara Bow, Joan Crawford, and Rudolph Valentino. According to movie legend, the critically acclaimed stage and screen actor John Barrymore would use no other shoemaker because Ferragamo had magically found a solution to provide comfort for his rather flat feet. In 1923, Ferragamo followed the movie industry to Hollywood, where he set up the Hollywood Boot Shop on Hollywood Boulevard in Beverly Hills, and screen siren Gloria Swanson began to inspire some of his most extravagant fantasies—it was for her that he created his famed corkscrew heels bedecked with Tahitian pearls. He joined Hollywood's inner circle, writing in his autobiography, *Shoemaker of Dreams* (1957), "Valentino would drop into my house on Brentwood Drive to eat a bowl of spaghetti as he had liked it in Italy. He was a beautiful boy, always impeccably debonair," although he realized that ultimately, "the world's stars do not come to my salon to buy my reputation; they come to buy shoes that fit and flatter them."

What began to set Ferragamo apart from other shoe designers was the wish to properly support women's feet when shod in his shoes. As he put it, "Women must be persuaded that luxury shoes need not be painful to walk in; they must be convinced that it is possible to wear the most refined and exotic footwear because we know how to design a supportive shoe modeled to the shape of the foot. Elegance and comfort are not incompatible, and whoever maintains the contrary simply doesn't know what he is talking about." To this end he studied physics, mathematics, and comparative anatomy at the University of Southern California and became an expert on the load-bearing properties of the foot's arch. Ferragamo realized that shoes had to be reinforced in that area and began to insert steel rather than the traditional leather shanks or cambrione into his designs for added support, a technique used in all of the company's shoes today. Similarly, many of his toe shapes were either overtly or subtly rounded during this period so that the foot could stretch and flex.

Ferragamo's daughter, Fulvia, recalls, "There was an ambition within my father to know everything he could about feet in order that he be able to then create shoes that would be as close as possible to perfection. Studying the anatomy of feet was no strange thing for him. It was simply part of his desire to be the best at what he did. What he discovered through his studies, was that the deformities of the feet so often attributed to hereditary factors were indeed attributable in a large part to poor shoemaking. Usually shoes were constructed so that the weight of your body went either to the toe or the heel. What my father discovered was that if shoes were designed so that the weight was put on the arch of the foot, many, many problems associated with the feet could be reduced or even eliminated. This was my father's discovery and his concept."

Soon the demand for Ferragamo footwear was such that it caused real problems for his business. Unwilling to sacrifice quality for quantity, and realizing that the skills of the U.S. shoe worker could not cope with the demands of production on a larger scale, Ferragamo moved back to Italy in 1927, settling in Florence. The city was home to dozens of small firms specializing in luxury leather goods and possessed the high level of expertise that he felt had been missing in California. Here the designer established what was to become one of the best-known shoe companies of the twentieth century, making the name "Ferragamo" synonymous with Florence and innovative

Below: Salvatore Ferragamo's daughter, Fiamma, with an array of Ferragamo shoes in 1968. **Bottom, from left**: 1. An F-shaped wedge heel in gold kid, *c.* 1940s. 2. One of Ferragamo's famous stilettos of the 1950s. 3. In this laced shoe, *c.* 1936, a layer of blue kid is placed over white and cut to give a scaled effect. 4. A mule of 1938 with "Oriental" toe in red suede and gold kid. 5. A "cage" heel stiletto, a metal framework design patented in 1956. 6. A black satin and gold leather sandal with a wedge covered in a mosaic of gilded glass, *c.* 1935.

shoe design. Italian shoemakers no longer produced imitations of French couture styles, but were defining an aesthetic of their own. Historian Stefania Ricci gives another reason for Ferragamo's move to the city; it was "the Mecca of international tourism; its allure did not just confine itself to art, but extended into the artisanal production of a range of unique consumer goods from embroidery to lace, straw hats, expensive glass and metal products. To relocate to Florence was a statement of distinction and quality as well as global influence. Ferragamo was perhaps one of the first to understand the power of the message that combined high-quality artisanal products with the historic and artistic past of the city." Thus any customer buying a pair of bespoke shoes from Ferragamo was also buying into the heritage culture that lived and breathed in Florence, from Michelangelo's *David* (1501-04) standing proud in the Accademia di Belle Arti to hand-marbled stationery from Giulio Giannini e Figlio.

Using U.S. techniques of mass production together with the craftsmanship of Italian luxury goods, Ferragamo created an assembly line of workers, each a specialist in one of the processes involved in the making of artisanal shoes. By the 1930s his footwear clearly stood out from the pack with its vivid color combinations, innovative materials, and unusual shapes, such as the inventive "hollow cage" heel of filigree brass, the inverted pyramid heel, and the turned-up oriental toe. His platforms were among some of the most flamboyant of the decade with their exaggerated arches and multilayered soles: a pair designed for celebrated actress and singer Judy Garland

had gold kidskin uppers and cork platforms covered in a rainbow of multicolored chamois; others were covered in mosaic mirror and indented with sparkling jewels.

The fame of Ferragamo was further enhanced by his experimentation with raw materials during the shortages of wartime, when the primary purpose of European shoes was to be functional and durable. The invention of the Ferragamo wedge was the direct result of the Italo–Ethiopian war after Mussolini's forces invaded Ethiopia in 1935. Economic sanctions were imposed on Italy by the League of Nations, making the steel cambrione used in Ferragamo's shoe arches difficult to source. His solution was to fill in the space between the sole and the heel with layers of Sardinian cork so that the wedge was light enough to wear. He said, "The comfort was in the cork. Rubber would have given a jerky springy step; cork makes the feet feel as if they're riding on a cushion." The cork had to be carefully worked to achieve the right result; a specialist craftsperson spent at least two days rubbing it down and then pressing it so it remained stable. The wedge shoe was revolutionary in that it gave height yet the wearer still retained their balance, and the designer created many innovative versions; in 1938, he combined the babouche—a Turkish design with a distinctive turned-up toe—with the backless mule, and attached a gold kidskin-covered wedge after a drawing by Oliver Messel for a production of the *Thief of Baghdad*; an oval-toed design in patchwork suede was created in 1942 with a four-tiered cork wedge covered in strips of turquoise blue, terra-cotta, mustard yellow, and deep-purple suede. The

> ## "The world's stars do not come to my salon to buy their reputation, [but] to buy shoes that fit and flatter them."
> Salvatore Ferragamo

wedge was Ferragamo's most influential shoe design and he filed for its patent in 1937—he was far too late, as he ruefully recognized, saying, "By that time every shoemaker in the world was making wedges and to have sustained my claims I would have been forced to sue everyone."

The designer's Invisible Shoe design of 1947 was another cutting-edge creation, featuring a slimline F-shaped wooden wedge heel with the wearer's feet held in by transparent nylon thread, giving a see-through effect to the shoe. Ferragamo had been inspired by the fishing line he had seen being used by anglers on the River Arno. This is just one example of the inspiration he found in and around Florence. Throughout his career Ferragamo kept coming back to the artisanal techniques of his homeland and using them in his shoe repertoire; Tavarnelle needlepoint lace from Tuscany was used to make uppers for mules, the seductive high-heeled slipper so popular in the 1930s; plaited raffia found in the villages nestled around Florence was employed in summer sandals using feather-light candy-colored cellophane. Ferragamo had been drawn to this unusual

material after hearing the rustling sound made when sweets were being unwrapped.

During the 1950s, the consolidation of Italy as an international center of fashion innovation continued with the help of the Italian government. Ferragamo became an ambassador of Italian style, working for the officially sanctioned "Made in Italy" promotion. This global campaign was set up to promote the Italian look and made household names of fashion designer Emilio Pucci and product designer Giò Ponti, as well as positioning Florence as a fashion center and general "home to good taste." As a rebranding exercise to help the country redefine itself as a center of design innovation after World War II, it could not have been more successful, and a process of cultural dissociation began. Italy changed from the country of Mussolini's Fascist project to a land of glamorous *dolce vita*, and the words "Italian design" became synonymous with stylish living. The stiletto heel took over from the wedge and court shoe, and a new sound could be heard in Florence: the click, click, click of the killer heel. Ferragamo's fantasy designs in gold kid and jewel-toned suede were a tonic to women who had been deprived of glamour during the war years. As journalist Anne Scott-James wrote, "As the last guns rumbled and the last all-clear sounded, all the squalor and discomfort and roughness that had seemed fitting for so long began to feel old fashioned. I wanted to throw the dried eggs out of the window, burn my shabby curtains, and wear a Paris hat again." In this decade, Ferragamo fashioned the most iconic of shoes, from Marilyn Monroe's red rhinestone metal spigot stilettos worn in the show-stopping number "Two Little Girls From Little Rock," sung with Jane Russell in the movie *Gentlemen Prefer Blondes* (1953), to Audrey Hepburn's black suede ballet flats with a low, oval heel and shell sole inspired by the Native American *opanke* or moccasin—she wore them both on and off stage. Monroe was such a fan she had more than forty pairs of custom-made flesh-tone silk Ferragamo heels that were worn with flesh-tone stockings to give length to her legs, remarking archly that his shoes "had given a lift" to her career. Another customer, Marlene Dietrich, was said by Ferragamo to be "the possessor of the most beautiful legs, ankles, and feet in the world."

After Salvatore's death in 1960, his wife, Wanda, and subsequently his six children took over the helm of what still remains a dynastic brand. Shoe production increased from the 350 pairs per day hand-crafted by 750 Italian artisans to 2,000 made in small factories around Florence. The family also expanded the operations of the company to include handbags, eyewear, silk accessories printed from drawings of flora and fauna, and a ready-to-wear fashion line. Today Salavatore's son, Leonardo, also runs boutique hotels under the name Lungarno.

Ferragamo's headquarters remain in Florence at the medieval Palazzo Spini Feroni, and the company's formal *tramezza* shoes are still handmade in a factory in the city, even though many of their competitors have switched operations to Asia to cut down on production costs. *Tramezza* is an artisanal technique traditionally used in the best of men's footwear and it comprises a thick yet flexible layer of leather set between the soft, vegetable-tanned leather insole and the leather sole, for durability and a perfect bonding of sole and hand-finished leather upper.

This model is considered one of the finest on the market today as it uniquely uses *tramezza* fashioned from leather softened by running water, rather than the more usual cork. The subsequent flexibility of the material allows it to take on the shape of the wearer's foot when put into contact with the warmth of the body. Despite the rigors of the modern marketplace, the company remains committed to excellence; significantly in 2008, Salvatore's son, Ferruccio, publicly announced that it was "written in stone" that all of the company's products would be manufactured in Italy to make sure that such quality was never compromised, including its most recent hit, the structured Sofia bag with its distinctive *gancini* bit clasp at the center of the flap. Today Ferragamo's output is still made in Italy using specially selected contractors with quality tightly controlled through its distribution center in Florence. In 2011, Massimiliano Giornetti, the newly appointed creative director of womenswear, gave a press conference and insisted, "I don't believe in fast fashion, that is not the spirit of Ferragamo."

1918
BALENCIAGA

Above: The great couturier
Balenciaga in a portrait taken by
photographer Boris Lipnitzki in
1927. **Right**: Balenciaga's black
silk ottoman tent coat with a large
square-cut collar (*c.* 1954) was
influenced by the silhouette of the

clerical dress he had seen in
Francisco de Goya's paintings.
Far right: In the 1940s, the couturier
experimented with the dramatic
effects of black and white satin in a
series of evening dresses, such as
this cleverly structured example.

"If a woman came in in a Balenciaga dress, no other woman in the room existed," wrote fashion maven Diana Vreeland in her fascinating autobiography *DV* (1984). She recognized the Spanish couturier's creations as, quite simply, sublime, and his austere architectural shapes in bold color combinations attracted wealthy clients, including the Duchess of Windsor and actresses Ingrid Bergman and Sophia Loren, who loved the way they were cut to fit and flatter their bodies. Billionairess Barbara Hutton was a loyal and somewhat extravagant customer—in one season she bought nineteen dresses, six tailored suits, and three coats (one suit would have cost approximately a quarter of the average national male wage in Britain)—and she would order her dresses in threes, one for each home to avoid packing.

Cristóbal Balenciaga Eizaguirre remains the best-known Spanish fashion designer of the twentieth century—"the master of us all" according to his couture contemporary Christian Dior—and he paid homage to the culture of his homeland throughout his career with designs such as the bolero based on the matador's "suit of lights," the *bata de colat* or tiered ruffled gown of the flamenco dancer, and the innovative use of mantilla lace. Vreeland described how "Balenciaga's inspiration came from the bullrings, the flamenco dancers, the loose blouses the fishermen wear, the cool of the cloisters," and the designer was also inspired by paintings of the Infanta by Diego Velásquez and of *majas* by Francisco de Goya. Born in the Basque fishing village of Getaria in 1895, Balenciaga grew up in a house run by his seamstress mother. It was overlooked by the Casa Torres, a hilltop mansion in which resided the marquesa, an elegant woman of fashion. According to fashion legend, the young Balenciaga saw her walking in the town in an

"[Balenciaga is] the master of us all."
Christian Dior

elegant ankle-length silk shantung suit from Paris and after he expressed his enthusiasm she challenged him to make a copy. It was such a success that the marquesa commissioned more work and Balenciaga used the money to finance an apprenticeship with a tailor at Casa Gomez in the fashionable resort of San Sebastián, the official summer haunt of the Spanish court. This was followed by a stint at the newly opened branch of the Grands Magasins du Louvre, a department store for which he was sent to Paris as a buyer. Balenciaga's first own-name atelier finally opened in 1919, with financial backing from his sisters, followed

by two more in Madrid (1932) and Barcelona (1938). Here he created his own designs while also importing Paris fashion and altering it for a clientele that included members of the Spanish royal family. The Spanish Civil War (1936-39) initiated a move to Paris where he opened the House of Balenciaga in 1937, working there in a monastic white studio until his retirement in 1968.

Balenciaga was a modernist in essence, obsessed with the properties of material and the myriad ways in which it could be cut and constructed. *Vogue* international editor at large Hamish Bowles described some of his techniques,

"Balenciaga made the slips of his dresses to fit the body like a second skin but made the garments fractionally larger. When the wearer moved, a current of air circulated between the layers, causing the dress alternately to float and caress the body, thus adding an element of mystery that blurred the reality of the figure beneath. A similar effect was created by a waist seam that arced gently upward from the natural waistline in front and swooped subtly down beneath it in back." Balenciaga's career revolved around such purity of vision—he was disinterested in seasonal trends and diffusion lines, preferring to redefine and explore his innovative cutting techniques. Sleeves were cut as one with the yoke and shortened to show an elegant display of wrist and hands; collars stood away from the neck to elongate its proportions and present a frame for a string of pearls; "middy" waists were dropped 1920s-style with a belt used to delineate the waist's natural position. As a counterpart to the work of Dior, whose New Look lines required considerable understructure and constriction around the waist to create the fashionable hourglass silhouette, Balenciaga preferred to hang the weight of a garment from the shoulders, and by refusing to focus on the waist he created the chemise, or *sacque,* dress in 1958, one of his variations on the theme of the T-shaped tunic. A shortened example fashioned from his signature tobacco-colored wool in 1957 prefigured the fashions of the early 1960s by anticipating the ubiquitous mini dress. In 1961, he created the "no seam" coat from a single piece of fabric semi-fitted to the body with an elaborate system of seams, darts, and tucks; it was a perfect example of how his aesthetic was impossible to reproduce as ready-to-wear. Balenciaga launched a fragrance, Le Dix, in 1947, with the couturier supervising every aspect of its branding from the design of the flacon through to the packaging. For many years Le Dix was sold exclusively in Paris, and such limited distribution gave the fragrance incredible cachet.

Hats were another significant part of Balenciaga's business, and from 1937 to 1940, were made by the well-known Parisian milliner Mme. Legroux, followed by Mme. Janine, Mme. Helene, and Mme. Ginette. The best-known Balenciaga hat was the revolutionary pillbox, based on a clerical cap or biretta and launched in 1951; it went on to become a millinery classic when popularized by Jackie Kennedy.

Far left: A poppy red linen Balenciaga suit with matching hat and white gloves photographed by Horst P. Horst for *Vogue* in 1952.
Left: A model wears a cowled robe gown in rose velvet by Balenciaga, photographed in the Château de Versailles in France in 1952.

Below: Balenciaga at a fitting in 1968 shot by Henri Cartier-Bresson.

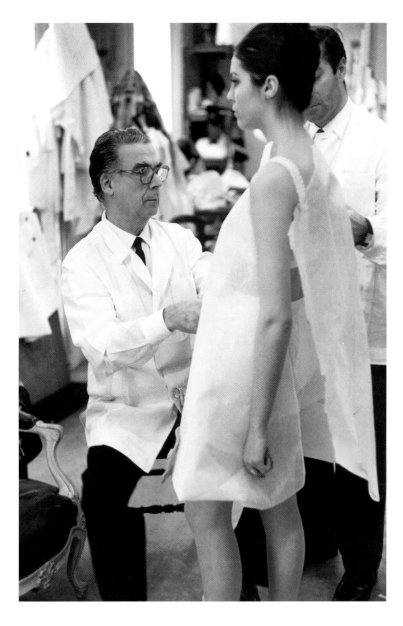

Balenciaga was the master of minimalist luxe; his designs may have had clean lines but the garments were worked in the most exquisite and costly materials. One client, Texan socialite Claudia de Osborne, bought a Lyons velvet ball gown in black, which Carmel Snow, editor of *Harper's Bazaar*, described as "so black it hits you like a blow." The flat-fronted dress had a bustle and short train decorated with more than 100 ermine tails, and a ziberline silk gown of 1967 had a deep neck and hemline in mink. Metallic threaded brocades and jewel-toned taffeta were bedecked with pearls, and Lesage embroidery was added to emphasize the lines and shapes of construction. In 1962 U.S. *Vogue* attempted to define what it dubbed "the Balenciaga Mystique"; "whatever it takes to hold vast numbers of women in the palm of your hand year after year, Balenciaga has it—to a degree that politicians and matinée idols might study with profit. Not that his clothes are easy to wear; on the contrary, they could hardly be more demanding—of elegance, wit, real clothes authority. Nor do they bristle with news; the changes he makes each season are just significant enough to make it dazzlingly clear that a woman in a this-year Balenciaga is a woman in touch with some of the soundest—and, possibly, most prophetic—fashion thinking of her time."

In 1968, the notoriously discreet couturier retired, having never granted an interview to the press; the event caused one of his distraught clients, the Countess Mona von Bismarck, to spend three days of mourning in her bedroom. Balenciaga had no interest in the youthquake that had become the driving force of fashion saying, "I am not made to dress people in the street." However, the space-age aesthetic that had invaded Paris couture through the work of the so-called ye-ye designers, including Paco Rabanne, Pierre Cardin, and Emmanuelle Khanh could not have developed without the minimalist experimentation of Balenciaga, not least because one of the style's most successful exponents was his protégé André Courrèges.

Balenciaga could well have been consigned to the archive of fashion history were it not for German chemical company Hoechst acquiring the rights to the name in 1978, followed by Jacques Bogart S.A., a holding company specializing in the manufacturing and licensing of fragrances, in 1986. Le Dix, a ready-to-wear line launched in 1987 designed by Michel Goma, and the designer stayed at the

Overleaf, clockwise from top left: 1. Backstage at the Balenciaga Paris ready-to-wear Spring/Summer 2008 show. 2. A mid-century Balenciaga gown worn by one of the world's renowned couture customers, Princess Liliane of Belgium, consort to King Leopold III. 3. This smooth white leather top-handled bag displays the minimalist feel that entered Balenciaga accessories for Spring/Summer 2013–14 under new creative director Alexander Wang.

house until 1992 when he was replaced by Belgian minimalist Josephus Thimister, who was succeeded by Nicolas Ghesquière, a former license designer in 1997.

Ghesquière had been apprenticed to Jean Paul Gaultier and Agnès B. and he brought a youthful cool to the brand by reinvigorating the house's design codes and attaining a new generation of celebrity customers that included Madonna and Chloë Sevigny. As he put it in 1999, "I look at all these images, and I learn and try to integrate them, but then I try to forget them. After all, I am twenty-eight and I can only see things through my eyes." Collections mixed a glacial androgyny with touches of eccentricity, such as the Alsatian sweater of Fall/Winter 2000, and many of his looks went mainstream, including the oversized cargo pants shown in Spring/Summer 2002 and the scuba-inspired outfits of Spring/Summer 2003 that remain an influential silhouette in womenswear today.

Shrunken black leather biker jackets and motocross pants spearheaded a return to the perennial rock-chick look, and the label scored hits with the multi-zipped Lariat it bag of 2001, with its distinctive braided handle, as carried by Kate Moss, and the gladiator sandal. Today the majority of young fashion consumers know the name Balenciaga because of Ghesquière's dynamic ready-to-wear and it bags rather than for the haute couture clothes that transformed the face of fashion in the 1950s. In 2001, the Gucci Group bought Balenciaga, and Ghesquière remained in position until 2013 when he announced his departure. Ten years earlier he had commented: "Perhaps I have saved the House of Balenciaga, but it has also saved me… I would like to do something under my own name at some point, but right now, I am very happy. Balenciaga is a perfect screen for me, for both showing my work and protecting it."

1921
GUCCI

In the fourteenth century, silk merchant Gregorio Dati wrote in his diaries, "A Florentine who is not a merchant, who has not traveled through the world, seeing the foreign nations and peoples and then returned to Florence with the same wealth, enjoys no esteem whatsoever." The Florentine entrepreneur Guccio Gucci certainly lived up to these expectations when in 1921 he opened a leather goods company in his native city. Like many Europeans with an interest in sartorial matters in the early twentieth century, Guccio Gucci was an Anglophile, having visited London in 1897 and worked at the Ritz and Savoy hotels after his father's straw-hatmaking business had foundered. Life as a bellboy was physically demanding but it gave him the opportunity to study the beautiful luggage of the wealthy guests, and he recognized that much of the fine leather from which they were fashioned came from his mother country. Gucci also spent four years working for the Compagnie Internationale des Wagons-Lits, the sleeping car company founded by Belgian Georges Nagelmackers in 1872 that crisscrossed Europe by rail. It was not at all surprising then, that when at home in Florence once more, he found work with Valigeria Franzi, a well-known manufacturer of luxury bags, trunks, suitcases, and wallets run by Felice Franzi since 1864. Franzi had its own factory with the latest tools, machinery, and artisans schooled in the latest techniques who trained

up the workforce. For anyone interested in the craft of leather goods, it was the place to learn the trade in Europe, and Gucci worked there from 1902 onward.

Gucci set himself up as an expert in fine luggage, and with a backer opened a leather goods company on Florence's Via della Vigna Nuova—Valigeria Guccio Gucci—and, later, as a sole trader, he opened Azienda Individuale Guccio Gucci in 1921. Luggage was sourced from the artisans of Tuscany, England, and Germany and he commissioned designs of his own, opening a workshop behind the shop to manufacture his own designs and repair the cases of his customers. Business was brisk, and a larger atelier on Lungarno Guicciardini provided the necessary space for sixty craftsmen. Gucci's children joined the family firm, making suitcases inspired by those Gucci had analyzed at the Savoy, as well as kidskin and chamois leather bags, gloves, and belts. In 1923, another Gucci boutique opened on Via del Parione and the original location was enlarged; in 1938, a two-story premises opened in Rome at 21 Via Condotti, at the heart of the city's most glamorous shopping district.

During the war years Gucci, like shoe designer Salvatore Ferragamo (see page 212), had an ingenious solution to the restrictions on material imposed by the League of Nations economic embargo; from a tannery in Santa Croce he sourced *cuoio grasso*, or veal skin, a soft and malleable hide with a ruffled surface that was treated with fish oil, which made it scratch-free, and used Neapolitan *canapa* or woven hemp, linen, and jute to create lightweight traveling bags that displayed a print of linked diamonds in dark brown against a tan background. In 1947, the iconic pigskin Bamboo bag, or Model 0633, with a burnished cane handle, was manufactured for the first time, taking inspiration from an equestrian saddle.

Right: The iconic Gucci 0633 Bamboo bag with its burnished cane handle, shaped in the traditional manner of the Piedmontese umbrella makers using heat and steam. **Below left**: The Model 175 Gucci loafer, in black or brown pigskin with horse-bit hardware and almond-shaped toe, launched in 1953.

On the death of Guccio Gucci in 1953, his sons, Aldo, Vasco, and Rodolfo, took over the running of the business, including the Milan store that had opened two years earlier on Via Montenapoleone. The company expanded to include stores in Rome and Florence, introducing a whole range of products that had incredible success spurred on by the global interest in Italian design. The most popular additions made old-world associations with equestrianism, pitching the relatively modern Gucci brand against the might of Louis Vuitton, Hermès, and Fendi, who had originally provided saddlery for the aristocratic families of Europe. The trademark green-red-green striped web was introduced in 1951, inspired by traditional saddle girth straps, and the horse bit began to appear on the brand's merchandise, first used in saddle-stitched handbags and later appearing as hardware on accessories, such as shoes and purses, and as a symbol on print design.

In 1953, the horse bit was used for the first time on Gucci's black and brown pigskin loafers for men known as Model 175 and worn by actors John Wayne and Clark Gable, and by singing legend Frank Sinatra. The female version launched in 1968, and had a stacked leather heel holding a narrow gold chain matched by one across the front vamp. It was available in a variety of exotic leathers, including alligator, lizard, and ostrich, in a rainbow of hues. By the 1960s, the almond-toed Gucci loafer was being sold in the New York store, a concession that had opened in the Savoy Plaza Hotel on East 58th Street in 1953 and had moved to Fifth Avenue in 1960. The Gucci loafer was considered a fashionable alternative to the traditional Oxford lace-up shoe; in 1979 Dustin Hoffman appeared sockless in Gucci loafers in the Oscar-winning movie *Kramer vs Kramer* (1979).

Today the Gucci loafer is a style classic made entirely in Italy by craftsmen in a workshop in Florence. The uppers are hand-sewn and nail lasted before being hand stained by brush in several coats of color to create a deep, rich, burnished tone; the next step is welting, then the long process of finishing begins, which includes several steps of polishing, hand staining, and drying before the horse-bit hardware is attached. In 2010, Frida Giannini, Gucci's creative director, said of the loafer, "It's an absolute classic. I play with the design each season, updating the shape, material, and details, but the shoe's essential beauty and functionality remain the same."

"I play with the design each season, updating the shape, material, and details, but the shoe's essential beauty and functionality remain the same."

Frida Giannini on the Gucci loafer

In 1960 the Hobo double-strapped shoulder bag with snaffle-bit decoration launched and was popularized by Jackie Onassis (it was renamed the Bouvier, and in its latest incarnation, the New Jackie, in her honor); it was a favorite of Nancy Reagan in the 1980s. The bag was a massive success, and store after store opened including in Montecatini, London, and Palm Beach in 1961, and in Paris in 1963. Gucci was becoming a global luxury brand and it developed an instantly recognizable logo to consolidate such success, the interlocking double G. Celebrities flocked to the stores, and in her history of the Gucci dynasty,

The House of Gucci (2000), Sara Gay Forden describes the luxurious items the brand began to develop for their affluent male customers: "Red Skelton had a set of maroon crocodile suitcases, Peter Sellers a crocodile attaché case, Lawrence Harvey commissioned a 'bar briefcase' complete with insets to hold bottles, glasses, and an ice bucket. Sammy Davies bought two white leather sofas like the one in the Beverley Hills store." In 1966, Gucci had a personal request from Princess Grace of Monaco for a scarf, after she visited the Milan boutique; artist Vittorio Accornero conceived a botanical illustration that was screen printed by Fiorio, a renowned Milanese silk scarf manufacturer, onto a 36-inch (90-cm) square of silk, and the Flora silk print scarf was born. Gucci also developed watches and its first ready-to-wear collections in the mid-1960s, featuring silk shirts with the double G logo and fur-trimmed leather coats; the monogrammed fabric was also used to create a line of luggage and bags.

The popularity of the designer accessory was such that by the 1970s counterfeiting was rife; the problem was exacerbated by advances in technology that enabled many of the craft skills to be overtaken by industrial processes. Convincing copies of designer bags were sold by street

Far left: Model Veruschka in 1971, wearing a entire outfit by Gucci.
Left: Tom Ford's reign as creative director saw Gucci transformed into an edgy and coveted brand.

Below: In her first solo effort as creative director of accessories, Frida Giannini created a line of Flora print bags inspired by a silk scarf pattern made for Grace Kelly.

GUCCI 231

vendors from Hong Kong to Berlin, tarnishing the reputation of many brands, including Gucci. The Gucci dynasty was also experiencing tumultuous internal conflict that brought the company to the edge of destruction; the rot was stopped with the appointment of Dawn Mello, formerly of Bergdorf Goodman, as executive vice president and creative director worldwide in 1989. She relaunched classics such as the Hobo bag, and appointed Texan designer Tom Ford as creative director in 1994; Domenico de Sole became chief executive in 1995. Gucci was now a burgeoning fashion conglomerate named The Gucci Group, and it acquired a succession of luxury brands including Yves Saint Laurent Rive Gauche, the leather goods firm Bottega Veneta, the historic jewelry house of Boucheron, footwear designer Sergio Rossi, and, in part ownership, fashion labels Stella McCartney, Alexander McQueen, and Balenciaga.

The über-sexy aesthetic of Tom Ford transformed the image of the company; it played with pleasure and danger in designs that referenced the decadent scene of 1970s Parisian and New York nightlife. Models strutted the catwalk in razor-sharp metal or rhinestone-studded stiletto heels, skinny rib sweaters, unbuttoned satin shirts, hipster velvet jeans in midnight blue, matching mohair coats, and, for evening, body-skimming cut-out silk jersey dresses with horse-bit belts. After one catwalk show, the fashion director of Neiman Marcus said, "It was hot! It was sex! . . . You just know that wearing those clothes would make you look like you were living on the edge—doing it and having it all!" Glossy advertising campaigns were shot by Mario Testino and featured deliberately incendiary imagery; in 2003, model Louise Pedersen displayed her pubic hair shaved into the Gucci logo and Tom Ford created the Gucci G-string, which sold out worldwide almost overnight. The designer said, "I think it's great. The G-spot is the ultimate in branding. I even considered selling a Gucci waxing kit in the stores. My goal when I make ad campaigns is to create an arresting image. Since 1995 we have been famous for being sexual and provocative. That's what we do."

In 2006, Frida Giannini, formerly Gucci's creative director of accessories, was appointed sole creative director of Gucci and, using the archives as a starting point, she reinterpreted several of the key house icons, including the Flora print and the Bamboo bag, which were morphed together to create the new Bamboo Flora Canvas bag, and the Jackie was enlarged to meet the demands of a modern audience. The rigid frame Stirrup bag, originally launched in 1975, has become the Soft Stirrup bag and takes two days to construct in a choice of calf, ostrich, painted python, or washed or shiny crocodile; the washed crocodile is created with two applications of hot wax color that are then worked by hand to achieve a chiaroscuro effect of light and shade and it is hand polished and washed to give an antiqued look. Every Gucci bag is finished with a number of processes that are obsessively detailed; each edge, for example, is hand-sanded, brushed, painted, and polished. The Flora print has had endless variations under Giannini's tenure, having been resized, recolored, abstracted, made up into dresses, applied to the surface of jewelry, and fashioned into evening bags. Today, despite the Gucci Group being the second largest fashion conglomerate in the world after LMVH, the original brand's leather goods are still made in Italy.

1924
LORO PIANA

Below: In 1924, Pietro Lora Piana set up the Loro Piana mill in Corso Rolandi, Quarona, Italy. **Bottom**: The family first began trading woolen fabrics as merchants in the early 1800s; in April 1924, the current Loro Piana company was established and is today run by Sergio and Pier Luigi Loro Piana. **Right**: The construction of a Loro Piana short-sleeved golf polo shirt in cotton pique.

For six generations the Loro Piana family has traveled the world seeking the best raw materials to transform into some of the most luxurious products on the planet: Tasmanian jackets that seem as light as a feather yet comfortingly warm; soft sweaters of baby cashmere gathered from the under fleece of hyrcus goat kids in Mongolia that are said to "float" on the body; and dresses of ultra-fine cotton jersey. Originally from Trivero, Italy, Loro Piana was a wool merchant in the early nineteenth century in Valsesia, a rugged region in the north west of Piedmont. In 1924, Pietro Lora Piana set up the Loro Piana mill in Corso Rolandi, Quarona, still the group's corporate headquarters today. In the early 1940s, Pietro's nephew, Franco Loro Piana, took over the management of the company and began exporting the finest of fabrics to the couture houses of Paris, including a fine and lightweight fabric trademarked as Tasmanian and renowned for its smooth finish and ability to drape.

The name Tasmanian was derived from the island of Tasmania; in 1820 Saxon merino sheep were introduced there from Australia where flocks had been established for some time. The fine wool of the island's sheep was much prized, and, after being sourced by Loro Piana, was used to manufacture a super lightweight yet strong and crease-resistant fabric weighing a mere 8 ounces (250 g) per yard. The fabric was eminently breathable yet able to retain the body's warmth by trapping air in the intersections in the threads of the fiber. From the 1960s, Loro Piana manufactured two types: the Tasmanian and the Winter Tasmanian, the acclaimed winter version in pure merino Super 130 wool weighing 11 ounces (320 g) per yard, a compact fabric with an almost perfect drop. In the same decade, the company opened up new markets outside of Europe and began selling high-quality fabrics, including

"We are always trying to find new ways to get the utmost quality and timeless elegance for fabrics and garments that can last more than a lifetime."

Loro Piana

cashmere in the United States and Japan. In the 1970s, Franco's sons, Sergio and Pier Luigi Loro Piana, took over as equitable chief executives of the company, alternating the role of chairperson every three years.

Today the company is a global luxury powerhouse and the world's largest cashmere manufacturer, supplying labels and also using it to create their own label knitwear fashioned by Italian artisans since the 1980s. Technology and tradition work hand in hand to ensure fabrics and cashmere goods are desirable items of incomparable quality and luxury. The *vicuña* is a case in point: a shy, wild creature and cousin of the alpaca that lives in the puna, a high treeless plateau in the Andes Mountains. Its soft cinnamon-colored coat has been prized since the time of the Inca because, after silk, it is the finest fiber in the world, with an average diameter of 12–13 microns. Instead of slaughtering the animal, an annual chaku, or ceremonial round-up, was held, the same ritual that exists today. Hundreds of Peruvian villagers march side by side across the Andean plains chanting while brandishing a rope hung with colorful steamers used to corral the vicuña into holding pens. Once sheared, the *vicuña* are then released back into the wild—but this has not always been the case. After the destruction of the Inca Empire in 1532, the Spanish conquistadors simply shot the animal until the species was close to extinction. In 1964, when it was estimated that only 5,000 *vicuña* remained, the Peruvian government established a sanctuary, the Pampa Galeras National Reserve, and a trade ban was imposed, which was held until 1994 when Loro Piana signed an agreement with the Andean communities for the reintroduction of the *vicuña* fabric to the world market. The company began liaising with the local population, teaching them how to safely shear the animal every two years to allow the *vicuña* to keep enough of its coat to survive the winter. Farmers' wages were increased, and a private sanctuary, the Franco Lora National Reserve, was set up in 2008.

This heritage brand continues to innovate, and the latest development is a fiber derived from the lotus flower formerly used only by the Intha, a.k.a. "children of the lake," for the robes of esteemed Buddhist monks. Using ancient techniques, 6,500 lotus stems, grown in the Inle Lake in eastern Myanmar, are transformed by hand into a single length of hand woven fiber that has the qualities of the finest thread of linen or silk. Today Loro Piana has become the largest cashmere manufacturer and the biggest single purchaser of the world's finest wools, which are fashioned into exclusive lines for men, women, and children, along with home furnishings, accessories, and gifts. The company has absolute quality control over every product as it is in charge of the entire production process through its vertical structure, starting from raw materials all the way through to finished products, in manufacturing facilities in Italy, the United States, and Outer Mongolia. As Lora Piana puts it, "For six generations, we have been working with the best raw materials available on Earth. We are always trying to find new ways to get the utmost quality and timeless elegance for fabrics and garments that can last more than a lifetime."

Left, clockwise from top left: 1. Spools of thread. 2. The weaving of cloth. 3. Super-fine woven knit is inspected over a light box to detect minuscule faults in the weave. 4. Ribbing being knitted into a garment by machine. **Above**: The Loro Piana Como Parka in navy made in collaboration with Canada Goose, featuring a wool outer shell with Storm System finish and white goose down insulation.

1925
FENDI

Italy has always had an unrivaled reputation for the artisanal creation of luxury leather goods. The fashioning of fur is also an important indigenous industry, and one of the best-known names associated with this lavish material is Fendi, a leather and fur workshop set up by Adele Casagrande on Via del Plebiscito in Rome. Fendi was an unusual Italian business in that it was run by a woman, and remained a matriarchal company inherited down the female line until 1999 when it became part of the LVMH stable of deluxe brands, although Adele's granddaughter, Silvia Venturini Fendi, is still actively engaged in the day-to-day operations of the company. The only act that had less of a nod to female independence in the early days was when the original company was renamed Fendi following Casagrande's marriage to Edoardo Fendi, and the couple moved in together above the shop. By 1932, Fendi occupied larger premises on the Via Veneto, the fur workshop was expanded, and the fame of the Roman furriers began to be known outside of the city itself. In 1946, the first Fendi daughter, Paola, joined the family business at the age of fifteen, followed incrementally by Anna, Franca, Carla, and Alda after they had finished their education. The sisters bought a youthful verve to the

now-established Italian house and during the post war years of Italian Ricostruzione, Fendi began to compete with other Italian firms that were benefiting from the Made in Italy campaign. This worldwide promotion of Italian fashion gave priceless publicity to brands such as Ferragamo, Gucci, and Pucci, and strengthened trading links with the United States.

After Edoardo's death in 1954, the five Fendi sisters took over, and one year later staged their first fashion show featuring leather and fur. By 1964, Fendi was a well-known name both within and outside of Italy's borders, and a boutique and office were opened on the historic Via Borgognona, known for its traditional artisans and neoclassical and Baroque façades. Anna Fendi was keen to preserve its heritage and set up the Associazione di Via Borgognona, an association of merchants of which she remains the president today. In 1965, Karl Lagerfeld was called upon to design the ready-to-wear line, and the kudos of employing the Parisian designer gave Fendi even more of an international profile. As the designer recalls, "It was still the family business with still the mother around with the five daughters who had to do what the mother said because the mother was tough, tough, tough, but divine. Really Roman matron, like in the book, divine."

Lagerfeld was responsible for the globally recognized FF logo, but his greatest contribution at Fendi was the complete change in the image of the fur coat. Post war fur was heavy and lacked flexibility, and the ubiquitous mink coat had become a status symbol of the middle-aged middle classes. Lagerfeld effected a transformation of this misbegotten garment by giving fur a liquid fluidity, treating it as if it were a woven material and transforming beaver, mink, fox, and squirrel into cutting-edge couture. The Fendi workshop became a hothouse of creativity

with endless experimentation in the tanning, dyeing, and shaping of pelts, and Lagerfeld's first fur collection for Fendi was launched in 1966. The designer was prepared to play with the most expensive skins, such as ermine and mink, by giving them an array of finishes and colors.

The classic Jacquard canvas featuring the abstract Fendi logo in black on a dark brown ground was introduced in 1965 as an alternative to leather, following the tradition set by Louis Vuitton's monogrammed canvas in the nineteenth century; three years later the company created its signature striped *caucciú* or waterproofed canvas fabric. In 1969 the first collection of ready-to-wear fur coats appeared on the catwalk at the Palazzo Pitti in Rome at much more accessible prices than the Fendi couture line, and the fruits of the fur experimentation were applied to leather. Bags appeared with prints, meshed tints, and methods of tanning to make them ultra-soft. In 1977, Fendi launched the first ready-to-wear womenswear collection, the 365, featuring clothes and accessories that could create an outfit for every day of the year, including black cashmere coats with detachable goat-hair collars; wool crêpe jackets with dramatic coq feather, sequin, and diamante trim; cotton lace midi dresses; and pieces in reversible leather and mink. In 1978, Fendi added footwear designed by Diego Della Valle to its repertoire.

By now, fur was being completely deconstructed by Lagerfeld and reworked in unconventional ways; it was quilted, knitted, and patchworked, and different furs such as beaver, fox, and Mongolian lamb were worked together in a kaleidoscope of color and technique. Most provocatively, lowly squirrel was treated to look like mink. A deconstructed fur coat of 1992 in green sheared muskrat with perforated green microfiber shell was described by fashion historian Harold Koda as "dramatically annulling all that is expected

"It was still the family business... and the five daughters... had to do what the mother said because the mother was tough, tough, tough, but divine."

Karl Lagerfeld

les mules à rayures Fendi

of the fur coat [creating] a new and unexpected beauty perhaps even greater than the old age resplendence of fur."

In 1979, each sister had her own place within the family firm; as Carla Fendi pointed out, "Paola is the eldest and technical expert on furs. Anna is the artist and follows all the leather production. Franca manages the shops; Alda is in charge of sales. And I coordinate all the departments." The sisters expanded the Fendi empire; in 1984, jeans, gloves, ties, glasses, lighters, foulards, and pens were added to its range of products, and in 1985, the first woman's fragrance was launched, followed in 1987 by Fendissime, a line that included furs, sportswear, and accessories. In 1989, the men's fragrance, Fendi Uomo, and its corresponding menswear line, Fendi Uomo (1990), could be bought at the company's first flagship store in New York on Fifth Avenue.

Entering the 1990s, Anna Fendi's daughter, Silvia Venturini, following her design process of "not to look at what's around you but dream of what's missing," realized that fashion was experiencing a momentary seizure; Prada had encouraged a new wave of "stealth utility," which made extravagant fashion seem outmoded, even vulgar, in an age hit by recession and environmental concerns. In 1997, Fendi realized that the aesthetic of minimalism was coming to a natural end and floated a bag design that was spot-on for such troubled times, the Baguette—it went on to become one of the most successful bags of all time. Cleverly conflating the idea of the bag as an exquisite one-off art object with the notion of luxury that was beginning to infiltrate high fashion of the new millennium, Silvia Venturini produced thousands of Baguette bags in 600 different choices of luxurious materials and luscious colorways, its interlocking double F logo forming the clasp, which was heavily embellished with crystal, paillette sequins, and beads. Fendi's flamboyant and increasingly outmoded 1980s look was salvaged by Venturini's maximalist bag. It was what every design house desired by the early 2000s—an instant classic, particularly when clutched under the arm of high-octane stars such as Madonna and Naomi Campbell. This small pochette could be purchased in silk velvet, fur, snakeskin, crocodile, woven raffia, or printed pony and was named the Baguette because its short strap meant it sat under the arm like a loaf of French bread, as an elite yet Bohemian accessory, a form of folk costume for the super-rich. Luxurious beadwork made global references to appeal to the "ethical" consumer by using Native American and Aztec motifs, which were in turn accented with materials that were pure old-school glamour: hot pink snakeskin, Swarovski crystals, and silver and gold distressed sequins. "Homespun" craft techniques such as Indian mirror work appeared on the outside of the Baguette, which flashed a wild citrus-python or apple-green-satin lining when opened. Classic tartan mohair or utilitarian denim was transformed with red sequins or old beads as tradition was coupled with sex appeal; in fiction, a Fendi creation was sported by fashion editor Miranda in Lauren Weisberger's novel *The Devil Wears Prada* (2003), and the label appeared in the HBO series *Sex and the City* (1998–2004). After Sarah Jessica Parker as Carrie Bradshaw sported a Fendi, Venturini noted, "Its popularity and prize status spiraled. Our store in Rome had Madonna in buying four or five bags. They called me and said come downstairs, but I'm really shy so didn't go downstairs to see her—but just knowing that she had come was enough for me."

Fendi continued to create innovative accessories, too; in 2004, the Fendi Spy became the it bag *du jour*, a double handled slouchy pleated bag in pebbled zucca leather with a hidden velvet coin purse with a snap closure that was available in a range of colors from tobacco brown to plum. The B Bag of 2006 designed by Lagerfeld continued the house's hits, hailing the return of the structured, tailored bag with two curved buckles on the front in white lambskin, red patent, and python through glossy black crocodile. The Selleria line, originally launched in 1925 and relaunched in 1996 by Venturini, is a limited-edition line of numbered accessories, such as the classic leather-lined Fendi Hobo with a woven hide handle, that are entirely cut and constructed by hand using techniques inherited from the Roman master saddlers. There are no obvious logos in this line; the most recognizable feature that unites all the products, apart from their high quality, is the white topstitching that proves a pleasing visual contrast with the heavy burnished leather.

1935
AUBERCY

In the 1930s, Paris was a cultural mecca for the avant-garde; Surrealism was redefining the boundaries of modern art with its decadent phantasmagorical imagery, and U.S. exiles reveled in the city's independent galleries and smoke-filled cafes. The business of haute couture and the luxury trades flourished in the heady days before the outbreak of World War II with architect Le Corbusier designing the modernist Villa Savoye in reinforced concrete on the outskirts of the city while extolling the virtues of bespoke. He saved special praise for the fine design of Hermès luggage, the Saderne straw boater, and handmade leather shoes. For him, the clean lines of the bespoke shoe showed its quality—shoddy workmanship was not hidden behind unnecessary decoration. As the architect put it, "Trash is always abundantly decorated; the luxury object is well made, neat and clean, pure and healthy, and its bareness reveals the quality of its manufacture."

Into the heady city of Paris came Aubercy, a luxury shoemaker opened by brothers Renée and André Aubercy in 1935 at 35 Rue Vivienne, formerly the location of a gentlemen's outfitters. The business was set up to cater to the demands of the fashionable boulevardier, or man about town, and the most devoted of modernists could not fail to be impressed with the clean, seamless lines of the Aubercy whole-cut shoe fashioned from a single piece of leather. It became clear that, for Aubercy, the difference was in the detail; every bespoke shoe was created to be aesthetically unique, yet certain elegant touches marked out its shoes, such as the beveling on the inside edge of the shoe or boot heel to prevent the hem of the trouser being damaged when walking, and the supporting arch stiffeners made from leather and sandwiched between the upper leather and the lining.

Left: The elegant second generation of the renowned Parisian shoemakers, Emile Aubercy. **Below left**: The exterior of the Aubercy shoe boutique and workshop in Paris. **Right**: The Aubercy André, a minimalist two-eyelet Derby, is the earliest of the firm's styles and named after its founder.

One of the company's most popular designs dating from the early period is the Barthold, which was inspired by Art Deco and featured the same decorative flourishes on a shoe that mixed the Oxford with the brogue. This innovative amalgamation of classic shoe styles—today considered a masterpiece of French shoe design—can still be ordered from Aubercy. In 1950, thanks to the patronage of Chilean businessman Arturo Lopez, Renée and André's successor, Emile Aubercy, traveled to London to learn the methods of bespoke shoemaking from the great English firms, including John Lobb (see page 118) and George Cleverley, with the remit to mix English methods of shoe construction with Italian flair. This was the making of Aubercy for the standard fashionable shoe tended to be style over substance, made for looks rather than durability or comfort. Aubercy's shoes could be trend-setting yet remained fit for purpose and stayed that way when, in 1970, the business passed into the hands of Emile's son, Philippe, and his wife who helped introduce a women's line that took classic Aubercy shoes and boots and modified them for their new female customers.

This hidden gem remains in the same premises today, and for those who appreciate the art of fine shoemaking, the Aubercy aesthetic is perfectly encapsulated in its ever-popular whole-cut Oxford in the evocatively named Cognac calf. The Aubercy Oxford, like all its shoes, is hand-lasted with Goodyear-welted construction, and unusually for a deluxe shoe, Aubercy uses Blake welting, too, a mechanical rather than hand-stitched technique that is used in much of Italian shoe manufacturing. In the Blake method of construction, named after its inventor, Lyman Reed Blake, in 1856, the insole is attached to the upper and the sole with a single row of stitching. As the stitching is internal, it is impossible for it to be done by hand and results in close-cut soles with no stitched edges on the outside of the shoe. The end product is a more flexible, lightweight shoe that is perfect for summer.

Aubercy continues to specialize in refined shoes under the direction of the fourth generation of the family, Xavier Aubercy, who took over in 1995. His refined classics with distinctive Aubercy accents include the five-eyelet William Derby; the bi-colored tasseled loafer mash-up

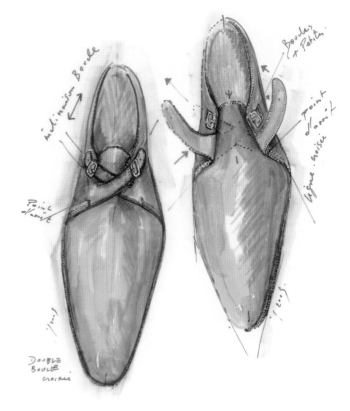

"The real luxury is what is not seen."

Emile Aubercy

with brogue detail at toe; and the Crazy Lace, a whole-cut shoe with asymmetric lacing that can be chosen from a range of rich colors, such as Empire Green made by Enzo Bonafe in Italy. Aubercy's artisans are so proficient that they are some of the few shoemakers to use shagreen, or sharkskin, a material that is notoriously difficult to work with because of its toughness. Shagreen is sourced by Roggwiller, which supplies exotic leather to the French luxury trades and today is owned by Hermès. The shoe with the most bling has to be the Phil, with diamonds embedded into the tip of the toe—the price is dependent upon the size and quality of the rocks chosen by the customer.

Aubercy is one of the few men's shoemakers to manufacture not only the Chukka and Chelsea boots but also the man's button boot, a style that has fallen out of favor in the twentieth century. From the mid-nineteenth century, boots, or bottines, were the accepted everyday footwear for all classes of men and women. Button boots were made of leather or a lighter canvas in the summer, and had a row of buttons that fastened over a flap of leather at the front and a low heel. The button closure gave the boot a tight fit that kept the foot warm and dry, plus it provided good ankle support. Aubercy's Lawrence model for men and women comes complete with working buttonholes instead of the more commonly used invisible zip, and customers are provided with their own button hook.

Recently, Aubercy has moved into other leather goods made in France and Italy, including ostrich briefcases, crocodile wallets, document holders, and the classic Mille Miglia leather travel bag created by Philippe Aubercy. Shoes remain at the heart of the business though, and each pair of bespoke, or *petit measure* as they are called, undergoes a staggering 390 separate processes, from the measuring of both feet to create an interior of the shoe that is as close to the replica of the owner's foot as is physically possible, to the hand-picking of the skin and the hand-punching of the seams. Each pair of shoes is worked on by one of only eight employees in Aubercy's workshop, taking at least two months to construct from start to finish. Xavier Aubercy remains ardent about his family firm saying, "We draw our strength from the beauty of our profession, from the generation that went before us, and all the people for whom exquisite shoes, beautiful objects, and craftsmanship are a passion or a dream. It's all this that gives us a sense of our accomplishments. This is the source of that extra something that we are so proud of."

Far left: From the hand-picking of leathers to the hand-punched seams, Aubercy's shoes are handmade with the utmost attention to detail.

Left: Aubercy Mesure Boucle or buckle shoes displaying the firm's sophisticated mix of Italian design flair and traditional techniques.

Below: Aubercy are known for the updating of classic shapes and the use of an extensive color palette, unusual in men's bespoke footwear.

Ref. TREVISE

1937
VALEXTRA

Valextra, a legendary luxury brand known as the "Italian Hermès," softly whispers rather than screams style. It was founded in 1937 by Giovanni Fontana in Milan's grand Piazza San Babila in the district known as the Quadrilatero d'Oro or "block of gold," the location of Italy's elite labels. Valextra can be recognized by a modernist approach to design combined with the Milanese traditions of fine leatherwork and saddlery. This results in seriously elegant leather goods, which by rejecting extraneous decoration remain classics outside of the historical moment. As the company motto runs—*sono la più bella e la più cara*—"I am the most beautiful and the most expensive."

From the beginning, Valextra had an extra-magical ingredient—glamour—evoked by the company's use of one of the key visual devices of 1930s moderne— streamlining. This design aesthetic was originally utilized for modes of transportation, but by the 1930s, clean surfaces, rounded corners, and flowing lines were applied to all manner of objects to express the exhilarating pace of urban life, thus giving the impression of speed to objects and communicating a modern, uncluttered style. Valextra's high-quality, hand-sewn luggage, including the iconic Avietta suitcase, had rounded corners and a dynamism in its structured lines that was exaggerated by the use of distinctive lacquered piping and was targeted at the first air travelers, wealthy globe-trotters who made up what became known as the international jet set. The emir of Kuwait, for example, ordered fourteen matching elephant-skin trunks, and other high-profile customers included the Duchess of Windsor and Rudolph Valentino who visited the store, drawn in by its reputation and extravagant window displays featuring leather goods fashioned from exotic animal skins, including crocodile,

hippopotamus, and, most unusually, sea lion, juxtaposed with all manner of exotica including elephant tusks.

Milan had always had a large artisan workforce, and many specialized workshops dotted around the outskirts of the city survived the industrial depression that hit the city in the 1930s. Valextra capitalized on the city's artisanal reputation by having its workshop in-store directly above a boutique that could be visited by its discerning customers. After World War I, Italian craftsmanship, including Valextra leather goods was showcased in a succession of Triennale exhibitions that made the country's products internationally desirable. A man wishing to display his wealth and business acumen drove an Alfa Romeo, wore a Brioni suit, and carried a Valextra Ventiquattro briefcase. Both Grace Kelly and Jackie Kennedy carried Valextra Pergamena or

parchment-white leather travel bags during this decade, and opera diva Maria Callas commissioned a hippopotamus -skin hatbox and matching vanity case. In 1954, the 24 Hour bag, a lightweight travel attaché case for overnight trips, won the Compasso d'Oro, the first award for industrial design in Europe set up the same year by the La Rinascente department store. Valextra built on its success with the steel-frame Avietta 48 Hour model in 1964, which was designed to accommodate a two-night stay with the same élan. The luxurious leather case was lightweight and elegantly compact, with a briefcase handle and brushed rhodium zippers and pulls with buckled interior straps to make sure the packing was secure. Other innovative designs created in this decade included the Grip sprung bi-fold wallet in grained leather and a leather and steel cigarette case designed to slot into the dashboard of a car.

Top: The Tric-Trac bag with hand-strap designed in 1960 by Valextra's founder, Giovanni Fontana, opened like a box to hold a man's wallet and keys. **Above**: Valextra's minimalist shapes are given visual punch with a vivid color palette. **Right**: There are many processes carried out by hand at Valextra. The signature Costa lacquered piping is constructed and the shear-cut edges are painted with ink three times by specially trained artisans.

In the 1960s, Valextra was one of the first leather goods brands to offer up a man bag. The general acceptance of the peacock male into fashion and the trend of pants becoming increasingly slimline around the hips made the use of a bag inevitable as men needed somewhere to keep their possessions safe without spoiling the lines of their pants. As writer Truman Capote put it, "I don't see how people can get along without some sort of little satchel." Valextra led the way by launching the Tric-Trac in 1960 designed by founder Giovanni, a wrist bag that opened like a box to hold the wallet and other daily essentials, and one visitor to Milan in the early 1970s remembers seeing "practically every man with a small bag dangling from his wrist. They were small, black leather, and zippered. Maybe because the culture was so macho they could get away with it. They never, ever caught on in England though."

In 1967, a U.S. journalist visited the store and was entranced by how "a man can buy a neat little bag to hold his tennis shorts, shoes, and racket. If he is staying at a hotel and hates the clutter of regular suitcases, Valextra can give him a traveling dresser in leather that stores his shirts in separate drawers, just as at home. A crocodile handbag for his wife or lady friend will cost him $1,000—'because,' explains sales lady Jenny Radice, 'we have to use four or five crocodiles.' Why so many crocs?

Well, to achieve the quality Valextra insists on for such fine articles, it seems only the mid-portions of a crocodile will do." However, he found Giovanni Fontana, seventy years of age at the time, increasingly despondent about the future of his company. In an age that celebrated obsolescence and fast fashion fads, Valextra appeared to be becoming anachronistic, and Giovanni's son, Giampiero, who was in charge of manufacturing said, "In the future there will be no more artisans sufficiently skilled to hand-craft our pieces and there will be no people left who can understand the glory of buying them. Eighty percent of our customers are Milanese. We Milanese are the English of Italy. We see the point of spending money on a fine case. We like the feel of it and the look of it. Valextra's products are not expensive because we are robbers but because we produce them with a devotion that is unique."

The family duly sold Valextra in 1970 and the company seemed to lose its identity during the ensuing decades by manufacturing goods under license for other high-end brands, including Dunhill and Armani. In 2000, help was at hand as architect and long time fan of the brand Emanuele Carminati Molina became a partner and president of Valextra. As a child growing up in Milan he had been entranced by the company's celebrated window displays and bought into it, as he put it as "an act of emotion; an act of love. I couldn't help thinking about

"I am the most beautiful and the most expensive."
Valextra's company motto

all the memories I had from my first years of school here in Milan when I first came to know Valextra." Molina's aim was to restore the company to its former glory by reinforcing its reputation as a purveyor of high-quality leather goods. To this end, he contacted the skilled artisans who had retired during the 1980s and asked them to rejoin Valextra and train up the next generation of craftsmen. Molina consulted the archives of the company and relaunched the Punch and Carita rigid-frame bags, both handmade using the finest leathers and immediately successful. Valextra has also more recently moved into collaborations with Blackberry after developing smartphone covers for the Curve and the ubiquitous tablet. As the company puts it, "Respecting our philosophy of interpreting the époque, we have been closely following the evolution of technology products that have become part of our daily lives. We will continue to study and create accessories that may connect in harmony with these tech gadgets. Our objective is not only to dress, but to modify the impact of the object by transforming it from a piece of technology into a symbol of elegance."

1941
COACH

SPRING – SUMMER

1967

1965

SPRING

COACH
PRESENTS A NEW
COLLECTION OF
"CASHIN CARRY"
BAGS AND ACCESSO-
RIES DESIGNED BY
BONNIE CASHIN

Bonnie Cashin's bags for Coach turned a wholesale leather company, established in 1941 in a Manhattan loft, into a global brand, famed for its luxurious leather bags. Coach was originally the Gail Manufacturing Company, an artisanal accessories manufacturer that employed six leather workers, to make billfolds or wallets throughout the 1950s in high-quality natural hide. Husband and wife team Miles and Lillian Cahn joined Gail in 1946 with Miles taking over as manager in 1950, and the couple eventually gained control of the firm in a leveraged buy out in 1961. They had considerable experience in the manufacture of leather goods and more importantly had inquiring minds and innovative ideas. In 1960, Miles Cahn began a series of investigations into the leatherwork and stitchwork normally used to manufacture baseball gloves. He was interested in how the leather became incredibly supple after abrasive handling on the pitch and innovated a method of processing hide so as to make it strong yet malleable and able to absorb saturated color. The Glove Tanned Cowhide, as it was named, is used to make many Coach bags today and is renowned for its practicality—these bags are built to last.

In the 1950s, Lillian decided to add a line of handbags to the firm's production, under the brand name Coach, to increase the small profits that were being made through wallet production. The first Coach bags were of high-quality natural tan and deep brown cowhide on which the grain could be clearly seen, and their functionality, durability, and distinctive double stitching marked them out from the cheap leather bags that had flooded the market after World War II; women had become used to buying so called "lather" bags, which were constructed out of a thin veneer of leather glued over cardboard. Coach's strategy was to ignore fast-moving fashion changes

Above: Two catalogs from Spring/ Summer 1965 and Spring 1967 presenting Bonnie Cashin's new designs for Coach with accompanying fashion illustrations.
Right, clockwise from top left:
1. A classic Coach glove-tanned leather shoulder bag with an inside zip pocket and brass hardware.
2. In 1978, Cashin designed the Duffle-Sac, a large, slouchy leather bag that was re-released in 2006.
3. Coach catalog spread, c. 1980s, featuring a Duffle-Sac (left).

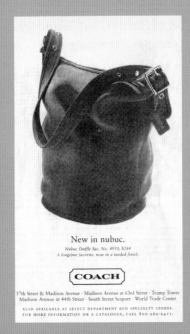

New in nubuc.

Nubuc Duffle Sac, No. 4950, 5284
A longtime favorite, now in a sueded finish.

COACH

57th Street & Madison Avenue · Madison Avenue at 63rd Street · Trump Tower
Madison Avenue at 44th Street · South Street Seaport · World Trade Center

ALSO AVAILABLE AT SELECT DEPARTMENT AND SPECIALTY STORES.
FOR MORE INFORMATION OR A CATALOGUE, CALL 800 262-2471.

"Sporting, practical,
and tough, geared to
the modern, mobile
lifestyle, geared to
city streets, geared
to traveling light."

Bonnie Cashin on her first handbag
collection for Coach in 1963

in favor of classic elegance, and when in 1959 the company premiered its nostalgic horse and carriage logo, it reflected Coach's burgeoning reputation as a leather goods firm by cannily making equestrian associations in the manner of Hermès. Bags were also numbered and stamped on the bottom with the Coach seal to validate their provenance.

In 1962 Coach made its best decision yet—to hire Bonnie Cashin, who had become a highly successful fashion designer with her sports-influenced clothes. Cashin was a non conformist, trained from childhood by her dressmaker mother who gave her scraps of fine textiles to play with. Cashin's first designs were costumes for the Fanchon and Marco dance troupes of Los Angeles in 1925, and from 1933 the Roxyettes, a chorus line who danced at New York's Roxy Theater; through this work Cashin began to understand, almost intuitively, how the body worked in motion but, constrained by the tight budgets, decided to move into costume design for film. Accordingly, the designer moved to Hollywood in the 1940s and worked on many successful films, including *Laura* (1944) starring Gene Tierney who, in one memorable scene, wore a Cashin skirt made of gray and white squirrel. In 1952, the designer set up her own company, Bonnie Cashin Designs, and began to gain

a reputation and win accolades for her womenswear, including the Neiman Marcus Award for Distinguished Service in the Field of Fashion and Coty Fashion Critics Award.

Cashin had always been interested in the properties of leather and her designs in this decade combined skin with textured fabric, such as chunky tweed, mohair knit, and jersey with hardware closures. She had developed a recognizable Cashin "look" by this time, influenced by a journey made to Japan where she had admired the method of layering clothes appropriately when the temperature changed. Her aim was to create a modular wardrobe of clothes that, as she put it, "were simple art forms for living in to be rearranged as mood or activity dictates." Cashin's layered capes, coats, and ponchos used lots of leather and suede in the design and structural elements of the garments, from whole skins to simple piped trim, and she applied her ideas of fashion innovation to Coach bags in a collaboration that lasted until 1974.

In the 1950s, the rigid handbag had held sway; writer Carol Shields evocatively described her mother's handbag as "big and black and aggressively pleated, with an enchanting clasp in the form of two parrots. The bag's richly dark interior held the mingled fragrance of

perfume and leather—calfskin probably—and a cotton handkerchief dabbed with 'Evening in Paris' wadded in one corner." Large, structured, and subtly expensive bags, such as those from Hattie Carnegie's store in Manhattan, dominated the decade, tastefully designed in black calf, alligator, or crocodile skin, and they were carried as a sign of class and social status. Handbags were conservative, with teenage girls dressing like their mothers in hats, gloves, and suits with lacquered hair and matching accessories.

Cashin's designs for Coach came just at the right time. Young women, spurred on by the writings of early feminists Simone de Beauvoir and Betty Friedan, began to reject the starchy etiquette of their mothers; British *Vogue* wrote in 1959, "Young is now the persuasive adjective for all fashions, hairstyles, and ways of life." Handbags expressed this air of liberation, an aesthetic spearheaded by Cashin at Coach. Her first collection, launched in 1963 under the witty name Cashin-Carry, was revolutionary, in the designer's words, "sporting, practical, and tough, geared to the modern, mobile lifestyle, geared to the city streets, geared to traveling light." The bags were flat-pack with wide straps and perfect for being flung into the back seat of a car by a go-getting woman on the move. They were closed with strong industrial zippers and brass toggles and came in "punchy" colors: a riot of rich lipstick reds and grassy greens with striped Madras cotton interiors. In 1964, Coach's first denim designs had geranium-red stitching and matching canvas lining; bags had built-in purses that were situated either inside or outside for ease of access, hung from belts on the hip, and closed with brass or silver turn-lock toggles inspired by the fixings used to fasten the roof of Cashin's convertible car. Leather totes were large and flat, based on paper grocery bags, and she experimented with packability, trying to refine the bag down to its most practical essentials. One Cashin concept was to have several bags of different colors layered one over the other on the arm banishing "the word 'match'" as she put it, for "that belonged to the previous generation." The pouch-like body bag of 1970 was one of Cashin's most innovative designs, an oversized pocket shape to rest against the curve of the body. It was one of her favorites too, as she described how "it feels so good next to me—I wear it under my coats and suits to foil bag-snatchers."

Cashin's non conformist work for Coach launched the label as a pioneer in women's accessories and was both critically acclaimed and universally popular. It was endlessly copied, too, but the designer was sanguine saying, "The moment you think an idea, it is no longer yours exclusively," and described her Duffle-Sac bucket-shaped bag of 1978 as "knocked off all over the world." The Duffle-Sac was one of the Coach Soft Sacs introduced in the 1970s and it was advertised as "wonderful, floppy, squashable, unconstructed shapes in magnificent glove tanned cowhide." The Sacs were a perfect match with the hippie-hobo slouchy vibe of the decade, and utility became the most important aspect of bag design. The Duffle-Sac was relaunched in 2006 with the Legacy range that today continues to update the designer's cutting-edge work.

By the early 1980s, Coach took over four floors of its business premises on West 34th Street, New York, employing skilled leather workers from Argentina. Soon demand for its products began to outstrip the limited supply but the Cahns refused to expand, wanting to remain in New York, keep the same staff, and maintain the same high quality and workmanship. In 1985, they sold the business after their children expressed no interest in taking over the long-standing family firm. It was bought by the Sara Lee Corporation , which expanded Coach into a powerful global brand driven by the concept of "affordable luxury" and opened new stores in San Francisco, Seattle, and Denver and a concession in Macy's department store. The Coach Lightweights Collection introduced lighter and smaller leather bags in taupe and navy, targeted at women who lived in the more temperate states of the United States, and a flagship store opened on New York's Madison Avenue. Business accessories such as document holders and diaries were targeted at the executive. In 2001, Coach was sold to its shareholders, gained its independence from Sara Lee, and is now known as Coach, Inc. It is indisputably the most recognizable U.S. leather brand, manufacturing handbags, luggage, accessories, and licensed items such as watches, footwear, jewelry, and furniture. Its impeccable leather bags, fashioned from buttery-soft, tumbled, fine-grain leather calf to smooth, firm cowhide, and inventive design remain true to Cashin's oeuvre, and the original Manhattan loft remains at the heart of the company as the corporate headquarters.

1947
DIOR

The fashion show is the promotional linchpin of a multibillion-dollar industry, yet remains ephemeral, a fleeting moment in time—performance art at its most spectacular and glamorous. Fashion is a form of visual language so seductive that its every twist and turn becomes imprinted on the bodies of women. Every decade has at least one fashion spectacular, a catwalk show that changes the way women dress; Lucile's Art Gown parades of 1904 were the first fashion shows conceived with a theme and house models; in 1947, Dior's mesmerizing Corolle line, or New Look as it was dubbed by the press, kick-started 1950s fashion after the grim austerity of the long war years.

In 1945, a fashion journalist wrote in *Harper's Bazaar*, "This year brings a new era and it follows as the peace of

war, that men want women, beautiful, romantic birds of paradise instead of hurrying brown hens." These were to be prophetic words; two years later, Christian Dior unveiled fashion's new direction, a tightly tailored collection that was haughty and high class, featuring the Bar jacket in shantung silk with sculpted basques to stand away from the body; heavily boned, wasp-waisted gowns with tiers of pleats; and huge crinoline skirts that mocked wartime sobriety and the restrictions on the use of materials. When the Corolle line was shown to the assembled fashion editors in Dior's salon in Paris, it entered the annals of fashion as one of the most defining moments. As fashion historian Lou Taylor writes, "The long frothy skirts of Dior's collection were so full that they brushed against the cheeks of the assembled crowd. The audience were shocked, enraptured, and captivated. Seasoned fashion journalists to this day remember that show as one of the most magical moments of their lives. Perhaps the huge quantity of Dior perfume that was sprayed over each member of the audience made everyone a little light-headed."

Dior's opulent designs were, for Janey Ironside, later to become professor of fashion at London's Royal College of Art, "like a new love affair, the first sight of Venice, a new chance, in fact a new look at life. Dior held a mirror up to women, in which they saw themselves as they wished to be; no longer Amazons but Nymphs; no longer Cinders but Cinderella." In Dior's hands, haute fashion reemerged, richly embellished and excessive, with full crinoline skirts hand-crafted out of yards of pale *café au lait* organza or champagne-colored tulle, all shimmering with embroidered mother-of-pearl. Elegant mannequins, throats lit by gleaming icy diamonds and sapphires, hair sparkling with gold dust, created a breathtaking scenario. The couturier later explained his approach: "We came from an epoch of war and uniforms, with

women like soldiers with boxer's shoulders. I designed clothes for flowerlike women, with rounded shoulders, full feminine busts, and hand-span waists above enormous spreading skirts."

The newly tightened waist, fitted bodice, padded hips, and bouffant skirts were accessorized by shoes designed by Roger Vivier who worked by Dior's side, complementing his romantic silhouettes. His high-heeled shoes, like the clothes, were the antithesis of the wartime utility look and challenged the conventional ideas of construction and silhouette. Taking the basic pump shape, Vivier cut curves into the vamp, thereby tailoring the shoe to fit more closely to the foot in the same way that Dior's tailoring held the body. Heels were sculpted into a variety of attenuated shapes, including the Choc, the Comma, the Spool, and some of the earliest stilettos. Vivier for Dior's shoes were such a success that a ready-to-wear line was launched, one of the first instances in which a couturier was prepared to join forces with another designer to explore the potential of a mass-market audience while retaining the magic of the luxury brand.

As the house gained rapid success, Dior perfume was developed in 1947, with Miss Dior launched as the first fragrance, followed by the first lipstick in 1953. Dior also paid attention to accessories—especially handbags—and he had very specific rules about the correct version a woman should carry. In his *The Little Dictionary of Fashion* (1954) Dior advised, "You can wear the same suit from morning to dinner—but to be really perfectly dressed you cannot keep the same bag. For morning it must be very simple, and for the evening it must be smaller and, if you wish, a little more fancy." Dior's insistence on simplicity by day belied the expense of what he was proposing; Dior day bags were painstakingly crafted out of luxurious skins such as python or ostrich. Dior's glamorous aesthetic was also demonstrated in the house's branded jewelry

commissioned from the leading practitioners of the day, including Henry Schreiner, Mitchel Maer who created the popular unicorn brooches from 1952 and 1956, Robert Goosens, Roger Semama, and Josette Gripoix. The style was neo-Victorian, nostalgic and opulent in tone, and the floral motifs were given a modern twist in their exaggerated dimensions and obviously faux stones. Dior kept strict quality control over the house's output and managed to create a mélange of sophisticated glamour and high-octane glitz with the use of large petal-shaped rhinestones, prong-set into hand-soldered settings in regal combinations of red, black, and gold.

By 1955, Dior was the largest house in Paris with more than 1,000 staff, and twenty-eight workrooms with wealthy customers from all over the world. Success followed success as Dior introduced a series of well-heralded silhouettes, including the Corolle and 8 lines (Spring/Summer 1947), the Winged line (Fall/Winter 1948), the Verticale line (Spring/Summer 1950) that emphasized the bust, the Oblique line (Fall/Winter 1950) that played with the curves of the body, the informal Sinuous line (Fall/Winter 1952), and the Tulip line (Spring/Summer 1953), described by the couturier as "the complete overthrow of proportion, the expansion of the bust, and the effacement of the hips." The couturier's architectural lines included the A line (Fall/Winter 1954), H line (Spring/Summer 1955), and Y line (Fall/Winter 1955). The press lapped it up and the house continued its resounding success until the unexpected death of its founder in 1957. Dior's successor, a young Yves Saint Laurent, launched his first well-received collection for the house in 1958; in 1961, however, his truly groundbreaking black leather Beat collection, inspired by the vibe of the existentialist Left Bank and anticipating the huge influence street style would have on fashion in the following decade, was too much for the established clientele. Saint Laurent was conscripted into the army and after suffering a breakdown Marc Bohan took over at Dior in 1960.

Bohan's first haute couture collection was launched a year later, featuring 1920s-style chiffon dresses with dropped waists in a flapper-revival style mixed with beautifully tailored double-breasted jackets. *The New York Times* wrote of a "shouting, clapping, surging mob at the

Above: A model wearing a Marc Bohan for Dior tweed suit with matching cap and scarf, from the Fall/Winter collection of 1961.
Right: Yves Saint Laurent posing with models after the successful launch of the Trapeze line in his Spring/Summer Collection for Dior in 1958. At this time, the House of Dior was responsible for nearly half of France's fashion exports, so there was a heavy burden of financial responsibility on Saint Laurent's shoulders.

Above left: John Galliano's extravagant Autumn/Winter 2004 collection for Dior Couture harked back to the doomed royal houses of turn-of-the century Europe, with a regal parade of mermaid-tailed robes accessorized with crowns, orbs, and diamonds. **Above right**: Dior Couture Spring/Summer 2004. Galliano explained how, "I imagined Princess Tutankhamun, Nefertiti, and put them together with the photos of Richard Avedon and Irving Penn. Et Voilà! It's très Dior." **Right**: In 1994, French First Lady Bernadette Chirac gave the Princess of Wales a quilted Dior bag. After the "Lady Dior," here shown in red crocodile, was consistently photographed on her arm by the paparazzi, 100,000 bags were sold in that year alone.

press showing [that] caused chaos in the elegant salon. M. Bohan was… kissed, mauled, and congratulated. Chairs were toppled." Bohan's Fall/Winter collection of 1966 was one of his most critically acclaimed and took inspiration from Julie Christie in the epic film *Doctor Zhivago* (1965), with its fur-trimmed belted tweed coats paired with long black boots.

In 1970, a menswear line was launched, an unprecedented success, later transformed into the Dior Homme line in 2001 after the appointment of Hedi Slimane followed by Kris Van Assche, who were key in the creation of cutting-edge fashion. In 1985, the launch of the phenomenally successful fragrance Poison gave Dior a new edge that was parlayed out into couture with the appointment of Gianfranco Ferré as artistic director from

1989 to 1996. The Italian-born Ferré proved a success with his love of fashion history and extensive research into the Dior archives. He later wrote, "The most prestigious *maison de couture* in France was a temple of rituals, traditions, codes of conduct, and rules, perhaps unwritten but no less hard and fast, no less binding for all that. For weeks I studied, analyzed and 'breathed' his style. And so I discovered affinities and analogies… that made it possible for me to meet the challenge—between my way of understanding and interpreting elegance and that of Monsieur Dior." Ferré caught the mood of the times with his tailored power suits, full-skirted coats, and high-octane cocktail dresses in pleated taffeta bedecked with huge bows. After Ferré left in 1996, John Galliano took the helm.

Born in Gibraltar, Galliano moved to London at a young age and immersed himself in the outrageous club scene of the early 1980s, mixing with key faces such as Boy George, Leigh Bowery, and Jeremy Healy, and learning lessons from Vivienne Westwood's use of historical pastiche. Galliano's work had always stood as a compelling conduit between fashion and art, and at Dior his catwalk became an extravaganza; the exaggerated silhouettes of his couture gowns were perfect for rebranding the stuffy Dior atelier as a hothouse of aesthetic innovation. The haute couture clothes may not have appeared in many women's wardrobes but millions of residual products did; today, Dior handbags, including the charm-bedecked Lady Dior of 1994, make up, and perfume such as J'adore, account for a massive increase in revenue for Dior's parent company LMVH.

Galliano's ignominious departure in 2012 led to a new appointment, Belgian Raf Simons, one of the most innovative fashion designers working today and known for his faultless tailoring. It was a move away from the historical theatricality of Galliano to a more contemporary cool, and Simons' first show reworked two Dior classics, the Bar jacket and Ligne A dress. *Vogue* fashion director Lucinda Chambers enthused, "It was what you hoped for and more—it was such a beautiful homage to Dior, a mix of the modern, clean, and unexpected with a real lightness of touch. Simons trod a brilliant line of being him and being respectful of Dior, I loved it."

"Dior today is just hipper, sexier, lighter, younger."
John Galliano

1948
LONGCHAMP

Toujours en tête du progrès!...

**LES PIPES
LONGCHAMP**
sont calorifugées

Turenne
Chevallereau

JEAN CASSEGRAIN & Cⁱᵉ. 20 RUE -SAINT-FIACRE . PARIS 2ⁱ . TELEPHONE CENTRAL 66-13

Above: In the 1940s Jean Cassegrain, founder of Longchamp, gave a deluxe air to the humble pipe by sheathing it in fine leathers such as calf, kid, and even crocodile. **Above right**: The first Longchamp Légende bag was launched in 2007, its elegant structure inspired by vintage doctor's bags.

When the brand name Longchamp is spoken today, we immediately think of beautiful canvas and leather bags, but this has not always been the case. The origins of Longchamp lie with the Cassegrain family and their mahogany-paneled tobacco shop, Au Sultan, situated on Boulevard Poissonnière in the center of Paris. After World War II in 1948, the enterprising Jean Cassegrain inherited the family business from his father, Gaston. Pipes had been incredibly popular among U.S. servicemen after the Liberation of Paris in 1944, and queues had snaked down the street from Au Sultan when the latest stock had been delivered from the pipe-makers of the Jura, where farmers turned to wood and leather work in winter as an additional source of income.

After the servicemen left Paris, Cassegrain had to rethink his ideas and decided to give a deluxe air to the humble pipe by sheathing it in fine leathers such as calf, kid, and even crocodile. It was a simple act but meticulously achieved; the leather worker used vegetable-tanned leather to make forms for both sides of the pipe, which were then soaked in water, shaped, and seamed tightly together using two needles simultaneously. Cassegrain's leather-clad pipes were so unique that people began to flock to the shop, so he branched out into selling them wholesale in 1948. Every pipe was stamped with the name Longchamp, after a mill based by the well-known Parisian racetrack. By associating itself with the racetrack, the company made all manner of fashionable equestrian associations, following in the footsteps of classic French leather goods companies such as Hermès. Certain stitching techniques taken from saddlery were being used in the production of the pipe so it seemed an obvious fit; Longchamp also had a corporate logo in the form of a jockey riding a galloping horse, designed by illustrator Turenne Chevallereau.

The entrepreneur also made sure that his elegant pipes were always seen in the right places, including at Paris's top hotels and, most significantly, in the PX stores that served U.S. military bases all over the world including Japan, where Cassegrain's products could be bought as early as 1955. The company expanded into small leather accessories such as purses, sealskin cigarette cases, and beautifully crafted passport covers with the letters hand-gilded in gold leaf. One important innovation was a garment bag crafted from black lambskin that was the precursor of Longchamp luggage.

The leather pipe coverings and other smoking accessories, such as leather tobacco pouches and cigarette cases, were originally crafted by artisans based in Paris and the Jura, but by the late 1950s, Cassegrain wanted to increase production. The first production unit opened in Segré in the Loire Valley in 1959 focusing on luggage,

and the fabled leather pipes began to be phased out as the popularity of this mode of smoking began to diminish in favor of cigarettes, ceasing altogether in 1978.

Longchamp became increasingly visible as a global brand when the South Terminal of Orly airport was opened by Charles de Gaulle in 1961, and the company opened a concession selling travel goods duty free, a novel idea that caught on as its products found their way across the world. The company duly expanded, opening boutiques in Hong Kong and Japan in 1979 and in New York in 1982. After the death of Jean Cassegrain, his son, Philippe, took over and decided to move into women's accessories, in particular leather bags, a design development that culminated in the LM range of luxurious embossed calfskin bags printed with Longchamp's horse and crossed belt motif, the LM standing for Longchamp Maroquinerie, or "small leather goods by Longchamp." The collection,

one of the first overtly emblazoned with a logo—a style that went on to dominate bag design in the 1970s—was extremely popular in the Japanese market and became the catalyst for the company's penetration throughout Asia. In 1982, the Derby collection of bucket- and pouch-shaped bags was launched, and Longchamp also expanded its range into scarves and clothing. In 1993, the company launched what continues to be its most popular line, the Le Pliage, a collection of lightweight folding travel bags in wipe-clean nylon usually used for military groundsheets, with Russian leather accents on the handles and flaps to give them a luxe feel. The leather was based on the cargo of antique skin discovered on board the shipwrecked *Die Frau Metta Catharina von Flensburg*, a ship that fell foul just short of Plymouth harbor in 1786. The leather was discovered by divers in the 1980s and was extremely unusual because the grain was a curious diamond shape. Philippe Cassegrain was inspired by both the pattern of the grain and the way in which the action of the sea had given the leather such a beautiful patination. He replicated the effect on the leather accents

of the Le Pliage bags, which gave a surreal feel when placed next to the hyper-modern gloss of the nylon. It was the catalyst for a revolution in luggage dominated by hard cases and leather. Nylon is now de rigueur for luggage.

Le Pliage became the cornerstone of the company, and the simplicity of the wide tote's design made it a vehicle for experimentation, acting as a planar surface on which imagery was created by a series of artists commissioned by the company to create something new. The tote was reconfigured in embroidered canvas in 1988, manufactured with a transparent lower half, and worked on most notably in 2003 by artist Tracey Emin, who customized it with a rosette in patchwork and slogans in appliqué, transforming a classic bag into what appeared to be a domestic craft project. In 1993, Longchamp also launched the Roseau leather tote bag with its distinctive bamboo toggle opening.

In the 2000s, Longchamp began to reposition itself as a fashionable but still classic brand, and targeted a younger audience with a series of iconic campaigns, featuring supermodel Kate Moss photographed by Mario Sorrenti, and collaborative projects with cutting-edge artists and designers, including Jeremy Scott and Thomas Heatherwick, who designed the Zip Bag and Longchamp's stunning brick-and-glass global flagship store in SoHo, New York. The building was an unusual choice, as the majority of the floor area was on the first floor with a very small ground-floor street frontage. Heatherwick came up with an ingenious design solution by cutting a three-story void through the building, thus allowing light in, and installing a stunning 55-ton staircase that brought people up to the store, fashioned from 1¼ inch (4 cm) hot-rolled steel and taking six months to build. Heatherwick describes the staircase as "an installation that divides and converges to form a topography of walkways, landings, and steps. The magnetic properties of the landscape stair enable movable lights and display stands to be attached with high-strength magnets. The transparent balustrades are fabricated using aerospace windscreen technology to create a series of individually formed panels that drape with the fluidity of fabric." The New York store displays the latest elegant Longchamp stock in fine leathers sourced from South America, France, and Italy; all skins have to be as near to perfect as possible before being hand cut by cutters who have been trained for at least two years to work with the grain so the pieces fit together perfectly. Many of the finishing processes are done by hand, down to the finicky coloring of the edges of the Longchamp label, which has to be done with a sable-hair brush. All crocodile bags are completely bespoke and made by one artisan from start to finish because of the unpredictability and expense of the hide.

Today Longchamp remains in family hands with Philippe's son, Jean, as chief executive and daughter, Sophie Delafontaine, who joined the business in 1995, in charge of the fashion range. In 2007, she collaborated with Kate Moss on the Légende, a shape reminiscent of a Victorian doctor's bag that went on to become one of the decade's so-called it bags. Moss has helped Longchamp's transition from a chic French luggage label to an international fashion brand, and since 2007 the company has launched seasonal ready-to-wear collections. Jean Cassegrain says, "I am grateful we evolved from pipes because I am not sure we would still be in business. It is the handbag that has become the fashion statement."

"I am grateful we evolved from pipes because I am not sure we would still be in business. It is the handbag that has become the fashion statement."
Jean Cassegrain

Far left: Le Pliage, a nylon fabric travel bag with leather handles that folds so it can be stored flat, designed by Philippe Cassegrain and Isabelle Guyon in 1993. **Left**: A wheeled suitcase in LM cuir showing the house logo of a galloping thoroughbred and intertwined belts. **Below**: Kate Moss models a bag from Neo-Vintage, her second collection for Longchamp launched in 2010.

1953
MISSONI

It was Missoni's confident assertion of pattern and color that almost single-handedly transformed the image of postwar European knitwear from that of homespun handicraft to one of catwalk prestige and luxury. In the 1950s, the brand built on the fashionable foundations laid by the Italian knitwear firms Avagolf, Avon Celli, and Mirsa and harnessed mechanical production to produce space-dyed knits in striking colors that went on to reach the height of popularity in the 1970s. By refusing to compromise on quality, Missoni broke through the conformity associated with identikit machine-knitted garments and introduced a modernism of expression that had been absent in knitwear since the 1920s. Today a Missoni knit is as redolent of Italian culture as a speedy Bugatti, a Giò Ponti lamp, or a streamlined stiletto heel by Salvatore Ferragamo.

In the late 1940s, Ottavio "Tai" Missoni set up a workshop to produce Venjulia tracksuits worn by the Italian team competing in the 1948 London Olympics, an event in which he had a vested interest—he was competing in the final of the 400 meter hurdles. While in London, he met Rosita Jelmini, the daughter of a family of shawl makers from Varese, Italy. They met for their first date under the statue of Eros in Piccadilly, and after a five-year courtship the couple were married in Golasecca, Italy. In that pivotal year, 1953, one of the world's most distinctive fashion brands was born.

The Missonis' first collaborative designs, under the label Maglificio Jolly, were created out of a cramped basement in Gallarate containing four knitting machines. Their success was by no means instant; Rosita describes how "we were doing everything ourselves at the time—mostly active sportswear. It took us at least ten years to find our way. We were kind of fortunate. We started with our knitting machines and found the fabric of the fifties—knitwear. It really was a field where there was a lot to be discovered."

The first collection to have the Missoni label was Milano-Sympathy, whose brightly striped shirtwaister dresses were shown in the windows of the department store La Rinascente in Milan in 1958. However, the couple's breakthrough did not occur until 1962 with the invention of the zigzag motif. Rosita explains, "We could only do stripes and then we started doing horizontal and vertical and little by little added more complicated stitches, plaids, and jacquards. Then we found the Raschel machines that do the zigzag and that was that." The Raschel knitting machine was developed in the nineteenth century to cater to the demand for lace, with its name derived from the popular French actress Élisabeth Rachel Félix, a.k.a. Mademoiselle Rachel. On stage she was well known for her naturalistic portrayals of the great classical roles; off stage she bedecked herself in the finest Valenciennes lace. The Raschel machine had multiple needles and was primarily

Below left: The late Ottavio "Tai" Missoni and his wife, Rosita, photographed in their Italian atelier in 1968, surrounded by garments and materials. **Right**: A Missoni coordinated outfit of 1975 comprising a herringbone-weaved scarf, striped top, and pleated maxi skirt in which the scarf and skirt's zigzag stripes match the welt-knitted top.

used to create a variety of knits quickly and more cheaply, ranging from sheer net to heavy carpets, and created vertical rows of chainlike loops with laid-in yarns. Rosita was familiar with this technique as it had been used in her family's firm to create open-work shawl patterns in which the horizontal yarns were held together by extremely fine threads, which gave a semi-sheer effect that looked very much like lace or a hand-crocheted fabric. In a revolutionary move the Missonis reconfigured their machines to create iconic knitted garments of an unprecedented combination of feather-weight, graphic patterning, and subtlety of color. An early enthusiast for their work was Anna Piaggi, the Milanese fashion writer and style icon, who, as editor and stylist of the monthly magazine *Arianna,* gave the fledging brand much-needed publicity.

In the early 1960s, the design duo collaborated with fashion designer Emmanuelle Khanh on the Missoni

Emmanuelle Khanh collection and launched their first catwalk show in 1966 at the Teatro Gerolamo in Milan, featuring what became their trademark separates, or "put-together look" as it was dubbed by the fashion press. Models took to the stage in lightweight rayon-viscose zigzag knits of a liquid fluidity that molded to the body, eminently suitable to the decade of sexual enlightenment. The director of the venue, Carletto Colombo, evocatively described the show as featuring "splendid girls armed with colored marker pens [who] drew marks and sketches on a backdrop that acted as a 'transparency' behind which the mannequins repeated, in a whirl of changing lights, the same gestures already made on the stage and changed almost in front of the audience's eyes."

Missoni's most infamous show took place in 1967 at the Pitti Palace, Florence. Inside the rusticated stonework of this Renaissance building, a catwalk taboo was broken

"[Missoni] knitted clothes have become international status symbols like Vuitton bags and Gucci shoes."

The New York Times, 1973

when Rosita asked her models to remove their underwear, fearing its visibility would detract from the lines of her body-skimming unlined knit dresses. Unbeknown to her, the bright lights of the catwalk rendered her work transparent, anticipating Yves Saint Laurent's "see-through" look by a year. The subsequent furore caught the attention of the legendary editor of U.S. *Vogue* Diana Vreeland who, impressed by the ingenuity of their color palette, championed the Missonis in the United States saying, "Look! Who said that only colors exist? There are also tones." Subsequently the first Missoni boutique was opened in Bloomingdales, New York, in 1970, and in 1973, *The New York Times* wrote that "[Missoni] knitted clothes have become international status symbols like Vuitton bags and Gucci shoes." Rosita and Tai moved operations to Sumirago where they set up a factory, studio, and home in a series of buildings designed by the architect Enrico Buzzi at the foothills of the Monte Rosa mountains where the company remains to this day.

The visual language created by the Missonis remains instantly recognizable by its chromatic compositions and combinations of shade, texture, and distinctive zigzag pattern. An earthy Missoni knit, as devised by color alchemist Tai, is more than just brown—his pre-production color combinations, carefully calculated on graph paper, create abstract tonal symphonies, which have particular impact when viewed on the large-scale wall hangings. Tai's play with the harmonies and dissonances created by laying one color next to another and the juxtaposition of planar shape with polychromatic warp-knitted stripes and zigzags find echoes in the dynamic works of early twentieth-century abstract art, in particular the work of Italian Futurist Giacomo Balla, whose paintings the couple collected before Tai's death in 2013. The relationship with early abstraction did not go unnoticed in 1973, when one Missoni knitted coat was described as "looking like a Mondrian had melted."

Missoni's space dyes are among the most innovative of its techniques, a method of dyeing yarn that produces a tonal virtuosity of light and shade in colors unprecedented in knitwear design before the 1960s. Lengths of yarn are dipped sequentially into a series of dye baths holding different colors, with the sequence then repeated. Thus a 6 inch (15 cm) length of blue can be followed by the same length of vermilion, then scarlet, creating a color repeat on a yarn that when woven creates unpredictable patterns, including stripes, diamonds, and zigzags that appear not unlike ikat. Missoni has also been a pioneer in CAD (computer-aided design), working in cotton, linen, and silk as well as wool and viscose to create ready-to-wear collections that defy seasonal trends.

Today the brand has become a twenty-first-century fashion powerhouse known for more than just its iconic graphic fine-gauge knits. The brand has over twenty-five sublines, which include Missoni Home, Missoni Menswear, fragrance, and the diffusion line M Missoni, plus boutique hotels in Edinburgh and Kuwait in partnership with the Rezidor Hotel Group. Rosita Missoni is responsible for the interior design of each hotel, which contains furniture by Eero Saarinen, Marcel Wanders, and Arne Jacobsen, with the brand's trademark zigzags, stripes, and flowers used throughout. The Missoni matriarch also heads up Missoni Home after having become disenchanted with the fashion line in the 1990s. Daughter Angela took over the overall creative directorship of Missoni fashion in 1998, and Luca Missoni, formerly the creative director for the Missoni Menswear and Missoni Sport collections, directs the Missoni archive.

BRAND DIRECTORY

An essential directory of a further 160 brands from all over the world that live up to the standard of a heritage fashion label by manufacturing high-quality garments and accessories. Brands such as these still exist in the modern marketplace because of their superb quality, superior craftsmanship, and timeless design appeal.

Left: A model wearing Balenciaga's three-quarter-sleeved evening dress with Van Cleef & Arpels jewels, 1953.

BRAND DIRECTORY

CLOTHING

HENRY POOLE & CO. 1806
UK

In 1806, James Poole opened as a linen drapers in Everett Street, Brunswick Square, London, and moved into military tailoring. By the 1850s, the firm had a magnificent showroom on Savile Row and was making bespoke suits for the elite of Europe, with branches in Paris, Vienna, and Berlin. Today the founders of Savile Row are located at No. 15 and are renowned for their excellent tailoring.

WOOLRICH 1830
UNITED STATES

In 1830, English immigrant John Rich built a woolen mill in Plum Run, Pennsylvania, and traveled by mule cart to the local lumber camps to sell wool socks, coverlets, fabric, and yarn to the woodsmen. By 1845, a new mill next to the Chatham Run became Woolrich, Pennsylvania, and it is still there today. Innovations include the first zippered men's pants, the Railroad Vest, and the Buffalo Check Shirt.

LODENFREY 1842
GERMANY

A company founded by weaver Johann Georg Frey, known for waterproofed woolen loden cloth that became fashionable for hunting clothes as worn by the Emperor Franz Joseph. The loden coat, a classic Bavarian garment that was finessed in the 1930s, is now made at the company's own factory, on the edge of the Englischer Garten in Munich.

AQUASCUTUM 1851
UK

An outerwear company founded in 1851 by Mayfair tailor John Emary. The name—*aqua*, "water," and *scutum*, "shield"—denotes the waterproofed range worn by King Edward VII and Greta Garbo. In 1987, when Prime Minister Margaret Thatcher visited the USSR, her entire wardrobe was supplied by the brand.

KNIZE 1858
AUSTRIA

This gentlemen's outfitter, the first ever menswear label, has been up and running since 1858 and is one of the historic names in European tailoring, catering to Habsburg archdukes and the well-heeled Viennese. It launched the first branded men's fragrance in 1924, Knize Ten, named after the top handicap in polo. Knize remains in its original concept store designed by modernist architect Adolf Loos in the 1910s.

CERRUTI 1881
ITALY

Antonio Cerruti started up the family-run weaving workshop in Biella, Italy, in 1881 and it has since become a leading fashion brand. The expansion happened in the 1950s when grandson Nino Cerruti took over the company and initiated garment production; the first menswear collection was launched in 1957. In 1978, Cerruti launched Nino Cerruti pour home, a phenomenally successful fragrance for men, followed by Nino Cerruti pour femme in 1987.

TURNBULL & ASSER 1885
UK

Turnbull & Asser was founded in 1885 by hosier Regan Turnbull and Ernest Asser, a salesman offering a bespoke service for the making of gentlemen's clothes from the highest-quality fabrics. During the 1920s, menswear became less formal and the dress shirt was worn without a jacket as an item of clothing in its own right. As demand grew for this new style, Turnbull & Asser focused its business on shirtmaking, for which it is best known today.

TRUZZI 1890
ITALY

Prized Milanese shirtmakers founded by Luigi Truzzi with a shop that opened under the arches of Corso Matteotti in 1928 and favored by distinguished gentlemen such as Clark Gable and the Duke of Windsor. Clients buy shirts with handmade collars and beautifully hand-stitched shoulders, buttonholes, and sleeves, plus side gussets at the hem for reinforcement.

BARBOUR 1894
UK

The classic Barbour waxed jacket has its origins in the Market Place in South Shields, England, where traveling draper John Barbour began supplying oilskins for the local fishing traders and fishermen. The Beacon Oilskin is the forerunner of the classic wax jackets still manufactured by hand in the factory in Simonside, Northumberland.

DAKS 1894
UK

DAKS is derived from the bespoke tailoring shop of Simeon Simpson in London, famed for it Simpson's suits. Simeon's son, Alexander, revolutionized pants design in 1934 by including an adjustable waistband that eliminated the need for belts and braces. In 1976 DAKS launched its distinctive House Check and it remains one of the UK's premier luxury brands.

FILSON 1897
UNITED STATES

C. C. Filson had a small logger's outfitting store in Seattle that took off with the Great Klondike Gold Rush. His mill manufactured Mackinaw clothing, blankets, and knitted goods, and sold boots, shoes, moccasins, and sleeping bags specially designed for the harsh outdoor life of the prospector. It became the premier destination for outdoorsmen, and the Filson Cruiser coat created in 1914 remains a best seller today.

DRIZA-BONE 1898
AUSTRALIA

A rugged authentic outdoors label that made its name with waterproofed outerwear worn on clipper ships and made from sailcloth soaked in linseed oil. The iconic Driza-Bone (dry as a bone) coat was designed for the homesteader when riding and it has a fantail in the back to cover the saddle, wrist straps to secure the sleeves and keep the arms warm, and leg straps to keep the coat secure.

AUSTIN REED 1900
UK

Austin Leonard Reed, the son of a men's clothing retailer from Reading, opened his own London store in 1900 on Fenchurch Street to appeal to the growing numbers of city commuters with its ready-to-wear menswear. In the 1920s, Austin Reed opened its flagship store on Regent Street, where it remains to this day.

J. PRESS 1902
UNITED STATES

In 1902, Latvian immigrant Jacobi Press sold menswear on Yale University campus in New Haven, Connecticut, the location of the company's largest store. J. Press introduced the three-button sack style suit and still stocks classic Ivy League or preppy styles, such as repp stripe ties and cashmere and camel-hair coats.

ANDERSON & SHEPPARD 1906
UK

A leading Savile Row firm established in 1906, known for its fluid English cut developed by Per Anderson. Fred Astaire, Noël Coward, and Gary Cooper were fans of A & S's natural body line, cut to show the style of the wearer rather than impose a rigid silhouette.

SORELLE FONTANA 1907
ITALY

Rome's oldest fashion house, Sorelle Fontana overlooks the Piazza di Spagna and was set up by three dressmaker sisters, Zoe, Micol, and Giovanna, from Traversetolo. In 1907 they opened Sorelle Fontana in Rome and created an Italian version of Dior's New Look, dressing Ava Gardner and Anita Ekberg, who wore a Sorelle Fontana dress in the fountain scene of *La Dolce Vita* (1960).

MADELEINE VIONNET 1912
FRANCE

The House of Vionnet opened in Paris in 1912 and revolutionized fashion through Madeleine Vionnet's bias-cutting, which molded evening gowns to the body, outlining its curves. In 2008, the brand underwent regeneration by Matteo Marzotto and Gianni Castiglioni, who acquired Vionnet so as to re-create its heritage looks within the context of modern fashion.

CARACENI 1913
ITALY

Caraceni, one of the great names of Italian tailoring, was founded in Rome by Domenico Caraceni, and it specializes in bench bespoke suits as worn by actors Humphrey Bogart, Gary Cooper, and Cary Grant. The original shop is under the management of Tommy and Giulio Caraceni, the nephews of Domenico, and branches are run in Milan by other members of the family.

LONDON FOG 1923
UNITED STATES

Established as the Londontown Clothing Company by Israel Myers in 1923, the company was later renamed London Fog and it made waterproof coats for the U.S. Navy during World War II. In the 1950s, thanks to a partnership with DuPont, they launched a successful range of raincoats out of a hard-wearing waterproof cloth with an inner barrier for protection.

BELSTAFF 1924
UK

Belstaff, run by Eli Belovitch and son-in-law Harry Grosberg, in Staffordshire, England, pioneered the use of waxed cotton in the design of all-weather motorcycle jackets, goggles, and gauntlets. The low-shine finish was distinctive and could be rewaxed instead of cleaned for durability. The Trialmaster jacket was launched in 1948.

HIMEL BROTHERS 1927
CANADA

In 1927, Ben, Isaac, and Leo Himel traveled from Piotroków Kujawski, Poland, to Canada and opened a clothing business in Toronto. They became leather specialists and today sell a small line of bespoke leather jackets made from start to finish by one tailor under the aegis of David Himel.

SCHIAPARELLI 1927
ITALY

A feisty single parent from an intellectual Roman background, Elsa Schiaparelli designed clothes and accessories in a Surrealist vein with shock-chic appeal. Her jewelry, fragrance, and accessories remained popular in the interwar years and there are avid collectors of her work today. Her house closed in 1954, but in 2013 it was announced that Christian Lacroix was to design a couture collection of fifteen looks for the fashion house to be shown in Paris.

CAMPAGNOLO 1933
ITALY

In 1922, at the age of twenty-one, Tullio Campagnolo began his amateur cycle racing career. During the 1927 Gran Premio della Vittoria race in the Italian Dolomite mountains his gears seized, prompting Campagnolo to develop the quick-release lever in 1930. His company created some of the earliest branded sportswear, which has been rereleased today in a series of heritage-inspired collections.

CANALI 1934
ITALY

Brothers Giovanni and Giacomo Canali founded a tailoring workshop in Triuggio, Brianza, in 1934. Emphasis is on the cut, and each suit is constructed around a core of camel hair, horse, and *peloncino* to keep the structure in shape. The firm is run by the third generation of the Canali family and all of the output is made in Italy.

NETOUSEK 1935
AUSTRIA

Founded by Viktor Netousek, this bespoke gentlemen's tailors remains family owned and is based in Vienna, providing the city's elite with English-style bespoke suits inspired by the Anderson & Sheppard line, as well as shirts, topcoats, leather accessories, and traditional Austrian Tracht clothing in Loden fabric. Netousek also provides a fitting service for ladies' evening wear.

BRIONI 1945
ITALY

When Nazareno Fonticoli and Gaetano Savini formed Brioni in Rome in 1945, formal dress followed the English mode of tailoring. Brioni, named after a Croatian island and playboy destination, put Italian tailoring on the map, holding the first men's fashion show in 1952 and dressing special agent James Bond, as played by Pierce Brosnan and Daniel Craig.

EDWIN 1947
JAPAN

After World War II, Japanese entrepreneur and denim fan Shuji Tsunemi imported jeans directly from the United States as no denim was manufactured in Japan at that time. The jeans were laundered, mended by hand, and sold to his customers; eventually Tsunemi created his own pair in 1961 and by the 1980s had developed the first "stone-washing" technique.

GITMAN BROS. 1948
UNITED STATES

Gitman Bros. is based in Ashland, Pennsylvania, and manufactures all-American-made shirts. In business since 1948, the company has a large archive that today has been sourced for Gitman Vintage, a line that features the company's distinctive button-down 3 inch (7.5 cm) collars, box pleats with locker hoops, and contrasting bottom buttonholes.

RENATO BALESTRA 1950
ITALY

Renato Balestra is a fashion designer who gained acclaim in 1952, when Italy was rebranded as *la dolce vita*. Today the atelier lies on Via Sistina in Rome and sells ready-to-wear, perfumes, menswear, furniture, and accessories. The house's first fragrance, Balestra, was launched in 1978.

ROBERTO CAPUCCI 1950
ITALY

One of the world's most innovative fashion designers, Roberto Capucci, a.k.a. the Givenchy of Rome, established his own house in 1950. He gained international fame for a signature style of sculpted dresses in unusual materials, including the Colonna of 1978, which was based on the Doric column. From 1980 onward, he formally withdrew from couture and presented only one collection each year in a selected city. Today he works as an artist and couturier in Rome.

GLOVERALL 1951
UK

Gloverall began as H & F Morris, a supplier of industrial work wear until the company realized the potential of the Duffel coat; in the 1950s it became the coat that was worn by the decade's Angry Young Men, beatniks, and trad. jazz enthusiasts. Gloverall moved from selling surplus Duffels to its own iconic design with its horn toggles and checked lining.

INCOTEX 1951
ITALY

Carlo Compagno Confezioni was a Venetian company that first started manufacturing pants and uniforms in 1951. In the 1970s, the company began focusing exclusively on pants and was renamed Incotex. Since then it has been manufacturing meticulously hand-crafted and precision-cut garments at its Industrie Confezioni Tessili factory, including standard chinos in 100 percent cotton.

PUCCI 1951
ITALY

Florentine aristocrat Emilio Pucci had an unexpected start in fashion after a photograph of a friend in the Swiss resort of Zermatt, wearing a ski suit he had designed in 1947, appeared in *Harper's Bazaar*. By 1950, Pucci had opened a boutique on the glamorous Italian island of Capri, selling designs that encapsulated *la dolce vita* with their multicolored print and body-conscious silk jersey.

CANADA GOOSE 1957
CANADA

Canada Goose, one of the greatest makers of outerwear, started as Metro Sportswear Ltd. in a small warehouse run by cutter Sam Tick. A down-filling machine transformed the company, and in 1982 it collaborated with the first Canadian to climb Mount Everest, Laurie Skreslet, on the Big Mountain jacket. One hundred percent of production is in Canada.

KNITWEAR

ROBERT NOBLE 1666
UK

Robert Noble was originally the Galashiels firm of David Ballantyne, which originated in 1666. In 1884, the firm built March Street Mills in Peebles, together with tied housing for its workforce, and a second mill was opened in Walkerburn to weave military tartan. In the 1920s, Ballantyne Sportswear was launched, and a factory specializing in knitwear started up at Innerleithen. In the 1960s, the businesses were consolidated into Scottish Worsted and Woollens and the weaving business was given the name of Robert Noble.

BALLANTYNE 1788
UK

In 1788 Henry Ballantyne established the Tweedvale mill to manufacture Scottish tweed, around which grew the village of Walkerburn. The firm pioneered intarsia knitting in the 1920s and popularized the argyle pattern that appeared in its sweater and sock designs. Today Ballantyne is a prestigious heritage brand known for the high quality of its cashmere knitwear.

JOHNSTONS OF ELGIN 1797
UK

A family-run mill established in Morayshire, Scotland, in 1797, and a pioneer of cashmere and vicuña weaving in Europe. The company is known for its historic manufacture of estate tweeds, including the Lovat mix. The company moved into fully fashioned knitwear in the 1960s, using its own yarns washed and milled in the River Teviot.

GAMMARELLI 1798
ITALY

Behind the Pantheon lies the ecclesiastical tailor, Gammarelli Sartoria, a family firm that has been outfitting popes, cardinals, bishops, and priests since 1798 and is known for its fine merino wool and cotton lisle socks; the ecclesiastical range contains cardinal red, archbishop purple, and priest black. Maximillian Gammarelli asks customers to clench their fist while the sock foot is curled around it, a method of measuring that guarantees a perfect fit.

PRINGLE OF SCOTLAND 1815
UK

Originally a hosiery manufacturer, Pringle of Scotland has always been at the forefront of knitwear innovation, including the intarsia argyle design as worn by the Duke of Windsor. Pringle also coordinated the sweater and cardigan to create the classic twinset. In 2000, the business entered a new era when Clare Waight Keller was appointed creative director and Pringle began to compete as a global luxury brand.

DEVOLD 1853
NORWAY

In 1853 Ole Andreas Devold founded a textile factory in Ålesund, manufacturing scarves, mittens, underwear, and knitted hats, including the traditional red cap, or Rødhua. The company then moved into work wear; the first garment was a fisherman's coarse-meshed sweater known as the Islender. In 1866, the Blaatrøie was introduced and, although originally designed for sailors, it became a popular leisure garment. Today Devold produces high-quality wool garments for the great outdoors.

SUNSPEL 1860
UK

Thomas A. Hill founded the company now known as Sunspel in Nottingham, England, in 1860 to manufacture undergarments from Egyptian cotton instead of the traditional wool. Sunspel is generally recognized to have invented the T-shirt, and during the war years was a supplier to the Royal Air Force. In 2005, the company was bought by Nicholas Brooke and Dominic Hazlehurst, who expanded the range by launching a womenswear line and opened retail stores.

ZIMMERLI 1871
SWITZERLAND

Pauline Zimmerli Bäurlin was a female entrepreneur who took advantage of the innovative Lamb knitting machine of 1866 and started manufacturing fine-gauge hosiery and men's socks, ribbed fabric, and underwear in Aarburg, Switzerland, using agents to sell her products around the world. Today the company manufactures luxurious underwear in materials such as mercerized cotton and fine twisted cotton yarn.

ANDERSON & CO 1873
UK

Anderson & Co is a long-established family firm, founded in 1873 by Thomas Anderson, which trades in classic seamless Shetland knitwear and hand-knitted Shetland shawls. The garments are made on a group of islands off the Scottish mainland, and traditional Fair Isle patterns are knitted in the round with designs handed down through the generations.

HAWICK CASHMERE 1874
UK

Hawick Cashmere was originally the Hawick Hosiery Company, founded in Trinity Mills in 1874, and it still manufactures every garment in the same factory today. It is known for its luxury knitwear made using the finest-quality yarns sold from its fifteen stores, including St. Moritz and Tokyo. Every style can be ordered in forty-nine colors.

SCHIESSER 1875
GERMANY

The first Schiesser hosiery workshop was founded by Jacques Schiesser in 1875 in a rented ballroom in the German town of Radolfzell. The initial nine circular knitting frames developed into a factory for weaving and dyeing tricot and employed nearly 300 workers. The company is known for its "second-skin" micro-fiber underwear and has more than 200 retail outlets across the world.

PETER SCOTT 1878
UK

Peter Scott, a former knitwear apprentice, founded his namesake company in 1878, at first manufacturing Pesco Knitted Underwear. Today it remains the largest privately owned knitwear manufacturer in the historic town of Hawick in Scotland and creates collections of classic styles for both men and women in cashmere, geelong, lambswool, and pure merino wool.

SAINT JAMES 1889
FRANCE

The classic Breton pure-wool striped sweater was created by Saint James, a firm established in Lower Normandy in the commune of Saint-James, close to Mont Saint-Michel in 1889. It was an item of work wear designed for deep-sea fishermen, but in the 1930s it was adopted by amateur yachtsmen and became a fashion item. Saint James has boutiques throughout France and also in New York, Tokyo, and Osaka.

CORGI 1893
UK

Tradesman Rhys Jones opened a small drapers, Ford Mills, in West Wales in 1893 and transformed his business after buying several second-hand Griswald hand-operated circular knitting machines to manufacture thick, thigh-high woolen socks for the local colliers and a finer version for chapel on Sundays. By the 1920s, the firm was exporting its fashionable argyle socks internationally, and Corgi Hosiery Limited was born. In 1989 Corgi was awarded a royal warrant by his Royal Highness, the Prince of Wales.

FALKE 1895
GERMANY

Franz Falke-Rohen founded his first knitting mill in 1895, which, when taken over by his son, also named Franz, in 1902, began to manufacture hosiery.

After World War I, the father-and-son team bought out the yarn-spinning mill of Carl Meisenburg based in Schmallenberg, now known as FALKE, and began the expansion of the label. FALKE is the leader in women's luxury knee-highs, stockings, and pantyhose, as well as men's knitted garments including sportswear.

BALTHASAR MERZ 1911
GERMANY

The German tradition of knitwear emanates from the Swabian Mountains, a result of the government providing knitting machines for farmers in the region after their land became infertile in around 1850. This is the lineage of the Balthasar Merz knitwear label, a company that began as Merz b. Schwanen in 1911 and is run by Peter Plotnicki today.

LE MONT SAINT MICHEL 1913
FRANCE

French label Le Mont Saint Michel, named after its location, was founded in 1913 to manufacture high-quality work clothes and became known for its traditional knitwear. After Alexandre Milan was appointed creative director in 2001, attracted by the brand's authenticity, the range was extended to include womenswear, menswear, childrenswear, and accessories.

AVON CELLI 1922
ITALY

Milanese knitwear brand Avon Celli was founded by Pasquale Celli, who used stocking looms to manufacture super-fine knitwear and went on to innovate a yarn composed of cashmere and silk woven on thirty-six gauge looms. Avon Celli knitwear has been worn by stars such as Grace Kelly, Sophia Loren, and Frank Sinatra, and Pablo Picasso was reputed to paint in an Avon Celli polo shirt.

HARLEY OF SCOTLAND 1929
UK

Peter Harley Buchan established Harley of Scotland in 1929 after being inspired by traditional Fair Isle knitting when visiting Orkney, Shetland, and the Fair Isles. Every sweater had unique colors and patterns that were used as a means of identifying the owner if lost at sea. Harley was set up to manufacture Fair Isle knitwear using super-soft, light yarns, including an innovative merino wool bouclé twist.

S.N.S HERNING 1931
DENMARK

In 1931 Søren Nielsen Skyt set up a business in Herning, Denmark, selling his own hand-knitted garments using a technique of "bobble" patterns that increased the garment's properties of insulation. He parlayed his ideas into the fisherman's sweater, created to withstand the harsh conditions at sea.

FEDELI 1934
ITALY

Originally a knit hat maker situated in Monza, run by father and son Luigi and Nino Fedeli. After studying knitwear manufacturing in Scotland, new machinery was introduced to produce their signature plait patterned sweater. From the 1960s, the brand gained a reputation for its high-quality cashmere items, sold through its now-historic Via Montenapoleone boutique in Milan.

ARMOR–LUX 1938
FRANCE

Armor-Lux is an underwear brand of exceptional quality manufactured by Bonneterie d'Armor, founded in 1938 by Swiss-German businessman Walter Hubacher. Its first ready-to-wear collection was launched in 1970 and showed Breton-style knits, striped mariner shirts, mariner jumpers, and reefer jackets. In 1982, Armor-Lux opened its own-brand shops, with all production carried out in France.

PANTHERELLA 1945
UK

The history of the hosiery manufacturer Pantherella can be traced back to 1937 when the former Midland Hosiery Mills, a manufacturer of women's hosiery, changed its name to Pantherella, and founder Louis Goldschmidt began to provide fine-knit socks for men. Pantherella socks are still 100 percent made in England at the production facilities in Leicester, England.

NORDSTRIKK 1963
NORWAY

In the town of Ålesund on the west coast of Norway lies a company that has been in the same family for fifty years, creating traditional knitwear using native wool for the Norwegian and international markets. Patterns include the well-known Selbu, and cardigans are fastened with the distinctive Norwegian pewter clasps.

VOLUND 1965
NORWAY

Volund is named after the ancient Nordic blacksmith who forged invincible arms and stunning jewelry; in its infancy, the business was a mill manufacturing hosiery in the village of Løkken Verk in Norway. The family-owned company, with only ten employees, now produces up to 20,000 traditional Norwegian sweaters per year.

FOOTWEAR

CHURCH'S 1675
UK

The Church family has made shoes since 1675. In 1873, Thomas Church and his three sons formally established the firm, and in 1884 it gained fame for its "Adaptable" shoe, "in six widths in every conceivable style and material," with a designated left and right fit instead of the usual "straights." In 1999, Prada acquired the brand.

MEINDL 1683
GERMANY

Meindl shoes are deeply rooted in their home country of Germany, in Kirchanschöring, where Petrus Meindl started working as the family's first shoemaker in 1683. The Meindl Company was established by Lukas Meindl in 1928 and gained fame for its Alpine hiking and nonskid waterproof hunting boots.

TRICKER'S 1829
UK

A Northampton-based shoe and boot manufacturer set up by Joseph Barltrop in 1829 and run by descendant Nicholas Barltrop today. The production is small and of extremely high quality, and the most well-known products are hand-welted bench-made brogues and brogued boots for both country and city wear.

FOSTER & SON 1840
UK

Foster & Son of Jermyn Street, London, is one of the few bespoke shoemakers to remain in private ownership and it is known globally for the highest standards of craftsmanship. In 1999 Foster joined forces with the leather goods name of Barrow and Hepburn Ltd. and the boot and shoemaker Henry Maxwell.

JOHNSTON & MURPHY 1850
UNITED STATES

Johnston & Murphy, founded by William A. Murphy in Newark, New Jersey, is known for the spectator shoe available in white buckskin with tan or black trim. Spectators were worn by African American jazz musicians in the 1920s, including Duke Ellington and Louis Armstrong; Johnston & Murphy references these roots by using Wynton Marsalis in its advertising.

GRENSON 1866
UK

The founder William Green, born in 1835, was taught how to make shoes by his mother before setting himself up as a factor, or middleman, taking orders for the client and relaying them to the craftsman. This provided the basis for his company, William Green & Son and he opened a factory in Northampton in 1874. The brand name Grenson was registered in 1913.

BLUNDSTONE 1870
AUSTRALIA

In 1853, James and Thomas Cuthbertson sailed from England on the *Corramandel* bound for Melbourne but were blown off course and landed in Hobart Town in Tasmania. They set up a shoemaking and importing business, buying out Blundstone and Son in 1902 and retaining the name. They are specifically known for their full-grain leather elastic-sided dress boot.

STACY ADAMS 1875
UNITED STATES

The Stacy Adams Shoe Company was founded in Brockton, Massachusetts, in 1875 by William H. Stacy and Henry L. Adams and created some of the most flamboyant spectator styles of the 1930s, including the Dayton. The revival of interest in swing dancing in the 1980s led to a rediscovery of the classic two-tone Dayton Wingtip.

G.H. BASS 1876
UNITED STATES

Maine-based G.H. Bass & Co. originated as a boot and moccasin maker catering to loggers and woodsmen. In the 1930s, Bass spotted an imported flat moccasin-topped slip-on shoe worn by Norwegian farmers. He adapted the shoe for casual wear with a hand-sewn front, leather soles and heels with a leather band in the front of the shoe. Launched in 1936, this was the Bass Weejun, a U.S. classic.

CROCKETT & JONES 1879
UK

Charles Jones and his brother-in-law, James Crockett, were given a grant of £100 each from the Thomas White Trust, created "to encourage young men of good character in the towns of Northampton and Coventry to set up business on their own." They opened a small bootmaking factory in Northampton and introduced Goodyear welting in the 1890s. The firm continues to make fine footwear today.

JUSTIN 1875
UNITED STATES

Justin started in 1875 as a small boot repair operation at the end of the Chisholm Trail, where cowboys would drop off one pair of boots to be mended and pick them up on the way back. Today Justin is an umbrella for a number of brands, including original competitor Tony Lama Boots, and still creates authentic U.S. boots for men and women.

BARKER 1880
UK

Northamptonshire boot maker Arthur Barker created peg-sole boots in which the pegs swelled when wet and made the sole waterproof. They became so popular that he employed other craftsmen in surrounding villages to satisfy the demand. After supplying the British army with boots during World War I, the brand expanded, and a new factory was built in Earls Barton in 1947. Barker manufactures 200,000 pairs of hand-lasted shoes per year.

ALDEN 1884
UNITED STATES

The Alden Shoe Company manufactures classic men's footwear and is known for its use of genuine shell cordovan, a hand-finished leather that undergoes a six-month vegetable tanning process. Alden works shell cordovan into hand-crafted shoes that retain a rich deep patina that improves with age.

LUDWIG REITER 1885
AUSTRIA

Karlsbad-born Ludwig Reiter I and his wife, Anna, founded the Ludwig Reiter shoemakers and workshop in Vienna in 1885, making dress shoes and boots for military officers. His son, Ludwig Reiter II, learned the shoe trade in Germany, England, and the United States, including the Goodyear welting technique. In 1909 Reiter returned to Vienna and it is still known today for its welted shoes.

CHEANEY 1886
UK

In 1886 Joseph Cheaney founded the J. Cheaney Boot and Shoemakers Company in Station Road, Desborough, England, and was joined by his sons, Arthur and Harold, in 1903. In 2009, John and William Church, who remain committed to making fine shoes entirely in the United Kingdom, bought out Cheaney.

CAPEZIO 1887
ITALY

The most renowned purveyor of ballet shoes is Salvatore Capezio, a native of Italy who had immigrated to the United States in the 1880s. He became a cobbler and opened a shop on New York's Broadway and 39th Street. The Metropolitan Opera House was directly opposite so Capezio began to repair theatrical shoes, including ballet pointes, eventually making his own as worn by Anna Pavlova. In the 1950s, a hard sole was added to the shoe and it became the ballet flat.

J.M. WESTON 1891
FRANCE

In homage to the reputation of traditional English shoemaking, a French company, founded in 1891 by Édouard Blanchard, was renamed J. M. Weston in 1922. These are the shoes worn by the political elite of France; François Mitterrand had thirty pairs of Weston's signature loafer, and Nicolas Sarkozy wears its Claridge Oxfords.

MASSARO 1894
FRANCE

Sébastien Massaro was the first in a dynasty of shoemakers working from 2 Rue de la Paix in Paris from 1894. Lazarus Massaro made bespoke footwear for the Duchess of Windsor and Marlene Dietrich, and worked with the couture house of Madame Grès. Raymond Massaro created the iconic two-tone slingback for Coco Chanel.

CLEVERLEY 1898
UK

George Cleverley was a London-born shoemaker who worked at Tuczec in Mayfair, where he remained for thirty-eight years. In 1958, Cleverley set up his own business, G. J. Cleverley & Co., in Cork Street. His trademark, the so-called Cleverley shape, was an elegant bespoke shoe with a chisel toe. Today the firm makes bespoke, semi-bespoke, and bench-made shoes.

ALFRED SARGENT 1899
UK

Established in 1899 by Alfred Sargent and his sons, Frank and Harry, the company has worked out of the same premises in Rushden, Northamptonshire, since 1915, making hand-crafted Goodyear-welted calf-leather and suede shoes and boots for more than four generations. It offers a full refurbishment service, ranging from a complete resole and reheel to a refinishing of the edges and uppers.

RED WING 1905
UNITED STATES

The Red Wing Shoe Company has built a reputation for making tough, comfortable footwear ever since shoe merchant Charles Beckman saw a gap in the market for durable yet wearable mining, logging, and farming boots. Today, premium Red Wing leather shoes and boots are tanned at the company's S. B. Foot Tanning Company and are triple stitched with waxed thread.

SANITA 1907
DENMARK

In 1907 a clog maker, Christian Meldgaard Andersen, opened a shop in Herning, Denmark, to manufacture wooden clogs with leather uppers, and traveled around the town by bicycle to sell his wares. Clog woods with a sheepskin lining were introduced in the 1970s. The firm sole and stapled upper has not changed since 1907.

GRAVATI 1909
ITALY

Gravati is a family firm of shoemakers based in Vigevano, Italy, whose classic handmade shoes for men and women use either Bologna, Goodyear, or the lighter Blake construction. All patterns are clicked, lasted, and finished by hand. Unusually, the firm does not maintain any stock; shoes are made entirely on commission.

QUODDY 1909
UNITED STATES

In 1909 Harry Smith Shorey embarked on a business making footwear with hand-sewn moccasin construction inspired by the Passamaquoddy of Maine. They were sold to local huntsmen and through retailers such as L. L. Bean. The Ringboot became the footwear of choice of members of the hippie movement in the 1960s.

BALDININI 1910
ITALY

Baldinini dates back to 1910 when the family firm began to make bespoke shoes in San Mauro Pascoli on Italy's Adriatic coast. Three generations later, the company has more than 100 stores around the world and employs more than 250 highly skilled craftsmen creating embroidered, painted, and hand-tooled footwear. The leather stack-heeled Baldinini Mule of 1974 is the firm's best-known design.

TONY LAMA 1911
UNITED STATES

At the turn of the twentieth century, cobbler Tony Lama joined the U.S. army to mend the boots of soldiers stationed at Fort Bliss, Texas. In 1911, Lama set up a business in El Paso making custom boots, which took off in the 1930s when Western-wear stores began to stock them in order to cater to tourists vacationing at dude ranches.

ARTIOLI 1912
ITALY

Severino Artioli was a master shoemaker in Ferrara, Italy, when he opened his business in 1912. He was an expert in fashioning leather and was committed to improving the tools of his trade. Vito Artioli was one of the first to develop a slip-on shoe with elastic under the tongue in the 1950s, so that it could be adjusted according to the width of the feet, and also elasticized lacing for city shoes such as the Oxford and Derby. Artioli pioneered "lost wax" cast metal trim to embellish vamps, heels, and outsoles.

WESCO 1918
UNITED STATES

John Henry Shoemaker learned the bootmaking trade at Rindgen, Kalmbach, Logie & Co. in Grand Rapids, Michigan, making boots for loggers, before working for the Goodyear Shoe Company. In 1918 he set up the West Coast Shoe Company (Wesco) to make good quality footwear, saying, "A shoe is no better than the leather it is made of—and all the leather on the market is not worth a 'whoop' where there is no shoemaking skill."

ALLEN EDMONDS 1922
UNITED STATES

Allen Edmonds is an upscale shoe manufacturer based in Port Washington, Wisconsin, dating from 1922 and specializing in men's dress shoes. The brand rose to prominence during World War II, when it supplied footwear to the U.S. army and navy and developed a loyal fan base. Its shoes are known for their durability, and the company offers a rebuilding service.

ANELLO & DAVIDE 1922
UK

A bespoke shoe shop founded in Covent Garden, London, in 1922 that specializes in handmade footwear. In the early 1960s, Anello & Davide adapted a Chelsea boot for The Beatles by adding a Cuban heel, leading to the birth of the Beatle boot. It was so successful that customers queued around the block. The boot was worn by Bob Dylan and, more recently, by the Kings of Leon.

NOCONA BOOTS 1925
UNITED STATES

Nocona Boots was founded by Enid Justin in 1925 to carry on the tradition started by her father H. J. "Daddy Joe" Justin, making high-quality Western boots in Spanish Fort, close to the Chisholm Trail. Daddy Joe started mending the boots of the cattle drivers and cowboys, and the coming of the railway in 1887 made him move to Nocona to increase trade. Daughter Enid joined her father at the age of twelve and after his death in 1918 went on to found Nocona Boots. In 1981, Nocona Boots merged with Justin Industries.

CASTAÑER 1927
SPAIN

A family firm that has been producing traditional espadrilles since 1927. After meeting Yves Saint Laurent in Paris in 1972, Lorenzo and Isabel Castañer converted their vernacular shoes into fashion accessories by using primary-colored canvas uppers, high wedges, and overlong cotton ties. Today Castaner is a high-end label making espadrilles for Hermès, Louis Vuitton, Christian Louboutin, Coach, and Kate Spade.

COLE HAAN 1928
UNITED STATES

Cole Haan was set up in Chicago and, after being bought out by Nike in 1988, still manufactures the original designs of the interwar period, including the spectator shoe: a two-tone Oxford shoe with black, brown, or tan leather at the toe cap, back quarter, and instep, and white or tan suede or buckskin at the front and sides.

ACME 1929
UNITED STATES

The Acme Shoe Manufacturing Company was founded in 1929 by father and son Jessel and Sidney Cohen, who manufactured children's sandals under the brand name Just-Kids. In 1935, after seeing expensive cowboy boots when on a business trip to Texas, Jessel Cohen began making cheaper versions on an assembly line. After being renamed Acme Boots, the company became the largest maker of cowboy boots from the 1940s to 1980s. In 2002, H. H. Brown bought the brand.

MAGRIT 1929
SPAIN

Established in Elde, Alicante, in 1929 by Spaniard José Amat Sanchez to manufacture women's shoes, Magrit is a family-owned high-end label that makes hand-finished shoes under its own label and collaborates with brands such as Bally, L.K. Bennett, and Donna Karan. Designs include sandals, peep toes, cork wedges, and pumps in python skin and water snake.

K. JACQUES 1933
FRANCE

This small workshop run by shoemaker Jacques Keklikian opened in 1933 in Saint-Tropez when it was a small fishing village, and catered to local fishermen who wanted sandals that could stand the wear and tear of the beach. Keklikian makes hand-stitched leather sandals, including the Darius gladiator that became well known after being worn by resident Brigitte Bardot.

MARIO BRUNI 1935
ITALY

In 1935, a small shoe-making operation manufacturing forty pairs of shoes per day was set up in Montegranaro, Italy, and by the 1970s had become the shoe brand Mario Bruni, which still uses many of its original production methods. Every process, from clicking through lasting to finishing, is carried out at the company's premises in Italy.

BRUNO MAGLI 1936
ITALY

The Magli family, including brothers Bruno and Marini and their sister Maria, began making women's shoes in a basement in Bologna, Italy, and the first workshop opened in 1936. The original Magli boutique opened in 1947 in Bologna, where the popular Magli moccasin was sold, and by the 1950s it was known for its stiletto-heeled winklepicker shoes. Magli is now privately held by an investment company and is a brand leader in exclusive men's and women's footwear, leather clothing, and accessories.

ROGER VIVIER 1937
FRANCE

Known as the Fabergé of footwear, Roger Vivier worked with Christian Dior in the early 1950s, designing shoes to complement the romantic silhouette of the New Look (see page 254). His immaculately tailored shoes fitted the foot perfectly and the heels were sculpted into an array of shapes, including the earliest stilettos. In 1965, Vivier created the Pilgrim Pump, still made by the firm today, a flat shoe with a square tapered toe and low stacked heel.

DAYTON 1946
CANADA

In 1965 the Dayton Black Beauty, a double-soled motorcycle boot, hit the market and it continues to be one of the firm's most popular models today. The Dayton double-soled classic Engineer boot with Goodyear-welted construction, reckoned to be the toughest ever made, debuted in 1978.

MINNETONKA 1946
UNITED STATES

The Native American moccasin was adopted by traders and European settlers, and by the twentieth century moccasins had become popular tourist souvenirs. Minnetonka, a company based in Minnesota, became the breakthrough manufacturer, and the Minnetonka Thunderbird, a hand-stitched moccasin in hide or deerskin with soft soles, was a best seller.

MORESCHI 1946
ITALY

Moreschi has grown from a small family-run shoe factory established in 1946 in Vigevano, a city in the province of Lombardy, into one of the most renowned of Italian brands. All production still takes place in Vigevano and includes handmade Goodyear-welted footwear, clothing, leather goods, and accessories.

SEBAGO 1946
UNITED STATES

The Sebago-Moc Company was established by Daniel J. Wellehan, Sr., William Beaudoin, and Joseph Cordeau. The Sebago hand-sewn penny loafer was inspired by the Native American moccasin and the shoe pioneered the company's patented welt construction. The Dockside boat shoe has become a shoe classic.

BERNARDO 1947
UNITED STATES

Bernardo is credited by some with the invention of the modern women's sandal and thus for helping to free up the foot. Around the same time as the company was established in 1947 by Bernard Rudofsky, the Miami sandal was launched, as later worn by Jackie O., Jane Birkin, and Twiggy. All sandals are handmade.

REPETTO 1947
FRANCE

The renowned Repetto Company was launched in 1947. Madame Rosa Repetto, at the behest of her son, dancer and choreographer Roland Petit, sought to design a more comfortable pair of ballet shoes. She came up with a new method of construction, the innovative "stitch and return" technique that gave an invisible join between the sole and the upper and was said to feel almost like wearing no shoes at all. The technique is still employed in Repetto's pointe shoes and ballerinas today.

GINA 1954
UK

Gina, formerly Mexico Shoes, was one of Europe's first manufacturers of the stiletto heel, and it still operates from the same premises in the East End of London today. In the early 1950s, owner Mehmet Kurdash used Hollis wood heels with a metal spigot to make the thinnest of heels. Today Gina handmakes high-end shoes, boots, and bags, and offers a couture service.

ATTILIO GIUSTI LEOMBRUNI 1958
ITALY

In 1958, Piero Giusti opened a small factory manufacturing footwear in Montegranaro, in the Marche region of Italy. After graduating from medical school his son joined the firm, and today Giusti's granddaughters, Sara, Vera, and Marianna, are in charge. Attilio Giusti Leombruni is known for its use of high-quality leather and artisan craftsmanship mixed with innovative technical solutions, as well as a commitment to eco friendly values.

BOCCACCINI 1959
ITALY

A family-run shoe business based in Milan that utilizes exotic leathers such as python, crocodile, and ostrich. In 1987, Alfredo Boccaccini launched L'Autre Chose, a successful range that was stocked at Barneys, New York, and the firm began a series of collaborations with Patrick Cox, Martin Margiela, and Alexander McQueen. The company has recently moved into ready-to-wear with collections designed by Michela Casadei, the first of which was launched in Autumn-Winter 2005.

UGGLEBO 1965
SWEDEN

In the late 1960s, Swedish company Ugglebo started to sell clogs to Eskil Gidholm, the founder of Eskil's Clog Shop, exporting their traditional footwear into the United States. Hippies loved this premium clog, and the company went from strength to strength as the style became fashionable all over the world. Today the Ugglebo wooden clog with leather upper can be bought in a variety of different styles.

ACCESSORIES

KURASHIKI KAGURAYA 1570
JAPAN

Kurashiki is the "Venice of Japan," an old market town at the foot of Mt. Tsurugata where fields of igura or rush reeds are harvested every year to make the traditional tatami mat. During the Edo period it was home to weavers such as Kaguraya, the world's earliest brand, which from 1570 wove the reeds into tatami mats. Today the same Edo weaving techniques are used in the production of the handmade Kaguraya bag.

GARRARD 1735
UK

George Wickes first entered his mark at Goldsmiths' Hall in 1722. He went into business on his own in 1735, and shortly after was appointed as goldsmith to the Prince of Wales. In 1802, Robert Garrard took control of the firm and was succeeded by his sons, Robert Garrard II, James, and Sebastian, in 1818. In 1843, Garrard became crown jeweler to Queen Victoria and in 1911 made Queen Mary's coronation crown, one of many important royal commissions.

CHRISTYS' 1773
UK

Scotsman Miller Christy traveled to London in 1773 after being apprenticed to a hatter in Edinburgh, and set up a firm of hat makers with Joseph Storrs in Whitehart Court selling silk hats; the firm also set up a factory in Stockport making wool and fur felt hats. Today Christys' is owned by Liberty of London and sells an extensive range of classic headgear.

BREGUET 1775
FRANCE

A. L. Breguet, born in Neuchâtel, Switzerland, founded this firm of fine watchmakers in Paris in 1775. He was a natural innovator, developing the first self-winding perpétuelle watches, and introducing gongs for repeating watches, the first shock protection for balance pivots, and the first carriage clock, which was sold to Napoleon Bonaparte. Breguet's early customers also included Louis XVI and Marie-Antoinette. The world's first wristwatch was designed by Breguet in 1810 for the queen of Naples, Caroline Murat.

DENTS 1777
UK

Dents has been hand-crafting leather gloves since 1777 in Worcester, England, and the skills of hand cutting and stitching are still practiced by the firm today; its best-known commission was for Queen Elizabeth II's embroidered leather coronation gloves. Today Dents still uses hand felling, a method of attaching the cuff of the glove to its lining with invisible stitching. Its collection also includes belts, handbags, hats, scarves, and serapes.

ASPREY 1781
UK

The luxury goods house of Asprey was founded in Mitcham, Surrey, by William Asprey in 1781 and a store was opened six years later in New Bond Street, London. Royal commissions followed, carried out by artisans including silversmiths, jewelers, leatherworkers, and watchmakers who, as today, operated in workshops above the store.

GOYARD 1792
FRANCE

Goyard evolved from the House of Martin, which was established by trunk-maker Pierre-François Martin in 1792. Former apprentice François Goyard took over the firm in 1852, opening workshops where he could control production from start to finish. Goyard still makes luggage, including handmade trunks, and customers have included Coco Chanel and Pablo Picasso.

TONAK 1799
CZECH REPUBLIC

Tonak is based in Nový Jičín, formerly in Hungary, and manufactures woolen and fur felt hats. The company was founded by Johann Nepomuk Hückel, who by 1865 had installed new felting machines for the production of headwear, including fezzes. In 1869 the business was taken over by a public company, J. Hückel and Sons, and remained so until it was nationalized and renamed Tonak.

PITTARDS 1826
UK

In 1826, Charles Pittard started up as a leather dresser in Yeovil, Somerset. The company went on to experiment with different leathers, including the soft cabretta skin used to create pilot's gloves in the 1940s, washable dress leather in the 1950s, and water resistant WR100 leather in the 1980s. It is renowned for its stunning leather gloves and sporting gloves used in golf, riding, and baseball.

CHRISTOFLE 1830
FRANCE

Christofle was the first firm to introduce electroplated silver and methods of coloring the metal through enamel, brass, and lacquer finishes. Due to Christofle's habit of commissioning avant-garde artists such as the Surrealists Man Ray and Jean Cocteau, and Italian designer and architect Giò Ponti to design its wares, the firm has a body of work that reflects the changing tastes of the last two centuries and beyond. Jewelery designers include Christian Ghion and Adeline Cacheux.

LONGINES 1832
SWITZERLAND

Auguste Agassiz made and sold pocket watches with crown-wheel escapements from a workshop in Saint-Imier, Switzerland, and crafted his first movement in 1867, winning an award at the Universal Exhibition in Paris. The firm pioneered the mechanization of watches, thus making Switzerland the center of the trade, and became a specialist in high-precision time keeping as displayed in its watches today.

TIFFANY 1837
UNITED STATES

The Tiffany jewelry brand and luxury store was founded in New York by Charles Lewis Tiffany and John B. Young. In 1902, Tiffany's son, Louis Comfort Tiffany, an accomplished designer and proponent of Art Nouveau in the United States, became the company's first art director. His work used themes from the natural world, including butterflies and wild carrot flowers; garnets were used to form blackberries and grapes. Tiffany is known for commissioning designs from names such as Frank Gehry, Paloma Picasso, and Elsa Peretti.

ROECKL 1839
GERMANY

Founded in 1839 by master leatherworker Jakob Roeckl, who invented a method of tanning leather to make it extremely soft that was used in the production of gloves. By the late nineteenth century, the company had a number of factories manufacturing gloves for home and abroad, and the first store opened in 1910 in Munich. Roeckl is known for its high-performance sports gloves.

A. LANGE & SÖHNE 1845
GERMANY

Ferdinand Adolph Lange set up the firm of Lange in Glashütte, Germany, in 1845. After his death, sons Emil and Richard crafted quality pocket watches and aviator watches during World War II. In 1948, the postwar Soviet administration expropriated the company's property and closed the brand, but after the fall of the Berlin Wall in 1989, the founder's great-grandson, Walter Lange, rebuilt the company, presenting its first range of wristwatches in 1994.

MARIA GASPARI 1850
ITALY

A family firm based in a medieval castle in Valenza, Italy, handmaking important jewelry. The tradition of Italian commerce meant that women could not own a business, so it was not until the twentieth century that the Cadabra family named the brand after Maria Gaspari. Today it is run by her daughter, Odile Gaspari, who has introduced a more affordable line that includes gem-studded watches.

BEERMANN 1856
GERMANY

The Hut-Atelier Beermann has been situated on Wandsbeker Marktstraße 18 in Hamburg since 1856 and it is run by the sixth generation of the family, Sabine Beermann. Beerman sells well-known hat brands, such as Borsalino, antique models, and takes commissions for bespoke. It also offers a repair and reblocking service.

BOUCHERON 1858
FRANCE

In 1858, this family dynasty was founded in Paris by Frederic Boucheron, who reputedly chose the sunniest side of the Place Vendôme in Paris so that the diamonds in the windows of his jewelry house would glitter in spectacular fashion. The house style comprised heavy floral designs picked out in diamonds, and in 1889 designer Paul LeGrand first conceived the idea of stringing pearls alongside diamond rondelle separators.

SZASZI 1858
AUSTRIA

Hungarian hatter Michael Szászy traveled to Vienna and set up shop in 1858 to manufacture bespoke silk top hats for the gentlemen of the city. In the early twentieth century, the shop fell into the hands of Franz and Josefine Caletka, who ran it for the next thirty years. With no heir, the business passed to former apprentice Shmuel Schapira, who continues the tradition of bespoke and thus exclusive gentlemen's hats.

CHOPARD 1860
SWITZERLAND

Louis Ulysse-Chopard set up a workshop in the Swiss town of Sonvilier to make fine watches for a refined clientele. The firm was inherited through the family, and in 1937 moved to Geneva. Louis's grandson, Paul, took the helm in 1943. The Scheufele dynasty took over in 1963 and has since expanded the brand into one of the leading names in deluxe watchmaking and jewelry.

PANERAI 1860
ITALY

Not only did Giovanni Panerai open his first watchmaker's shop on Ponte delle Grazie in Florence, but he also inducted the city's first watchmaking school. In 1916, Officine Panerai invented Radiomir, a radium-based powder used by the Italian navy to make the dials of their sighting instruments luminous, and it was used for the first time in the frogman's watch of 1936.

TAG HEUER 1860
SWITZERLAND

Twenty-year-old Edouard Heuer opened a workshop in the Jura, Switzerland, in 1860, and an outlet in London sixteen years later. In 1887, Tag Heuer patented the oscillating pinion for stopwatches, which is still used in some of the firm's movements, followed by the waterproof watch casing of 1895. In 1911, the brand launched the Time of Travel, the first dashboard chronograph for the airplane and automobile, and in 1912 moved into women's wristwatches. Tag Heuer stopwatches also became the official timers used in the Olympic Games and in 1992 the company became the official time keeper of the Formula One World Championships.

JUNGHANS 1861
GERMANY

After the company was founded by Erhard Junghans in the Black Forest town of Schramberg in 1861, it went on to become the largest watchmaker in Germany, launching its first quartz wristwatch, the Astro-Quartz, in 1970. From 1956, Junghans collaborated with modernist designer Max Bill on a range of time keeping devices that have become icons of German design—one of his wall clocks is featured in the collection of the Museum of Modern Art in New York.

BULOVA 1875
UNITED STATES

Joseph Bulova was a young Czech immigrant who opened a jewelry shop on Maiden Lane in New York City. By the early twentieth century, it sold clocks and pocket watches, and in 1912 Bulova set up a factory in Bienne, Switzerland, to manufacture components. In 1919, the firm introduced the first line of men's jeweled wristwatches, followed by ladies' in 1924, and in 1961 the innovative Accutron, the first electronic watch.

CHANTELLE 1876
FRANCE

A French lingerie brand that dates back to 1876 and is known for a series of revolutionary innovations, including the use of two-way stretch elasticized fabrics in corsetry and the first girdle in 1902. In the 1950s, the Chantelle girdle was advertised as the one "that never rides up"; Chantelle's first bras were launched in 1960.

WITTING 1876
NETHERLANDS

In 1876, H. Witting founded a cap factory on Oosterstraat 51 in Groningen to manufacture high-quality caps, which attracted attention because of their excellent fit. Witting moved into fashion accessories, and in the 1930s the firm was first taken over by the Nissink family and then by former employee Arnold Frits Bakker in 1960. His sons, Sietze and Arnold, now run the concern.

BREITLING 1884
SWITZERLAND

Breitling is a leader in watch technology and remains the only watch brand to give all models precise chronometer-certified movements developed and manufactured in its own workshops. It was founded in the Jura, Switzerland, in 1884 by Leon Breitling, who went on to design the first chronograph push-piece used in timers for sport and in aviation. The firm continues to pursue technical innovation.

FABERGÉ 1885
RUSSIA

Known as the purveyor of luxury jeweled eggs for the Russian royal family, Peter Carl Fabergé was a jeweler of international renown, particularly for designs that combined hand enameling with machine-made guilloché metal backgrounds and rose-cut diamonds. In 2009, Tatiana and Sarah Fabergé, great-granddaughters of the founder, launched the first Fabergé jewelry collection for ninety years, Les Fabuleuses.

ADLER 1886
TURKEY

In 1886 Jacques Adler of Vienna opened an atelier in the goldsmiths' quarter of Istanbul and it gained fame with its *haute joaillerie*, combining themes from the East and West. Today the firm is run by the third and fourth generations of the family and the center of operations is in Switzerland.

WALTER WRIGHT 1889
UK

Walter Wright came from a long line of Huguenot hatmakers who settled in London in the seventeenth century. The firm of 1889 initially supplied wholesalers and shops, concentrating on the philosophy of volume but always with good quality. Today Philip Wright creates bespoke headwear, aside from the wholesale business, with a team of highly skilled milliners in Luton, England.

EL CABALLO 1892
SPAIN

El Caballo is a Spanish business that originated in 1892 from a family firm in the Arenal port of Seville selling agricultural equipment, followed by hunting and riding equipment. The firm transitioned to equestrian-style handbags and footwear inspired by riding boots made of naturally tanned cowhide. Stores are in Spain, Portugal, and Panama.

DUNHILL 1893
UK

The Dunhill family originally ran a saddler business in Euston Road in London, but when Alfred Dunhill took over in 1893 he turned it into Dunhill Motorities to provide "everything for the car but the motor," including leather driving coats, goggles, car horns, picnic sets, and timepieces. In 2005, the brand was revamped by Savile Row tailor Richard James and leather supremo Bill Amberg, among others, and has become a global menswear brand.

SWAROVSKI 1895
AUSTRIA

A global name that grew out of a family business, a small nineteenth-century glass foundry in Bohemia. In 1892, Daniel Swarovski developed a way of precisely cutting and multifaceting glass crystals mechanically, producing a prismatic chaton that sparkled with the intensity of a diamond. It was later to be used in jewelry by Chanel, Schiaparelli, and Dior.

GLOBE-TROTTER 1897
UK

Globe-Trotter, a purveyor of top-quality luggage, was established in 1897 by native Englishman David Nelken in Saxony, Germany, until it moved to the United Kingdom in 1901; it now resides in Broxbourne, Hertfordshire. The cases are manufactured using the same nineteenth-century methods, and leather is sourced from British tanneries. The distinctive leather corners are pressed for five days using the original Victorian machinery. Captain Robert Falcon Scott took a Globe-Trotter on the Antarctic expedition in 1912, and in 1947 Queen Elizabeth II took the company's luggage with her on honeymoon.

VOLLERS 1899
UK

Vollers has a long pedigree, established in Portsmouth by Harry and Nelly Voller in 1899 under the name Madame Voller, specializing in handmade corsets. Son Bertrand took over the company after his parents' retirement in 1919, and as corsets fell out of favor the girdle took over. In the 1980s, the corset enjoyed a revival as outerwear, giving Vollers a new lease of life. Ian and Corina Voller are now the fifth generation to run the family firm, creating designs inspired from the original patterns, as worn by brides and burlesque stars.

ROLEX 1905
SWITZERLAND

In 1905 Wilsdorf & Davis was set up by Hans Wilsdorf and his brother-in-law, Alfred Davis, in London, to import Swiss movements and mount them in high-quality watchcases. The Rolex trademark dates from 1908, and after the company moved to Geneva, Switzerland, it became renowned for its innovations, such as the waterproof Oyster wristwatch of 1926 and the two time-zone wristwatch, or Rolex GMT master, of 1954. A Rolex watch has become one of the world's best-known status symbols.

J. W. HULME 1905
UNITED STATES

This U.S. leathergoods company started life as a tent and awning maker founded by John W. Hulme in 1905; in 1917, Hulme constructed tents out of cotton canvas for U.S. soldiers fighting in World War I. In the 1920s, Hulme began to manufacture hand-cut leather and canvas sporting bags and accessories; in 2003, it reduced its output, refusing to compromise on quality over quantity by shipping work overseas. Every item continues to be individually hand crafted by U.S. artisans.

VAN CLEEF & ARPELS 1906
FRANCE

A great jewelry dynasty was born on the marriage of Estelle Arpels, the daughter of a gemstone dealer, and Alfred Van Cleef, the son of a stone-cutter, as the couple went on to found Van Cleef & Arpels in Paris in 1906. The company has been at the forefront of jewelry trends throughout the twentieth century, including Art Deco geometry in the 1920s and the cartoon-inspired Winking Cat brooches in the 1950s.

BORBONESE 1910
ITALY

The Borbonese family established its jewelry and accessories business in Turin, Italy, in 1910, with the workshop run by milliner Lucia Lorenzoni Ginestrone. In the 1960s, the house collaborated with many fashion houses, including Fendi, Valentino, and Yves Saint Laurent; in the 1970s, Borbonese joined with Redwall to create a line of bags featuring the iconic eye of the partridge print.

SAMSONITE 1910
UNITED STATES

Luggage salesman Jesse Shwayder set up the Shayder Trunk Manufacturing Company in Denver, Colorado, in 1910; it became Samsonite, the name derived from the biblical character of Samson, known for his great physical strength. Samsonite's hard-shell luggage was summarily advertised as "strong enough to stand on," and the first suitcase was advertised in Macy's window in New York in 1918 with half a ton of sugar resting on top.

AKUBRA 1911
AUSTRALIA

Englishman Benjamin Dunkerley emigrated and started a hatmaking business in Hobart, Tasmania. He developed a machine to remove the hair tip from the underfur of a rabbit to create felt, thereby speeding up the process. The business moved to Surrey Hills, Sydney, and in 1904 was joined by English hatter Stephen Keir; in 1912 the Akubra trade name was used for the first time. The firm remains in family hands and manufactures leather-trimmed fur felt hats—it remains the only complete fur-felt manufacturer in Australia.

EBEL 1911
SWITZERLAND

Husband and wife Eugène Blum and Alice Lèvy established the watchmaking firm of Ebel in La Chaux-de-Fonds, Switzerland, in 1911; Ebel stands for Eugène Blum et Lèvy. The couple were contemporaries of Swiss architect Le Corbusier, who was the son of a watch-face enameler. The links between modernist architecture and watchmaking are made explicit in Ebel's work, and in 1986, in celebration of the brand's seventy-fifth anniversary, it bought Le Corbusier's Villa Turque in La Chaux-de-Fonds.

MELIN TREGWYNT 1912
UK

Melin Tregwynt is a traditional Welsh wool mill in Pembrokeshire that manufactures Welsh wool blankets, throws, and hats, bags, and scarves. The original mill has stood since the seventeenth century, when local farmers would bring the wool fleece to be spun into yarn for the family's blankets. Owners Eifion and Amanda Griffiths are the third generation of the same family who have owned the mill since 1912.

OLNEY HEADWEAR 1914
UK

Olney Headwear is recognized all over the world as a manufacturer and supplier of fine quality hats. The company has been based in Luton, the traditional center of the millinery trade in the United Kingdom, since 1914, when Albert E. Olney set up the business. Olney remains a family firm, owned and run by its fourth generation.

LACO 1925
GERMANY

Laco was founded in 1925 by Frieda Lacher and Ludwig Hummel; in 1936, Frieda's son, Erich, took over the helm. From 1936 to 1945, Laco gained a reputation as the finest watchmaker in Germany, with designs such as the *Beobachter Uhr* (observer watch) used by the German Luftwaffe. Today Laco continues to make highly accurate watches and since 2000 has re-released many heritage styles.

OLIVER GOLDSMITH 1926
UK

Oliver Goldsmith offered an alternative to the mass-produced government-subsidized glasses available in the 1950s and 1960s. Founded in 1926 by P. Oliver Goldsmith, the company has always been at the forefront of eyewear development, being one of the first to recognize that innovative materials such as plastic could revolutionize the industry and take over from the customary (and cumbersome) tortoiseshell and metal. The Space Wraps of 1969 and the Pyramid of 1972, commissioned by hairdresser Vidal Sassoon, demonstrate the innovative Goldsmith approach.

HARRY WINSTON 1932
UNITED STATES

One of the best-known jewelers in the world, Harry Winston opened its doors in 1932 and became the destination of choice for both Hollywood and high society. The business collaborated with De Beers so as to acquire the most renowned gems, including the Hope diamond in 1949: 45.52 karats of shimmering blue with a list of former owners that included Louis XIV.

LEJABY 1930
FRANCE

France is known for its fabulous lingerie created by many female entrepreneurs; Lejaby was one such brand, set up by seamstress Gabrielle Viannay with businessman Marcel Blanchard in 1930 in Lyon, making some of the world's first bras—the Miss Top launched in 1965 was a huge success. Lejaby pioneered new material, such as nylon, in the 1960s, followed by the revolutionary micro-fiber. The couture line is 100 percent handmade in France.

RAY-BAN 1937
UNITED STATES

The Ray-Ban Aviator antiglare metal frame was created in 1936 in collaboration with the U.S. Air Force to aid flyer safety. It had contacted Bausch and Lomb to craft lenses that would block the sun without impeding the pilots' sight, and Bausch and Lomb responded with a series of goggles with teardrop-shaped lenses that evolved into a much simpler pair of lightweight sunglasses. The Ray-Ban Aviator model still carries the same lens today.

KANGOL 1938
UK

The "K" comes from silk, "ANG" from angora, and "OL" from wool, delineating the materials of the hats made by the Cumbrian company Kangol, set up by Jacques Spreiregen in 1938. During World War II, the company supplied military headwear, and in the postwar years, beatniks adopted its black beret. In the 1980s, Kangol gained instant credibility when its headgear was adopted by the B-boys of New York, in particular Grandmaster Flash and Run-D.M.C.

SIMONE PÉRÈLE 1948
FRANCE

A year after Dior's revolutionary New Look was launched to an enraptured press in Paris, corsetière Simone Pérèle established her luxury lingerie label with the Soleil lace bra and its distinctive pointed half-cups. In the 1960s, she introduced the Sole Mio bra, the first lace bra in lycra. The Pérèle look is hand-tailored, and when a new style is

introduced, the process from concept to precision pattern making for the prototype can take up to six months. The Heritage collection is a modern reworking of archival pieces.

LISE CHARMEL 1950
FRANCE

Lyon, the traditional center of silk weaving in France, was the original home of the lingerie brand Lise Charmel, founded in 1950 and known for its use of luxurious materials, such as inlaid guipure lace, silk, Swarovski crystal, and tulle. Today the label consists of five brand names: Lise Charmel, Éprise by Lise Charmel, Epure by Lise Charmel, Antinéa by Lise Charmel, and Antigel by Lise Charmel.

LA PERLA 1954
ITALY

Ada Masotti opened a corsetry boutique in Bologna, Italy, in 1954 under the name La Perla, and designed foundation garments in skin tone until the 1960s, when the brand branched out into color and graphic woven checkered prints in Op art monochrome. Swimwear was introduced in 1971, and the company pioneered the use of elastic lace in 1978. La Perla is now a leading international brand of luxurious underwear.

INDEX

PICTURE CREDITS

Every effort has been made to trace all copyright owners, but if any have been inadvertently overlooked, the publishers would be pleased to make the necessary corrections at the first opportunity. (Key: **t** = top; **c** = center; **b** = bottom; **l** = left; **r** = right; **tl** = top left; **tr** = top right; **tc** = top center; **tcr** = top center right; **cl** = center left; **cr** = center right; **ctl** = center top left; **cbl** = center bottom left; **bl** = bottom left; **br** = bottom right)

2 © Massimo Listri/Corbis **4/5** © Massimo Listri/Corbis **8** Gamma-Rapho via Getty Images **11** © Condé Nast Archive/Corbis **12/13** Pooch Purtill Photography **15t** Pooch Purtill Photography **15b** Pooch Purtill Photography **16t** Pooch Purtill Photography **16b** © Bettmann/CORBIS **17** Pooch Purtill Photography **18t** Pooch Purtill Photography **18bl** Pooch Purtill Photography **18br** Pooch Purtill Photography **19** Pooch Purtill Photography **20l** Pooch Purtill Photography **20r** Pooch Purtill Photography **21** © Bettmann/Corbis **22** Copyright Swaine Adeney Brigg **23tl** Pooch Purtill Photography **23tr** Pooch Purtill Photography **23br** Pooch Purtill Photography **23bl** Pooch Purtill Photography **24l** Copyright Gieves and Hawkes **24r** Copyright Gieves and Hawkes **25** Pooch Purtill Photography **26t** Pooch Purtill Photography **26b** Copyright Gieves and Hawkes **27l** Pooch Purtill Photography **27c** Pooch Purtill Photography **27r** Pooch Purtill Photography **28** Copyright Gieves and Hawkes **29l** Copyright Gieves and Hawkes **29r** Copyright Gieves and Hawkes **30** Camera Press/Figarophoto/Gyslain Yarhi **33tl** © Thierry Orban/Sygma/Corbis **33tr** Camera Press/Figarophoto/Deschamps **33b** © Paul Almasy/Corbis **34t** © Christie's Images/Corbis **34b** Camera Press/Figarophoto/Caroline Menne **35** © Stephane Cardinale/People Avenue/Corbis **36** Copyright John Smedley Ltd. **37** Copyright John Smedley Ltd. **38tl** Copyright John Smedley Ltd. **38tc** Copyright John Smedley Ltd. **38tr** Copyright John Smedley Ltd. **38br** Copyright John Smedley Ltd. **38bl** Copyright John Smedley Ltd. **39** Copyright John Smedley Ltd. **40tl** Pooch Purtill Photography **40bl** Pooch Purtill Photography **40r** Pooch Purtill Photography **43tl** Copyright John Smedley Ltd. **43tr** Copyright John Smedley Ltd. **43b** Pooch Purtill Photography **44** ©RIA Novosti/TopFoto **45** Gamborg Collection/The Bridgeman Art Library **46** State Russian Museum, St. Petersburg, Russia/The Bridgeman Art Library **47tl** ©RIA Novosti/TopFoto **47tr** ©RIA Novosti/TopFoto **47br** ©RIA Novosti/TopFoto **47bl** ©RIA Novosti/TopFoto **48/49** Photo by Peter Rigaud **50tl** Photo by Peter Rigaud **50tc** Photo by Peter Rigaud **50tr** Photo by Peter Rigaud **51** Photo by Peter Rigaud **52** Photo by Peter Rigaud **53tl** Photo by Peter Rigaud **53tr** Photo by Peter Rigaud **53b** Photo by Peter Rigaud **54l** Copyright Brooks Brothers **54cl** Copyright Brooks Brothers **54c** Copyright Brooks Brothers **54cr** Copyright Brooks Brothers **54r** Copyright Brooks Brothers **55** Copyright Brooks Brothers **56** Copyright Brooks Brothers **57** c.Warner Br/Everett/Rex Features **58tl** Copyright Brooks Brothers **58tr** Copyright Brooks Brothers **58b** Copyright Brooks Brothers **60** © Peter Marlow/Magnum Photos **61** © Andrew Butler/Alamy **62l** © Jorge Royan/Alamy **62r** © Jorge Royan/Alamy **64** Pierre Ballif/ Mes Chaussettes Rouges **65** Virgile Dureuil/ Mes Chaussettes Rouges **66l** Courtesy of Antigua Casa Crespo **66r** Courtesy of Antigua Casa Crespo **67l** Courtesy of Antigua Casa Crespo **67tr** Courtesy of Antigua Casa Crespo **67br** Courtesy of Antigua Casa Crespo **69t** © Bettmann/CORBIS 69B © Rune Hellestad/Corbis **70** Photo by Apic/Getty Images **71t** © Sergio Gaudenti/Kipa/Corbis **71b** Bloomberg via Getty Images **74** Camera Press/Paul Delort /Le Figaro **74br** Camera Press/Figarophoto/Ceccarini **74bl** Copyright Charvet, 28 Place Vendôme, Paris **75** Copyright Charvet, 28 Place Vendôme, Paris **76t** Camera Press/Figarophoto/Ceccarini **76b** © Burt Glinn/Magnum Photos **77** Camera Press/Figarophoto/Delort **78** Pooch Purtill Photography **79t** Pooch Purtill Photography **79b** Pooch Purtill Photography **80** Pooch Purtill Photography **81** Pooch Purtill Photography **82** courtesy of Elke Franck, Hamburg 2013 **83l** courtesy of Elke Franck, Hamburg 2013 **83tr** courtesy of Elke Franck, Hamburg 2013 **83br** courtesy of Elke Franck, Hamburg 2013 **84tl** courtesy of Elke Franck, Hamburg 2013 **84tr** courtesy of Elke Franck, Hamburg 2013 **84b** courtesy of Elke Franck, Hamburg 2013 **86** Getty Images **87** © Philippe Eranian/Corbis **88t** Time & Life Pictures/Getty Images **88b** Time & Life Pictures/Getty Images **90b** Camera Press/Madame Figaro/Ivan Soldo **91** © Corbis **92** © Burt Glinn/Magnum Photos **93t** Photography by Guy Hills for Huntsman **93bl** Pooch Purtill Photography **93br** Pooch Purtill Photography **94tl** Photography by Guy Hills for Huntsman **94ctl** Photography by Guy Hills for Huntsman **94cbl** Photography by Guy Hills for Huntsman **94bl** Photography by Guy Hills for Huntsman **94l** Photography by Guy Hills for Huntsman **95** Photography by Guy Hills for Huntsman **96** Photo by Apic/Getty Images **97** Camera Press/ Jean Michel Turpin/Le Figaro Magazine **98** White Images/ Scala, Florence **99l** Roger-Viollet/Topfoto **99r** Roger-Viollet/Topfoto **100l** AFP/Getty Images **100r** AFP/Getty Images **101r** © Condé Nast Archive/Corbis **102** © Miguel Medina/AFP/Getty Images **103t** Miguel Medina/AFP/Getty Images **103b** Miguel Medina/AFP/Getty Images **104l** Courtesy of www.thedapperslowth.com **104r** Courtesy of www.thedapperslowth.com **105** Courtesy of www.thedapperslowth.com **106** Courtesy of www.thedapperslowth.com **107t** Courtesy of www.thedapperslowth.com **107bl** Courtesy of www.thedapperslowth.com **107br** Courtesy of www.thedapperslowth.com **108** Copyright Burberry **109** Copyright Burberry **110tl** Copyright Burberry **110cl** Copyright Burberry **110bl** Copyright Burberry **111** Copyright Burberry **112t** Copyright Burberry **112b** Copyright Burberry **113** Copyright Burberry **114** Courtesy of Borsalino **115t** Courtesy of Borsalino **116tl** Courtesy of Borsalino **116cl** Courtesy of Borsalino **116bl** Courtesy of Borsalino **117l** Courtesy of Borsalino **117r** Courtesy of Borsalino **118tl** Pooch Purtill Photography **118tr** Pooch Purtill Photography **118tcr** Pooch Purtill Photography **118b** Pooch Purtill Photography **119** Pooch Purtill Photography **121t** Pooch Purtill Photography **121cr** Pooch Purtill Photography **121cl** Pooch Purtill Photography **121br** Pooch Purtill Photography **121bl** Pooch Purtill Photography **122t** Pooch Purtill Photography **122b** Pooch Purtill Photography **123t** Pooch Purtill Photography **123b** Pooch Purtill Photography **124tl** Courtesy of William Lockie of Scotland **124tr** © Shannon Tofts Photography **124br** Pooch Purtill Photography **128bl** Pooch Purtill Photography **129** Pooch Purtill Photography **130** Courtesy of Aubade **131** Courtesy of Aubade **132** Courtesy of Aubade **133tl** Courtesy of Aubade **133tr** Courtesy of Aubade **133br** Courtesy of Aubade **133bl** Courtesy of Aubade **134** Courtesy of Aubade **135** Courtesy of Aubade **136t** Photographer Erlend Angelo **136b** Courtesy of Dale of Norway **137t** Courtesy of Dale of Norway **137b** Courtesy of Dale of Norway **138** Courtesy of Dale of Norway **139l** Photographer Lars Botten **139r** Photographer Lars Botten **140** Courtesy of E.Vogel Inc. **141t** Courtesy of E.Vogel Inc. **141bl** Courtesy of E.Vogel Inc. **141br** Courtesy of E.Vogel Inc. **142t** Courtesy of E.Vogel Inc. **142b** Courtesy of E.Vogel Inc. **142c** Courtesy of E.Vogel Inc. **143l** Courtesy of E.Vogel Inc **143tr** Courtesy of E.Vogel Inc. **143br** Courtesy of E.Vogel Inc. **144t** Courtesy of Dinkelacker **144bl** Courtesy of Dinkelacker **144br** Courtesy of Dinkelacker **146t** Courtesy of Dinkelacker **146b** Courtesy of Dinkelacker **147t** Courtesy of Dinkelacker **147b** Courtesy of Dinkelacker **147r** Courtesy of Dinkelacker **148** Photo by Anthony Cake/Photoshot/Getty Images **149t** © How Hwee Young/epa/Corbis **149b** © Axel Koester/Corbis **150l** © United Archives /Topfoto **150r** © United Archives / Topfoto **151t** The Cecil Beaton Studio Archive at Sotheby's **151b** Publifoto/Olycom **152** DUfoto/Foto Scala, Florence **153t** Bloomberg via Getty Images **153cl** Gamma-Rapho via Getty Images **153cr** Gamma-Rapho via Getty Images **153bl** Gamma-Rapho via Getty Images **153br** Gamma-Rapho via Getty Images **154** Snap/Rex Features **155** Photography by Erik Gould, courtesy of the Museum of Art, Rhode Island School of Design, Providence. **156** Nigel R. Barklie/Rex Features **157l** © Jeff Gilbert/Alamy **157r** © Jeff Gilbert/Alamy 158 Courtesy of Lucchese Boot Company **159t** Courtesy of Lucchese Boot Company **159cl** Courtesy of Lucchese Boot Company **159bl** Courtesy of Lucchese Boot Company **159bc** Courtesy of Lucchese Boot Company **159br** Courtesy of Lucchese Boot Company **160r** © Christie's Images/Corbis **161t** Courtesy of Lucchese Boot Company **161bl** Courtesy of Lucchese Boot Company **161br** Courtesy of Lucchese Boot Company **162l** Roger Viollet/Getty Images **162r** © 2006 TopFoto/RogerViollet **163tl** © 2006 TopFoto/RogerViollet **164** Photo by Laure Albin-Guillot/Roger Viollet/Getty Images **165tr** Photo by Chicago History Museum/Getty Images **165tl** Photo by Chicago History Museum/Getty Images **165br** Photo by Chicago History Museum/Getty Images **165bl** Photo by Chicago History Museum/Getty Images **166** UIG via Getty Images **167** © Paolo Pellegrin/Magnum Photos **168** Courtesy of Edward Green **169t** Pooch Purtill Photography **169cl** Pooch Purtill Photography **169c** Pooch Purtill Photography **169cr** Pooch Purtill Photography **170** Pooch Purtill Photography **171t** Pooch Purtill Photography **171b** Pooch Purtill Photography **172** Sipa Press/Rex Features **173** Sipa Press/Rex Features **174t** Sipa Press/Rex Features **174b** Sipa Press/Rex Features **175** © Marianne Rosenstiehl/Sygma/Corbis **176/177** Pooch Purtill Photography **178** © Bettmann/Corbis **179t** Courtesy of Chippewa **179bl** Chippewa Falls Public Library **179br** Chippewa Falls Public Library **180t** Courtesy of Chippewa **180b** Vintage Chippewa Boots catalogue courtesy of Chippewa **181l** Courtesy of Chippewa **181r** Copyright Alaska State Library **182** Courtesy of Scully Sportswear Inc. **183t** CSU Archives/Everett Collection/Rex Features **183b** Courtesy of Scully Sportswear Inc. **184** Courtesy of Scully Sportswear Inc. **185t** Moviestore Collection/Rex Features **185b** Moviestore Collection/Rex Features **186** Copyright Troentorp Clogs **187** IBL Bildbyra, Landskrona Museum/HIP/TopFoto **188tl** Copyright Troentorp Clogs **188r** Copyright Troentorp Clogs **188bl** Copyright Troentorp Clogs **189tl** Copyright Troentorp Clogs **189cl** Copyright Troentorp Clogs **189bl** Copyright Troentorp Clogs **190** Getty Images **191l** The Granger Collection/TopFoto **191r** © Condé Nast Archive/Corbis **192l** © ullsteinbild/TopFoto **192t** Image Courtesy of The Advertising Archives **193t** Gamma-Keystone via Getty Images **193c** © Douglas Kirkland/Sygma/Corbis **193b** ©ullsteinbild/TopFoto **194** AP/Press Association Images **195tl** © Victoria and Albert Museum, London/V&A Images **195tr** ©Victoria and Albert Museum, London/V&A Images **195br** ©Victoria and Albert Museum, London/V&A Images **195bl** ©Victoria and Albert Museum, London/V&A Images **196** © Ferdinando Scianna/Magnum Photos **197** Getty Images **198** Photo by George Strock/Time Life Pictures/Getty Images **199t** Copyright LL Bean **199b** Photo by George Strock//Time Life Pictures/Getty Images **200l** Photo by George Strock/Time Life Pictures/Getty Images **200tr** Photo by George Strock/Time Life Pictures/Getty Images **200br** Photo by George Strock//Time Life Pictures/Getty Images **201** Copyright LL Bean **202** Camera Press **203** Alinari/Rex Features **205l** Camera Press **205r** Camera Press **206** Miu Miu Paris Ready to Wear. Autumn/Winter 2013/2014. **207** © Fairchild Photo Service/Condé Nast/Corbis **208l** Courtesy of E. Marinella, Napoli **208r** Courtesy of E. Marinella, Napoli **209** Roberto Sorrentino per E. Marinella **210t** Roberto Sorrentino per E. Marinella **210b** Courtesy of E. Marinella, Napoli **211tl** Courtesy of E. Marinella, Napoli **211tr** Courtesy of E. Marinella, Napoli **211bl** Courtesy of E. Marinella, Napoli **211br** Courtesy of E. Marinella, Napoli **212** © 2003 Credit:Topham Picturepoint **213** © David Lees/Corbis **214** © Banca Dati dell'Archivio Storico Foto Locchi Firenze **215l** ©2006 Alinari/TopFoto **215r** Photo by Fratelli Alinari/Alinari Archives, Florence/Alinari via Getty Images **216t** © David Lees/Corbis **216b** © 2003 Credit:Topham Picturepoint **217t** © 2003 Credit:Topham Picturepoint **218t** © Interfoto/Alamy **218b** Camera Press/ Renaud Wald/Madame Figaro **219l** © Elbardamu/Alamy **219r** Photograph By Camera Press London **220** Photo by Lipnitzki/Roger Viollet/Getty Images **221l** Ted Blackbrow/Associated Newspapers /Rex Features **221r** Roger-Viollet/Rex Features **222l** © Condé Nast Archive/Corbis **222r** © Condé Nast Archive/Corbis **223** © Henri Cartier-Bresson/Magnum Photos **224t** © Christopher Anderson/Magnum Photos **224c** © Christopher Anderson/Magnum Photos **224b** © Christopher Anderson/Magnum Photos **225** © Christopher Anderson/Magnum Photos **226t** Camera Press **226b** Retna/Photoshot **227** Photo by Francis Demange/Gamma-Rapho via Getty Images **228** © 2013 Bata Shoe Museum, Toronto, Canada **230l** © Condé Nast Archive/Corbis **230r** © Condé Nast Archive/Corbis **232l** Copyright Loro Piana **232r** Copyright Loro Piana **233** Copyright Loro Piana **234tl** Copyright Loro Piana **234tr** Copyright Loro Piana **234cr** Copyright Loro Piana **234b** Copyright Loro Piana **235** Copyright Loro Piana **236** ©Vittoriano Rastelli/Corbis **237t** ©Vittoriano Rastelli/Corbis **237b** ©2006 Alinari/TopFoto **238** Camera Press/Ivan Soldo/Madame Figaro **239** Camera Press/Ivan Soldo/Madame Figaro **240t** Copyright Aubercy, Paris **240b** Copyright Aubercy, Paris **241** Copyright Aubercy, Paris **242tl** Copyright Aubercy, Paris **242bl** Copyright Aubercy, Paris **242r** Copyright Aubercy, Paris **243tl** Copyright Aubercy, Paris **243tr** Copyright Aubercy, Paris **243b** Copyright Aubercy, Paris **244t** Copyright Aubercy, Paris **244b** Courtesy of Valextra **245** Courtesy of Valextra **246t** Courtesy of Valextra **246b** Courtesy of Valextra **247l** Courtesy of Valextra **247c** Courtesy of Valextra **247r** Courtesy of Valextra **248** Courtesy of Coach, Inc. **249tl** Courtesy of Coach, Inc. **249tr** Courtesy of Coach, Inc. **249br** Courtesy of Coach, Inc. **249bl** Courtesy of Coach, Inc. **250** Courtesy of Coach, Inc. **251** Courtesy of Coach, Inc. **252tl** Courtesy of Coach, Inc. **252tr** Courtesy of Coach, Inc. **252bl** Courtesy of Coach, Inc. **252br** Courtesy of Coach, Inc. **254** Roger-Viollet/Topfoto **255t** © Condé Nast Archive/Corbis **255b** Rex Features **256** © John French/V&A Images **257** Photo by Sabine Weiss/Gamma-Rapho/Getty Images **258l** Camera Press/Mitchell Sams **258r** Camera Press/Mitchell Sams **259** Courtesy of Dior **261** Camera Press /Jerome Laurent/Madame Figaro **262l** © Robert Mora/Alamy **262r** Camera Press/Renaud Wald/Madame Figaro **263** Image Courtesy of The Advertising Archives **264** Giuseppe Pino/Mondadori Portfolio via Getty Images **265** Getty Images **266** Camera Press/ Caroline Menne/Madame Figaro **267** © Ferdinando Scianna/Magnum Photos **268/269** © Condé Nast Archive/Corbis **270** Pooch Purtill Photography **271** Pooch Purtill Photography **272** Pooch Purtill Photography **275** Pooch Purtill Photography **277** Pooch Purtill Photography **278** Pooch Purtill Photography **280** Pooch Purtill Photography **281** Pooch Purtill Photography **282** Pooch Purtill Photography **283** Pooch Purtill Photography **285** Pooch Purtill Photography

Author acknowledgments
This book is dedicated to Lionel Marsden. Thanks to Ruth Patrick, Jane Laing, Mark Fletcher, and all at Quintessence; and also Sheila Ableman, Maggie Norden, Mary Patterson, and Joanna and Clive Ball.

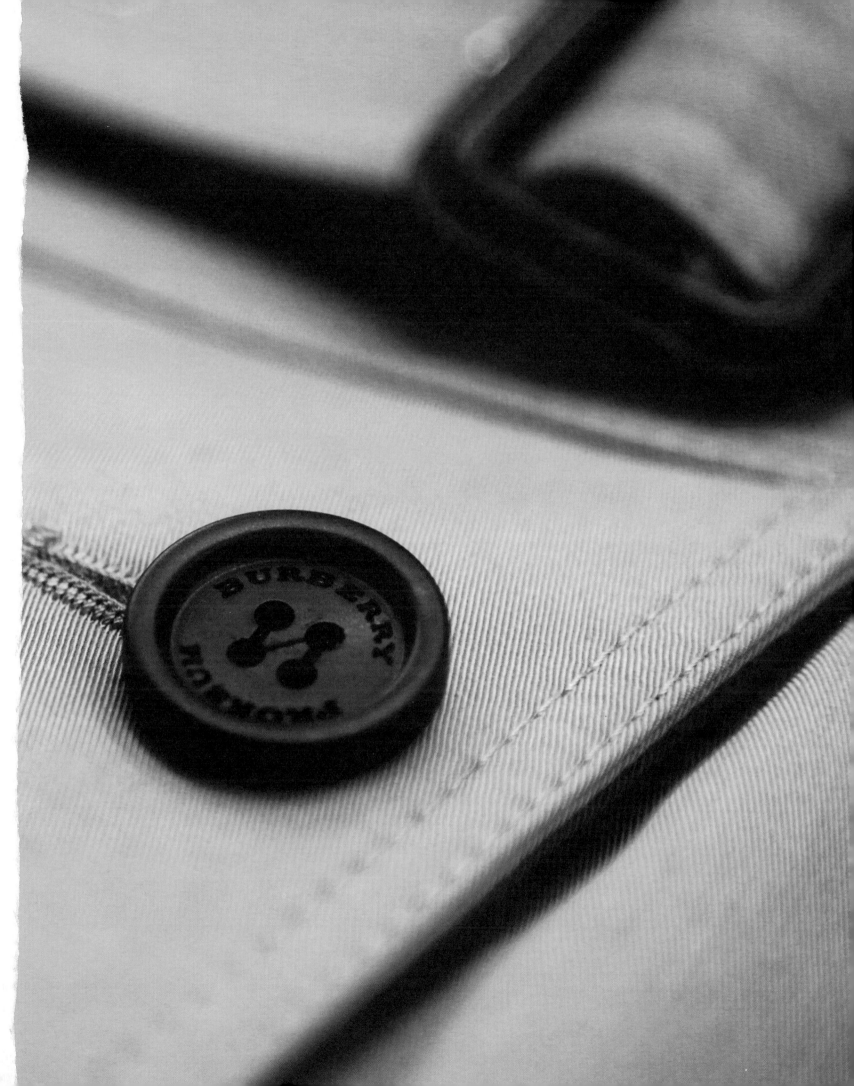